W9-CQI-637

BOUNDARIES

readings in

DEVIANCE, CRIME AND CRIMINAL JUSTICE

A Customized Reader

General Editors

Bradley R.E. Wright
University of Connecticut

Ralph B. McNeal, Jr.
University of Connecticut

Compiled by

SOC 216: Criminology
University of Connecticut
Sociology

PEARSON

Custom
Publishing

Director of Database Publishing: Michael Payne
Sponsoring Editor: Robin J. Lazrus
Development Editor: Catherine O'Keefe
Editorial Assistant: Ana Díaz-Caneja
Marketing Manager: Kathleen Kourian
Operations Manager: Eric M. Kenney
Production Project Manager: Marianne C. Groth
Database Project Specialist: Elizabeth MacKenzie-Lamb
Rights Editor: Francesca Marcantonio
Cover Designer: Renée Sartell and Kristen Kiley

Cover Art: "Chain with Broken Link," courtesy of Emanuele Taroni/PhotoDisc. "Fence," courtesy of PhotoDisc. "Cubed Face," courtesy of Getty Images.

Please visit our website at *www.pearsoncustom.com*
Attention bookstores: For permission to return any unsold stock, contact Pearson Custom Publishing at 1-800-777-6872.

ISBN: 0536142394

PEARSON CUSTOM PUBLISHING
75 Arlington St., Suite 300
Boston, MA 02116

SOCIOLOGY READERS FROM PEARSON CUSTOM PUBLISHING

Create the reader that matches **your** syllabus!

Effective pedagogical apparatus - headnotes. end-of-selection questions.
and optional introductions included with all selections!

Intersections: Readings in Sociology
www.intersectionsreader.com

An archive of 380 of the best classic
and contemporary readings in sociology.
Readings not only elucidate the discipline.
but also help spark student interest in the
entire area through the richness. diversity.
and breadth of its readings. Select only
the content you wish to use in your
course to reflect your teaching methods
and course perspective.

Inequalities: Readings in Diversity and Social Life
www.inequalitiesreader.com

The most comprehensive collection
of high-quality readings on multiple
forms of inequality and how they intersect.
More than 175 classic and contemporary
articles reflect theoretical. conceptual.
and global perspectives to match the
goals and objectives of your sociology or
interdisciplinary —oriented course.

Crossroads: Readings in Social Problems
www.crossroadsreader.com

An essential source of over 300 essays
and readings that illuminate and help
explain central ideas and issues in the study
of social problems. Choose from a rich and
diverse archive of high quality articles that
cover topics and present perspectives
germane to your course.

Boundaries: Readings in Deviance. Crime and Criminal Justice
www.boundariesreader.com

More than 350 classic and contemporary
readings that cover all the topics
addressed in deviance. criminology and
criminal justice courses. The richness of
this repository of readings provides
unlimited flexibility and timely solutions
to create a reader that fits your course and
teaching style.

Reading Women's Lives: The Customizable Reader for Women's Studies
www.readingwomenslives.com

Nearly 500 selections are available
including literature. pieces that reflect
multicultural and cross-cultural diversity.
readings drawn from the social sciences
and third-wave feminism readings.
Nineteen optional thematic introductions
to key topics in Women's Studies – themes
such as The Body. Difference and
Inequality. Feminism and the Women's
Movement. Sexualities.
and Socialization.

Contents

Reading List for Sociology 216

#	Date	Theory of Crime	Issues of Crime	Readings
1	Jan 17	Class Introduction	What is Crime?	
2	Jan 24	What is a theory?	Survey	MST, Chap 1 Akers
3	Jan 31	Biological	Overview of Crime in US	MST, Chap 3 Mednick
4	Feb 7	Psychological	Serial Murders	MST, Chap 4 Jenkins
5	Feb 14	Rational Choice	Death Penalty	MST, Chap 2 Radelet
6	Feb 21	Social Control	Drugs	MST, Chap 8 Becker
7	Feb 28	Midterm	Midterm	None
8	March 7	Spring Break	----	----
9	March 14	Social Learning	How to Burgle	MST, Chap 6 Wright
10	March 21	Strain Theories	Culture of Fear	MST, Chap 7 Glasner
11	March 28	Labeling	Gun Control	MST, pp. 153-56 Stolzenberg
12	April 4	Routine Activities	Analysis of UConn	MST, pp. 81-88 Cohen
13	April 11	Social Ecology	Broken Windows	MST, Chap 5 Wilson
14	April 18	Conflict	Is U.S. CJ Racist?	MST, pp. 149-61 Tonry
15	April 25	Feminist	Gender & Crime	MST, pp. 161-68 Chesney-Lind

Introduction to Criminological Theory

RONALD L. AKERS
University of Florida

In this introduction to his book Criminological Theories, *Ronald Akers discusses the place of theory in criminology. He examines three separate questions: 1) What is theory? 2) What different types of criminological theories exist? 3) What makes for a good theory? In answering these questions, he distinguishes between theories of law-making and those of law-breaking. He also discusses evaluative concepts such as theory testability, score, parsimony, and validity.*

☺ What Is Theory?

To many students, criminal justice practitioners, and other people, theory has a bad name. In their minds, the word *theory* means an irrelevant antonym of *fact*. Facts are real, while theories seem to involve no more than impractical mental gymnastics. Theories are just fanciful ideas that have little to do with what truly motivates real people. This is a mistaken image of theory in social science in general and in criminology in particular. Theory, if developed properly, is about real situations, feelings, experience, and human behavior. An effective theory helps us to make sense of facts that we already know and can be tested against new facts.

Consider the situation of a young girl's child abuse and her later involvement in prostitution. What about the relationship between the limited opportunities for legitimate work and the selection of a career in crime? Think about the fact that members from a significant proportion of

"Introduction to Criminological Theory," by Ronald L. Akers, reprinted from *Criminological Theories: Introduction, Evaluation, and Application,* Third Edition, 2000. pp. 1–13. Copyright © 2000 by Roxbury Publishing Company.

immigrant groups have become successively involved in organized crime, such as Jews, Irish, and Italians, Puerto Ricans, African Americans, and Latinos. Or consider the fact that some kinds of behavior are legally defined as criminal, while others are not. Theories are tentative answers to the commonly asked questions about such events and behavior. Why? By what process? How does it work? The answers may provide explanations of one set of events by referring to other events.

> In general, scientific theories make statements about the relationships between observable phenomena. (Vold et al., 1998:2)

> Theories, then, are really generalizations of a sort; they explain how two or more events are related to each other. (Williams and McShane, 1988:2)

> A theory is a set of interconnected statements or propositions that explain how two or more events or factors are related to one another. (Curran and Renzetti, 1994:2)

Note that these and other definitions of theory (see Gibbs, 1990) refer to statements about relationships between actual events; about what is and what will be. They are not answers to questions of what ought to be, nor are they philosophical, religious, or metaphysical systems of beliefs and values about crime and society.

Criminological theories are abstract, but they entail more than ivory-tower or arm-chair speculations. They are part of the broader social science endeavor to explain human behavior and society. Understanding why people conform to or deviate from social and legal norms is an integral part of a liberal education. Moreover, such understanding is vital for those who plan to pursue specialized careers in the law or criminal justice. Virtually every policy or action taken regarding crime is based on some underlying theory or theories of crime. It is essential, therefore, to comprehend and evaluate the major theories of criminology, not only for the academic or research criminologist, but also for the educated citizen and the legal or criminal justice professional.

◉ Types of Criminological Theories

Edwin H. Sutherland (1947) defined criminology as the study of the entire process of law-making, law-breaking, and law-enforcing. This definition provides us with a starting point for classifying criminological theories. One such major type of theory addresses the first and third part of this process: the making and enforcing of the law. Theories of this kind attempt to account for why we have laws and why the criminal justice system operates the way it does. Another major type of theory explains law-breaking. Such theories account for criminal and delinquent behavior. They are usually extended to explain any deviant behavior that violates social norms, whether or not such behavior also violates the law.

There are not as many different theories of the first kind (theories of law and criminal justice) as there are of the second kind (theories of criminal and deviant behavior). Therefore, while both are important, more attention will be paid here to the second type of theory. Conflict, labeling, Marxist, and feminist theories are examples of theories that attempt to shed light on both criminal behavior and the law.

Theories of Making and Enforcing Criminal Law

Theories of making and enforcing criminal law (also herein referred to as theories of law and criminal justice) offer answers to questions of how or why certain behavior and people become defined and are dealt with as criminal in society. Why is a particular conduct considered illegal and what determines the kind of action to be taken when it occurs? How is it decided, and who makes the decision, that such conduct is criminal? And how are the resources of the public and state brought to bear against it? Theories try to answer these questions by proposing that social, political, and economic variables affect the legislation of law, administrative decisions and rules, and the implementation and operation of law in the criminal justice system.

This does not refer to philosophies regarding what kind of legal system we should have; nor is it a theoretical statement, for instance, to argue that we should have a fair, just, and effective criminal justice system. Such a statement offers desirable social goals that citizens may debate and vote on, but it provides no scientific explanation of law and criminal justice. Arguments over the goals and purposes of the system—such as whether it should focus on crime control rather than due process, should provide just deserts for law violators or only take actions that deter crime, or should rehabilitate or severely punish serious offenders—are not theoretical arguments. Philosophical and pragmatic debates over society's control of crime may be informed by theory or have relevance to the application of theory, but they are not themselves theoretical explanations of why laws are formulated and enforced. Theories attempt to explain the behavior of the participants in the legal system and the operation of the system itself. They produce hypotheses about the factors that account for legal and criminal justice actions and decisions. Theories do not tell us what are the correct, proper, and desirable values that should be exemplified in the system.

This is not to imply that the theorists themselves are totally unaffected by philosophical and value judgments. There is a significant relationship between theories of crime and criminal justice and philosophies that define the desirable goals of a just, effective, and well-managed criminal justice system. Such goals partially direct which theories will be considered important, and those theories will help to develop strategies to reach these goals.

For example, one of the reasons that conflict theory is important in criminology is that its theoretical propositions about the operation of the system are relevant to the political and moral debate over the justness of that system. The goal of a just system is to treat everyone equitably based on legally relevant factors such as the nature of the criminal act and the laws relating to it. Conflict theory hypothesizes that actions taken in the criminal justice system may be decided differentially based on such factors as the race, class, and gender of offenders, rather than on the type of crime. The decisions of a criminal justice system that relies more on such social characteristics than on the nature of the crime is not a just system. Therefore, the extent to which conflict theory is supported or refuted by research evidence is critical to the debate over the fairness of the criminal justice system.

Theories of Criminal and Deviant Behavior

Theories of criminal and deviant behavior try to answer the question of why social and legal norms are violated. This question has two interrelated parts: (1) Why are there variations in group rates of crime and deviance, and (2) why are some individuals more likely than others to commit criminal and deviant acts?

The first question poses the problem of trying to make sense of the differences in the location and proportion of deviant and criminal behavior in various groups and societies. For example, why does the United States have such a high rate of crime compared to Japan and many of the Western

6

European countries? Why do males as a group commit so many more violent and criminal acts than females? How do we explain the differences in homicide and drug use among different classes and groups within the same society?

The second question raises the issue of explaining differences among individuals in committing or refraining from criminal acts. Why are some individuals more likely to break the law than others? By what process or under what circumstances do people typically, and not just in a specific, individual case, reach the point of obeying or violating the law? Why does one person commit a crime, given a certain opportunity, while another does not, given the same opportunity? Why are some people more likely than others to commit frequent crimes or pursue criminal careers?

The first set of questions focuses on societal and group patterns, the second on individual differences. A theory that addresses broader questions about differences across societies or major groups in society is called a "macro" theory. Conversely, one that focuses specifically on small group or individual differences is referred to as operating on the "micro" level of analysis (Orcutt, 1983; Alexander et al., 1987). Other terms have also been used to make a similar distinction between theories. Cressey (1960) refers to "epidemiology" (the prevalence and distribution of crime across groups and societies) and "individual conduct." Akers refers to such different theories as social structural or processual (Akers, 1968; 1985). These distinctions between macro and micro, structural and processual, refer not only to questions about groups and individual behavior, but also to the kinds of answers a theory offers. For example, a theory that tries to answer the question of the differences between male and female crime rates by relying on innate biological differences between men and women would still be operating on the micro level.

In actuality, the two major questions of group and individual behavior are really just subtypes of the same general question: Why do or do not people commit crime and deviance? This is why theories of criminal behavior are neither strictly structural nor processual, although each will emphasize one or the other. Theories emphasizing social structure propose that the proportion of crimes among groups, classes, communities, or societies differ because of variations in their social or cultural make-up. Most structural theories, however, also include implicit or explicit statements regarding the process by which these structural conditions produce high or low crime rates. Processual theories assert that an individual commits criminal acts because he or she has experienced a particular life history, possessed a particular set of individual characteristics, or encountered a particular situation. Such theories also consider the deviancy-producing structures that an individual must encounter in order to increase the probability of his or her committing a crime.

There are other ways to classify criminological theories. One common way is to refer not just to micro or macro, but to several levels of explanation that ascend from the smallest to the largest unit of analysis. Such a classification typically categorizes the theories according to the general scientific discipline from which the explanatory variables are drawn. The most common classifications are: biological theories that explain crime with one or more genetic, chemical, neurological, or physiological variables; psychological theories based on personality, emotional maladjustment, mental retardation, psychic disturbance, or psychological traits; social psychological theories that account for crime by reference to behavior, self, and cognitive variables in a group context; and sociological theories that explain crime with cultural, structural, and socio-demographic variables. (See Nettler, 1984; Gibbons, 1979; Williams and McShane, 1988; Shoemaker, 1990; Jensen and Rojek, 1998; Vold et al., 1998; Liska and Messner, 1999.)

Just as the categories of structure and process overlap to some extent, some theories will draw from two or more disciplines. For instance, contemporary biological theories do not rely exclusively on genetic or biochemical factors, but also draw from psychological or sociological variables as well. Other theories, such as social learning, are clearly social-psychological, utilizing both sociological and psychological variables.

· · ·

❀ Criteria for Evaluating Theory

How do we know if a theory offers a sound explanation of crime or criminal justice? The various theories that will be explored provide different, sometimes contradictory, explanations of crime. How do we judge which explanation is preferable over another, or which is the best amongst several theories? The weakest reason for accepting or rejecting a theory of crime is how well it conforms to one's own beliefs, ideologies, or preferred policies.

If criminological theories are to be scientific, then they must be judged by scientific criteria. The most important of these is empirical validity, the extent to which a theory can be verified or refuted with carefully gathered evidence. But there are several other major criteria by which theories can be assessed. These include internal logical consistency, scope and parsimony, testability, empirical validity, and usefulness and policy implication. (For discussions of the criteria for evaluating criminological theories, see Gibbons, 1979; Chambliss, 1988; Shoemaker, 1990; Barlow and Ferdinand, 1992; Tittle, 1995; Vold et al., 1998.)

Logical Consistency, Scope, and Parsimony

The basic prerequisite for a sound theory is that it has clearly defined concepts and that its propositions are logically stated and internally consistent (Budziszewski, 1997). For example, a theory which proposes that criminals are biologically deficient and that deficiency explains their criminal behavior cannot also claim that family socialization is the basic cause of criminal behavior.

The scope of a theory refers to the range of phenomena which it proposes to explain. For instance, a theory that accounts only for the crime of check forgery may be accurate, but it is obviously very limited in scope. A better theory is one which accounts for a wide range of offenses including check forgery. A theory of juvenile delinquency that does not relate as well to adult criminality is more restricted than one that accounts for both juvenile delinquency and adult crime. A theory that explains only the age distribution of crime has a more limited scope than one that explains the age, race, sex, and class distributions of crime.

Parsimony, the conciseness and abstractness of a set of concepts and propositions, is also a desirable characteristic in a scientific theory. Scope and parsimony are interrelated, in that a theory which explains a wide scope of events with a few, succinct statements is scientifically preferable to one which relies on a complex set of propositions and variables that accounts for only a small range of events. The principle of parsimony is to use as few propositions as possible to explain the widest range of phenomena. For example, a theory which proposes that all crime and delinquency is caused by low self-control is much more parsimonious than a theory that requires a different set of multiple hypotheses to explain crime and delinquency, depending upon the type of offense and the age, sex, or race of the offender.

Testability

A scientific theory must be testable by objective, repeatable evidence. If a theory cannot be tested against empirical findings, it has no scientific value. Gibbons (1979:14) argues that, "In the final analysis, the acid test of a scientific theory is testability; that is, the extent to which it can either be verified or disproved by appropriate empirical evidence." It is not enough for a theory to fit known facts about crime or contain empirical evidence consistent with its propositions. It must also be possible to subject the theory to empirical falsification; in other words, it must be open to evidence that may counter or disprove its hypotheses with negative findings. If it is not falsifiable in this sense, it is not testable (Stinchcombe, 1968).

A theory may be untestable because the definitions of its concepts and its propositions are stated as a tautology. A tautology is a statement or hypothesis that is true by definition or involves circular reasoning (Budziszewski, 1997). If, for example, one begins with the definition of low self-control as the failure to refrain from crime then proposes low self-control as a cause of law violation, then one's proposition is tautological. Given the definition of low self-control, the proposition can never be proven false, because self-control is defined by the very thing it is hypothesized to explain. It simply says that a person who has low self-control has low self-control, or that a person who violates the law violates the law. A variation on a tautology that is true by definition is seen in the practice of placing a label on some behavior, then using that label to explain the same behavior. For instance, one may label serial killers as psychopaths, then assert that people commit serial murders because they are psychopathic. Such a statement does no more than repeat the label. Similarly, we may observe that a person drinks excessively and has problems with alcohol, so we theorize that the person overdrinks because he is an alcoholic. How do we know he is an alcoholic? We know because he drinks excessively and has problems with alcohol. We have come full circle.

Another way in which a theory may be untestable is that its propositions are so open-ended that any contradictory empirical evidence can be interpreted or re-interpreted to support the theory. For example, a theory may propose that males who rob banks are motivated by an irrational and unconscious impulse to resolve their guilt over their childhood sexual attraction towards their own mothers. This is a testable explanation of male bank robbery because it is not true by definition. If research finds enough bank robbers who fit this description, then the theory is supported. If research uncovers other cases where bank robbers claim their only motive is money and they have no such feelings towards their mothers, then that can be taken as falsifying the theory. However, the theory cannot be falsified if the claims of the latter bank robbers are dismissed by asserting that their very denial of these feelings in effect supports the theory, because the same unconscious impulse that motivated them to rob banks also rendered them unconscious of their true motivations. Similarly, a theory may contend that criminal laws always serve the interests of the ruling capitalist elite. Even if laws are enacted to serve the interest of the working class, one could always reinterpret them with the argument that such laws only appear to serve the working class but in fact serve the ruling class. There is no way to falsify the theory. Hence, a theory that can never be proven wrong, regardless of the findings, is not a testable theory.

A theory may also be untestable because its concepts are not measurable by observable and reportable events. A theory's concepts and propositions identify the explanatory events or independent variables that account for variations in the dependent variables, which are events or behavior to be explained. Even a non-tautological theory cannot be tested if it is not possible to find observable events that can be taken as objective and repeatable measures of these concepts. Without such measures, the hypothesized relationships cannot be checked against actual events. If a theory proposes that people commit crimes because they are possessed by invisible demons, there is no way to prove whether or not such demons are responsible for the crime. If we cannot measure the existence of demons separately from the occurrence of criminal behavior, we may simply assume the existence of the demons from the existence of the crimes. We have a similar tautology if the dependent and independent variables are measured by the same events. For example, it is tautological to explain delinquent behavior as the result of social disorganization, if one of the indicators of social disorganization is the delinquency rate itself. Both the events to be explained and the events used to explain them are the same thing. It is tautological to interpret an event as the cause of itself.

Not all concepts must be directly measurable for a theory to be testable, but one must be able to relate them in a logical and clear way to measurable

11

phenomena. For instance, one part of social learning theory proposes that an individual's exposure to admired models who are involved in deviant or delinquent behavior will increase the chances that person will imitate those same behaviors. Imitation is defined as one engaging in acts after he or she has watched them being engaged in by others. It is quite possible to directly observe the behavior of adult or peer models whom adolescents are in a position to imitate, or to ask adolescents to report exposure to such models then observe the extent to which their behavior matches that of the models. The concept of imitation refers to observable, measurable events; therefore, propositions about modeling are testable.

Empirical Validity

This is the most important criterion for judging a theory. Empirical validity simply means that a theory has been supported by research evidence. For a theory to be logical, parsimonious, and non-tautological means little if it turns out to be false. It is seldom the case, however, that a theory is found to be entirely true or entirely false. Falsifiable theories may encounter some negative evidence without being judged as wholly invalid. The question is, what degree of empirical support does the theory have? Do the findings of research provide weak or strong support? Does the preponderance of evidence support or undermine the theory? How does its empirical validity compare with that of other theories?

For instance, deterrence theory proposes in part that offenders will not repeat their crimes if they have been caught and given severe legal punishment. If research finds that this is true for only a small minority of offenders or that punished offenders are only slightly less likely to repeat crimes than unpunished offenders, then the theory has some, but not much, empirical validity. Labeling theory, on the other hand, proposes that the experience of being caught and processed by the criminal justice system labels offenders as criminal. Hence, the label promotes their self-identity as criminals and makes them more likely, rather than less likely, to repeat their crimes. If research finds that, other things being equal, apprehended offenders are more likely to recidivate than those who have not been caught, then labeling theory has more empirical validity than deterrence theory.

Empirical Validity and the Concepts of Causality and Determinism

Notice the terms "more likely" and "less likely." Empirical validity does not mean that a theory must identify variables that always cause criminal behavior to occur or always explain the decision to arrest an offender. The traditional concept of causality in science is that cause X must precede and produce effect Y. To be a cause, X must be both a "necessary condition," the absence of which means that Y will not occur, and a "sufficient condition," so that Y always occurs in the presence of X. No criminological theory can meet these two traditional causation criteria of necessary and sufficient conditions. But that makes little difference, since a probabilistic concept of causality is more appropriate for assessing the empirical validity of criminological theories. The probabilistic concept of causation simply asserts that the presence of X renders the occurrence of Y more probable. That is, contemporaneous variations or changes in criminal behavior are associated or correlated with variations or changes in the explanatory variables identified in the theory. The presence of the variables specified in the theory precede the occurrence of crime and delinquency, thereby predicting when they are more likely to occur or reoccur. The stronger the correlations and associations, the greater the theory's empirical validity.

Interpreting correlations as causation even in the probabilistic sense remains a problem, because the direction of the relationship between two correlated variables may not be the same as specified in the theory. For instance, a theory may hypothesize that an adolescent engages in delinquent conduct as a result of associating with other adolescents who are already delinquent. Finding a correlation between one's own delinquent behavior and the delinquency of one's friends, therefore, could be taken as evidence in support of the theory. But the relationship may exist for converse reasons; that is, the adolescent first becomes delinquent and then seeks out delinquent associates. Thus, the association with other delinquents may be the dependent variable, resulting from one's own prior delinquency, rather than the independent variable that increases the probability that the adolescent will commit delinquency. Further research would be needed to find out which direction the relationship typically runs. The probabilistic concept of causality suggests that human behavior is neither completely determined by external forces nor completely an outcome of the unfettered exercise of free will choices. Rather, behavior is best understood from the middle-ground perspective of "soft determinism" (Matza, 1964). Soft determinism recognizes that various factors influence and limit actions but leave room for individual choices that cannot be completely predicted. Increasingly, criminological theorists have come to adopt this view (Gibbons, 1994; Akers, 1998).

> . . . [B]iological, sociocultural, and developmental factors may influence—but not determine—behavior because the systematic processes underlying criminal behavior are complex, dynamic, and self-reinforcing. A key reason for the effective unpredictability of these and similar non-linear systems is their extreme sensitivity to initial conditions. (Vila, 1994:329)

> Numerous theorists, however, have come to advance similar arguments in recent years. Versions of soft determinism or indeterminism are now advocated by control theorists, rational choice theorists, social learning theorists, conflict theorists, and others. . . . [P]eople may transcend previous experience through reflective thought altering their preferences and developing unexpected and sometimes novel strategies for acting on those preferences. (Agnew, 1995a: 83, 88)

$\mathcal{U}$(sefulness and $\mathcal{P}$olicy $\mathcal{I}$mplications

Finally, the value of a criminological theory can be further evaluated by its usefulness in providing guidelines for effective social and criminal justice policy and practice. Every criminological theory implies a therapy or a policy. The basic assumption in theory-guided practice is that the better the theory explains the problem, the better it is able to guide efforts to solve the problem.

All major criminological theories have implications for, and have indeed been utilized in, criminal justice policy and practice. Every therapy, treatment program, prison regimen, police policy, or criminal justice practice is based, either explicitly or implicitly, on some explanation of human nature in general or criminal behavior in particular (Barlow, 1995b; Gibbs, 1995).

Every recommendation for changes in our legal and criminal justice system has been based on some underlying theory that explains why the laws have been enacted, why the system operates as it does, and why those who are in the system behave as they do.

The question, then, is not whether policy can be or should be based on theory—it already is guided by theory—but rather, how well is policy guided by theory and how good is the policy and the theory on which it is predicated? In most public discourse about criminal justice policy, the underlying theoretical notions are ill-stated and vaguely understood. A policy may be adopted for political, economic, or bureaucratic reasons, then a theoretical rationale is formulated or adopted to justify the policy. Typically, the theoretical underpinnings of a program are not a single coherent and tested theory, but rather a hybrid mixture of several, sometimes conflicting, theoretical strands (Wright and Dixon, 1978). This understandably results from the effort to try any number of things to see what works. Utility and effectiveness, not theoretical purity, is the standard in policy and practical application.

Criminological theory has implications not only for official public policy and programs, but also for what can be done informally in families, peer groups, neighborhoods, and communities. From a sociological perspective, this informal control system embedded in everyday life and interaction has more impact on behavior than formal criminal justice policy (Felson, 1998). Of course, there is an interdependence of formal and informal actions and activities to combat crime and delinquency. In either case, the policy should not rest solely on its theoretical or philosophical plausibility or simply conform to common sense. Just as theories must be shown empirically to be valid, policy and practice must be shown empirically to work and produce the outcomes they are intended to have (prevention, control, or reduction of crime and delinquency). They must also meet ethical, legal, and moral standards of fairness, equity, due process, and appropriateness for a democratic society.

A clear, parsimonious, non-tautological, and empirically valid theory has even more to recommend it if it can also guide programs and practices. If a program guided by that theory is instituted and is successful in achieving its goals, we gain additional confidence in the validity of the theory. However, this is an indirect and imprecise way to judge the empirical validity of a theory. The program may be a poor adaptation of the theoretical principles to the actual situation. There may be practical or ethical roadblocks against carrying out the actions that the theory implies are needed to change criminal behavior, reduce recidivism, or make the system operate better. There may be political or economic factors that come into play to enhance or retard the effectiveness of the program that have nothing to do with the validity of the theory. Therefore, the success or failure of policies and programs cannot be used by themselves to test theory.

· · ·

● Summary

Criminological theories are both theories of the making and enforcing of criminal law and theories of breaking the law. The former attempts to explain the content of the laws and the behavior of the criminal justice system; the latter tries to explain the commission, occurrence, and patterns of criminal and deviant behavior. Structural or macro theories focus on differences in group and societal rates of crime, while processual or micro theories address individual differences and social processes. The aim of criminological theory is to gain an understanding of crime and criminal justice. Theories are useful for addressing the issues of which policies are more or else likely to work, but they are not philosophical statements about what ought to be done. A theory may be evaluated, either on its own or by comparison with other theories, on the criteria of clarity and consistency, scope and parsimony, testability, practical usefulness, and empirical validity. Of these, the focus here will be on a theory's empirical validity and on its usefulness for guiding policy and practice.

References

Agnew, Robert. 1995a. "Determinism, indeterminism, and crime: an empirical exploration," Criminology 33:83–110.

Akers, Ronald L. 1968. "Problems in the sociology of deviance: social definitions and behavior," Social Forces 46:455–465.

————. 1985. Deviant Behavior: A Social Learning Approach. Third Edition. Belmont, CA: Wadsworth. Reprinted 1992. Fairfax, VA: Techbooks.

————. 1998. Social Learning and Social Structure: A General Theory of Crime and Deviance. Boston: Northeastern University Press.

Alexander, Jeffrey C., Bernhard Giesen, Richard Munch, and Neil J. Smelser, eds. 1987. The Micro-Macro Link. Berkeley: University of California Press.

Barlow, Hugh. 1995b. "Introduction: public policy and the explanation of crime," pp. 1–14 in Hugh Barlow, ed., Crime and Public Policy: Putting Theory to Work. Boulder, CO: Westview Press.

Barlow, Hugh D. and Theodore N. Ferdinand. 1992. Understanding Delinquency. New York: HarperCollins Publishers.

Budziszewski, J. 1997. Written on the Heart: The Case for National Law. Downers Grove, IL: Intervarsity Press.

Chambliss, William J. 1988. Exploring Criminology. New York: Macmillan Publishing Co.

Cressey, Donald R. 1960. "Epidemiology and individual conduct: a case from criminology," Pacific Sociological Review 3:47–58.

Curran, Daniel J. and Claire M. Renzetti. 1994. Theories of Crime. Boston: Allyn and Bacon.

Felson, Marcus. 1998. Crime and Everyday Life. Second Edition. Thousand Oaks, CA: Pine Forge Press.

Gibbons, Don C. 1979. The Criminological Enterprise: Theories and Perspectives. Englewood Cliffs, NJ: Prentice Hall.

_____. 1994. Talking About Crime and Criminals: Problems and Issues in Theory Development in Criminology. Englewood Cliffs, NJ: Prentice Hall.

Gibbs, Jack P. 1990. "The notion of a theory in sociology," National Journal of Sociology 4:129–158.

_____. 1995. "The notion of control and criminology's policy implications," pp. 71–89 in Hugh Barlow, ed. Crime and Public Policy: Putting Theory to Work. Boulder, CO: Westview Press.

Jensen, Gary F. and Dean G. Rojek. 1998. Delinquency and Youth Crime, Third Edition. Prospect Heights, IL: Waveland Press.

Liska, Allen E. and Steven F. Messner. 1999. Perspectives on Crime and Deviance. Third Edition. Upper Saddle River, NJ: Prentice Hall.

Matza, David. 1964. Delinquency and Drift. New York: Wiley.

Nettler, Gwyn. 1984. Explaining Crime. Third Edition. New York: McGraw Hill.

Orcutt, James D. 1983. Analyzing Deviance. Homewood, IL: Dorsey.

Shoemaker, Donald J. 1990. Theories of Delinquency: An Examination of Explanations of Delinquent Behavior. Second Edition. New York: Oxford University Press.

Stinchcombe, Arthur L. 1968. Constructing Social Theories. New York: Harcourt Brace and World.

Tittle, Charles R. 1995. Control Balance: Towards a General Theory of Deviance. Boulder, CO: Westview Press.

Vila, Bryan. 1994. "A general paradigm for understanding criminal behavior: extending evolutionary ecological theory," Criminology 32:311–360.

Vold, George B., Thomas J. Bernard and Jeffrey B. Snipes. 1998. Theoretical Criminology, Fourth edition. New York: Oxford University Press.

Williams, Franklin P. III and Marilyn D. McShane. 1988. Criminological Theory. Englewood Cliffs, NJ: Prentice Hall.

Wright, William E. and Michael C. Dixon. 1978. "Community prevention and treatment of delinquency," Journal of Research of Crime and Delinquency 14:35–67.

❧ ❧ ❧

Questions

1. According to Akers, what is a theory?

2. What are the two main types of criminological theories?

3. Which type of theory is most common? Why do you think that is?

4. Define the following terms as used in this selection: "logical consistency," "parsimony," "scope," "testability," "empirical validity," and "policy implications."

5. In your opinion, do individuals' own beliefs and values influence their belief in a theory? Explain your thinking.

Genetic Influences in Criminal Convictions

SARNOFF A. MEDNICK, WILLIAM F. GABRIELLI, JR.
AND BARRY HUTCHINGS

In this large-scale study, the authors examined the criminal records of more than 14,000 adults who had been adopted as children. They also examined the records of their adoptive and biological parents. The authors found something interesting: The criminal histories of adoptees significantly correlated with those of their biological parents—but not with the records of their adoptive parents. This finding supports the possibility of a genetic component in criminal behavior.

*T*his study of the role of genetic factors in the etiology of criminal behavior is based on a register of 14,427 nonfamilial adoptions in a small northern European nation between 1927 and 1947. The register was established by a group of American and European investigators (1) and includes information on the adoptee and his or her adoptive and biological parents.

Court convictions were used as an index of criminal involvement. The data exclude minors below the age of 15, who are exempt from court convictions. Court records were obtained for all persons for whom data and place of birth were available (N = 65,516). The subjects' occupations permitted the coding of socioeconomic status (2).

Cases were excluded from the study if there was no record of place or date of birth, if the identity of the biological father could not be established, if the adoption was by a single woman, or if the birth date was prior to 1 January 1895. Exclusion of an adoptee resulted in exclusion of the entire adoptive family but, if a parent was excluded, the remaining subjects were retained for analysis. Data on individuals not fully identified are shown in Table 1.

"Genetic Influences in Criminal Convictions," by Sarnoff A. Mednick, William F. Gabrielli, Jr., and Barry Hutchings, reprinted from *Science*, vol. 224, no. 4651, 1984, pp. 891–894.

TABLE 1 *Conviction rates of completely identified members of adoptee families*

Family member	Number identified	Number not identified	Conviction rate by number of convictions			
			0	1	2	> 2
Male adoptees	6,129	571	0.841	0.088	0.029	0.049
Female adoptees	7,065	662	0.972	0.020	0.005	0.003
Adoptive fathers	13,918	509	0.938	0.046	0.008	0.008
Adoptive mothers	14,267	160	0.981	0.015	0.002	0.002
Biological fathers	10,604	3,823	0.714	0.129	0.056	0.102
Biological mothers	12,300	2,127	0.911	0.064	0.012	0.013

Conviction rates of completely identified members of the adoptee families are also shown in Table 1. Rates for biological fathers and male adoptees are considerably higher than those of adoptive fathers. The adoptive father rate (8 percent) is a bit below that of the population average for men of the same age range and time period (3). Most of the adoptive fathers convicted of criminal activity were one-time offenders, while male adoptees and their biological fathers were more heavily recidivistic.

Conviction rates of the women in the three categories are lower than those of the men but follow the same pattern. Adoptive mothers are just below the population average for women of this age range and time period (2.2 percent) with respect to rate of conviction (4).

In most of the analyses that follow, the relation between parent and adoptee court convictions will be considered. If either mother or father (biological or adoptive) had a court conviction, the parents for that adoptee will be considered criminal. In view of the low number of convictions among female adoptees, analyses will concentrate on male adoptees.

The size of the population permits segregation of subgroups of adoptees with combinations of convicted and nonconvicted biological and adoptive parents in a design analogous to the cross-fostering model used in behavior genetics. If neither the biological nor the adoptive parents are convicted, 13.5 percent of the sons are convicted. If the adoptive parents are convicted and the biological parents are not, this figure rises only to 14.7 percent. However, if the adoptive parents are not convicted and the biological parents are, 20.0 percent of the sons are convicted. If the adoptive parents as well as the biological parents are convicted, 24.5 percent of the sons are convicted. These data favor the assumption of a partial genetic etiology.

20

However, simply knowing that an adoptive parent has been convicted of a crime does not reveal how criminogenic the adoptee's environment has been (5). At conception, the genetic influence of the biological father is complete. This is not a fair comparison between environmental and genetic influences but indicates only that sons whose biological parents have court convictions for criminal offenses have an increased probability of becoming convicted. Adoptive parent criminality was not found to be associated with a statistically significant increment in the son's criminality, but the effect of biological parent criminality was. A log-linear model, when only the additive effects of the biological parents and the adoptive parents is considered, shows that these two factors leave almost no room for improvement of the model fit by interaction effect.

The relation between criminal law convictions in the sons and degree of recidivism in the biological parents (6) is positive and relatively monotonic (Fig 1). A log-linear analysis shows a statistically significant relation for property crimes but not violent crimes. The chronic offender is infrequent but commits a markedly disproportionate number of crimes. This high rate of offending suggested the hypothesis that genetic predisposition plays a substantial role in these cases.

FIGURE 1 *Percentage of adoptees convicted of violent and property offenses as a function of biological parents' convictions (6)*

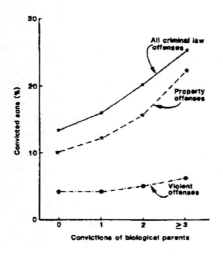

In one U.S. birth cohort study (7), the chronic offender was defined as one who had been arrested five or more times; these chronic offenders, who consist of 6 percent of the males, had committed 52 percent of the offenses. In our adoption cohort we recorded court convictions rather than arrest data. If we select as chronic offenders those with three or more court convictions, they were 4.09 percent of the male adoptees. This small group of recidivists accounts for 69.4 percent of all court convictions for all the male adoptees, a high concentration of crime in a small fraction of the cohort.

Table 2 shows how chronic offenders, other offenders (one or two convictions), and nonoffenders are distributed as a function of amount of crime in the biological parents. The proportion of chronic adoptee offenders increases as a function of recidivism in the biological parents. Note, however, that a genetic influence is not sufficient to produce criminal convictions in the adoptee. Of those adoptees whose biological parents have three or more convictions, 75 percent never received a court conviction. Another way of expressing this concentration of crime is that the chronic male adoptee offenders with biological parents having three or more offenses number only 37. They make up 1 percent of the 3,718 male adoptees in Table 2 but are responsible for 30 percent of the male adoptee convictions. The mean number of convictions for the chronic adoptee increases sharply as a function of biological parent recidivism.

There are instances where a biological mother, a biological father, or both contributed more than one child to this population. Some of these children, who were full or half-siblings, were placed in different adoptive

TABLE 2 *Proportion of chronic offenders (3 convictions), other offenders (1 or 2 convictions), and nonoffenders in male adoptees as a function of number of convictions in the biological parents. Cases in which adoptive parents have been convicted of criminal law violations are excluded.*

Male adoptee convictions	Biological parent convictions			
	0	1	2	≥ 3
None	0.87	0.84	0.80	0.75
1 or 2	0.10	0.12	0.15	0.17
> 3	0.03	0.04	0.05	0.09
Number of adoptees	2492	574	233	419

22

homes. The probability of any one male adoptee's being convicted is 0.159; the probability of at least one of a pair of unrelated, separated male adoptees' being convicted is 0.293. The probability of both of a pair's being convicted is 0.025. Thus the concordance rate for pairs of unrelated, separated male adoptees is 8.5 percent. This can be viewed as a baseline.

There were 126 male-male half-sibling pairs placed in separate adoptive homes. Of these, 31 pairs had at least one member of the sibship convicted, and of these 31 pairs, 4 pairs were concordant for convictions—a concordance rate for half-siblings of 12.9 percent. There were 40 male-male full sibling pairs placed in different adoptive homes. Of these, 15 pairs had at least one member of the sibship convicted; of these 15 pairs, 3 pairs were concordant for convictions—a concordance rate for full siblings of 20 percent. The numbers are small but indicate that as the degree of genetic relationship increases, the level of concordance increases.

Of 98 biological fathers with at least one pair of male-male separated adoptee children, 45 had received at least one court conviction (8). Of the 45 sibling pairs (half and full sibs) contributed by these fathers, 13 pairs had at least one member with a court conviction; of these 13 pairs, 4 pairs were concordant for convictions—a concordance rate of 30.8 percent (9). The results suggest that a number of these separated adoptee siblings inherited some characteristic that made both vulnerable to criminal behavior. In those instances in which the biological father is criminal, the effect is enhanced.

Convictions of females for criminal law violations are infrequent (Table 1). Perhaps women whose criminal behavior prompts a court conviction have a predisposition for such behavior. Criminal involvement in many men, on the other hand, may be more socially or environmentally induced. It is possible, therefore, that criminal behavior in the biological mother will be more closely related to the adoptees' convictions than criminal behavior in the biological father.

In all our analyses, the relation between biological mother conviction and adoptee conviction is significantly stronger than that between biological father and adoptee convictions. In comparison to the biological fathers, crime in the biological mothers is more closely related to crime in the daughters. This result is statistically significant, but in view of the relatively low frequency of female convictions, the findings must be interpreted with caution.

We have previously reported (10) the variance ascribable to "genetic" social class and "rearing" social class, examining adoptee crime as a joint function of biological parents' social class and adoptive parents' social class. Male adoptee crime varied as a function of both genetic and environmental social class; log-linear analyses revealed both effects to be statistically significant. Our finding that environmental aspects of social class life influence the relation between social class and crime suggests that regardless of genetic background, improved social conditions are likely to lead to reductions in criminal behavior.

There is also a correlation between adoptive parent socioeconomic status (SES) and biological parent SES, representing an attempt by the adoption agency to match certain characteristics of the two sets of parents. However, the relation between biological parent and adoptee criminal convictions exists at each level of adoptive parent SES. Stepwise multiple regression analyses, which varied the order of entry of biological parent convictions and SES and adoptive parent convictions and SES, indicate that independent of SES, biological parent criminality is significantly related to adoptee criminality.

Before generalizations can be made, biases introduced by loss of subjects in specific analyses should be considered (Table 1). In addition, the transfer history of the adoptees, as well as the possible effects of labeling of adoptee children of convicted biological parents, should be considered.

First, our consideration of characteristics of those not fully identified suggests that their inclusion would not have altered the nature of the results presented here. Perhaps the most critical facts in this judgment are that the adopted-away sons of parents not fully identified have levels of criminal law convictions and rearing social status that are approximately the same as for the sons of those parents fully identified. The observed differences are small; it is difficult to formulate any manner in which the lost subjects might have had an impact on the findings reported.

Second, among the adoptees, 25.3 percent were placed immediately in an adoptive home; the remainder were placed in orphanages. Of those placed in orphanages, 50.6 percent were placed with an adoptive family in the first year, 12.8 percent in the second year, and 11.3 percent after the age of 2. Analyses showed that age of transfer did not interact with genetic influence so as to alter significantly the relation observed with the full population (11).

Third, prospective adoptive parents were routinely informed about criminal convictions of biological parents. This information could result in the labeling of the adoptee and affect the likelihood that the adoptee would commit criminal acts. Of the convicted biological parents, 37 percent had their first conviction before the adoption; thus the adoptive parents were likely to be informed of the conviction. In 63 percent of the cases, the first conviction of the biological parent occurred after the adoption; in these cases the criminality information was not transmitted to the adoptive parents. In cases in which the biological parent was first convicted before adoption, 15.6 percent of the male adoptees received convictions. In cases in which the biological parent was first convicted after the adoption, 16.1 percent of the male adoptees received convictions. The conviction rate of female adoptees was 4 percent in each group. A similar result was obtained by studying the effect of timing of the initial arrest of the biological father (12). The fact that the adoptive parents were informed of the biological parents' criminality did not alter the likelihood that the adoptive son would be convicted of a crime.

In summary, in a population of adoptions a relation was found between biological parent criminal convictions and criminal convictions in their adoptee children. No evidence was found that type of crime of biological parents was related to type of adoptee crime. A number of potentially confounding variables were considered; none proved sufficient to explain the genetic relation. We conclude that some factor transmitted by criminal parents increases the likelihood that their children will engage in criminal behavior. This claim holds especially for chronic criminality. The findings imply that biological predispositions are involved in the etiology of at least some criminal behavior.

References and Notes

[1] S. S. Kety, D. Rosenthal, P. H. Wender, F. Schulsinger in *The Transmission of Schizophrenia*, D. Rosenthal and S. S. Kety, Eds. (Pergamon, Oxford, 1978), p. 345. At the request of relevant agencies, the country has not been named.

[2] K. Svalasto a, *Prestige, Class and Mobility*, (Gyldendal, Copenhagen, Denmark, 1959).

[3] S. Hurwitz and K. O. Christiansen, *Kriminologi* (Gyldendal, Copenhagen, Denmark, 1971).

[4] P. Wolf, *Br. J. Criminol.* 13, 5 (1962).

[5] Recall the preponderance of one-time offenders in the adoptive parents. It was a condition of adoption that the adoptive parents not have a conviction for the 5 years preceding the adoption.

[6]Only cases in which neither adoptive parent is convicted were included. In view of the low frequencies of court convictions and recidivism among the adoptive parents and in order to simplify interpretation, analyses include only cases in which adoptive parents have no criminal law convictions.

[7]M. E. Wolfgang, R. J. Figlio, T. Sellin, *Delinquency in a Birth Cohort* (Univ. of Chicago Press, Chicago, 1972), p. 88.

[8]It should be noted that this is a significantly higher rate of convictions (45.9 percent) than the conviction rate (28.6 percent) for the total population of biological fathers ($X^2(1) = 14.6$, $P < 0.01$).

[9]For a full report on how these siblings were identified, see T. Teasdale and D. Owen, *Behav. Genet.* 11, 577 (1981).

[10]K. Van Dusen *et al., J. Crim. Law Criminol.* 74, 249 (1983).

[11]Among males, there was a statistically significant association between adoptee criminality and amount of time spent in the orphanage waiting for adoption. This effect, which was not true for females, may be due to institutionalization. Or it may be a function of selection bias ("less desirable" boys adopted later and also being convicted).

[12]B. Hutchings and S. A. Mednick, in *Biosocial Bases of Criminal Behavior*, S. A. Mednick and K. O. Christiansen, Eds. (Gardner, New York, 1977), p. 127.

[13]Supported by PHS grant 31353 from the Center for Studies of Crime and Delinquency and by a fellowship from the Netherlands Pure Science Foundation to S.A.M.

● ● ●

Questions

1. What percentage of the adoptees in this study had criminal convictions?

2. Why did the adoptive parents in the study have fewer criminal convictions than the biological parents?

3. Why do you think the criminal records of adoptees correlated with those of their biological parents in terms of property crimes but not violent crimes?

4. How else might the findings of this paper be interpreted? For example, how could the findings result from early environmental rather than genetic factors?

A Murder "Wave"? Trends in American Serial Homicide

PHILIP JENKINS

Since the 1960s, police and media in the United States have reported a substantial increase in the number of serial murders. But have serial murders actually worsened, or is it only awareness of them that has increased? In this article, Philip Jenkins addresses this question by examining serial murder rates over a 50-year period. His study illustrates the all-too-common difficulty of accurately measuring crime and its change over time.

*J*t is widely agreed that the frequency of serial murder in the contemporary United States is very high in comparison with similar societies, and probably in relation to most historical periods as well (Egger, 1990; Jenkins, 1988; Levin & Fox, 1985; Lindsey, 1984; Newton, 1990). It is common to write of an American "wave" of serial murder that began in the late 1960s. Murder sprees and serial homicide careers were by no means new in the 1960s, but events of this sort seemed to begin occurring with greater frequency and severity, establishing a macabre trend that continues unabated. Holmes and DeBurger (1988) have suggested a surge in "multicide" dating from about 1960. Norris (1988) comments, "Since 1960 not only have the number of individual serial killers increased but so have the number of victims per killer, and the level of savagery of the individual crimes themselves" (p. 19). Leyton (1986) suggests that reported acts of multiple homicide in the United States were 10 or 12 times more frequent after the 1960s than before. On a related topic, Fox has remarked that 1966 marked "the onset of the age of mass murder" (quoted in "Experts Say," 1988, p. A3).

"A Murder 'Wave'? Trends in American Serial Homicide," by Philip Jenkins, reprinted from *Criminal Justice Review*, vol. 17, no. 1, 1992, pp. 1–19.

27

However widespread it may be, perceptions of an "epidemic" leave a number of unanswered questions about the reality of the phenomenon and its causation. First, recent conditions are not without parallel in American history; in an earlier study, it was suggested that serial homicide little below the present scale and frequency did in fact occur in the United States in the early twentieth century, between about 1900 and 1940 (Jenkins, 1989). On the other hand, repeat homicide appears to have become much rarer between about 1940 and 1965. This is a matter of some importance for our understanding of recent developments. If the frequency of serial murder activity fell in midcentury and then increased sharply during the 1960s, this suggests that this type of crime is connected to wider social conditions that require explanation. We might explore factors that affect the prevalence of extremely violent behavior, the nature of criminal justice responses, or the availability of a victim population. Alternatively, we might hypothesize that apparent changes in multiple homicide merely reflect fashions in recording or reporting rather than substantive changes in behavior; the increase of reported cases from the late 1960s onwards would thus reflect new perceptions by the police or the mass media, and the "wave" might be a myth or an artificial construct.

Whichever approach proves more accurate, the historical study of serial murder offers significant theoretical lessons. It is particularly useful for examining the constructionist approach in sociology, which stresses that social problems are rarely as novel as they sometimes appear (Best, 1989, 1990). In this view, behaviors such as the use of violence against children or the elderly are endemic in society, but they ultimately come to be perceived and defined as new problems with names such as "child abuse" and "elder abuse." The task of the sociologist is to determine the social, political, and bureaucratic forces that lead to this new recognition and definition and to identify the claims-makers who shape the debate. A constructionist approach would favor the view that serial murder activity remained high throughout the century but that the phenomenon was only recognized (or rediscovered) in the mid-1960s. If indeed these years marked a real and significant increase of the behavior itself, this would provide an important exception to the constructionist model.

If there was a real and sudden growth in multiple homicide after 1960, then explaining it offers a challenge for sociologists and criminologists, and it is disappointing that so few of the current accounts have attempted a systematic explanation. One notable exception is that of Leyton (1986), who presents an ambitious chapter entitled "Towards an Historical Sociology of Multiple Murder." Leyton accepts the idea of a surge, which is attributed to the changing life opportunities of certain social groups and classes. The growing closure of avenues of opportunity in the 1960s led some to frustration and to consequent outbursts of violent protest, of which multiple murder was one dramatic manifestation. The theory may or may not have substance, but at least it attempts to place the observed phenomenon in a context of known social theory. It also marks a vital shift away from the largely individualistic and psychodynamic explanations that have long dominated the analysis of multiple homicide. An authentic increase in serial murder in the 1960s would have significance for policy makers no less than academics. Understanding the social context of offenders such as Ted Bundy or John Wayne Gacy might provide an opportunity for intervention, with the goal of removing or reducing the factors that promote this sort of crime.

These questions can only be answered by tracing the frequency of serial murder in the United States over a lengthy period before and after the apparent upsurge in offenses in the mid-1960s. Obviously there are major methodological difficulties in such an endeavor, and a comprehensive history would be impossible. However, it will be argued that the resources do exist for an admittedly tentative account that favors the objectivist approach to this problem. It will be argued that serial homicide was indeed rare in midcentury and has become much more frequent in recent years. This change will be explained chiefly in terms of the weakening of social control mechanisms from the mid-1960s onwards.

◉ Methodology

The most important stage of this research involved compiling a list of all serial murder cases recorded in the United States between 1940 and 1990. Each case involved an offender associated with the killing of at least four victims over a period greater than 72 hours. Excluded were cases in which the offender acted primarily out of political motives or in quest of financial profit. Organized and professional criminal activity was thus excluded, although this limitation would not be accepted by all researchers. Of course, the list cannot include cases that did not come to the attention of law enforcement or in which neither the police nor the media recognized a linkage in a series of homicides. Also, the exact number of cases in a particular series is a highly controversial subject.

The issue of "association" poses a large and probably insurmountable problem. It is rare for any serial killer to be formally charged and convicted in all the cases in which he or she is a strong suspect, and we thus have to rely on much less certain evidentiary criteria to assess the real number of victims. In one well-known case, Ted Bundy was executed in 1989 for a murder committed in Florida, and the same state had tried and sentenced him for only two other homicides, but it has been suggested that Bundy was guilty of anywhere from 25 to 100 other murders across the United States. In the present study, an individual was included if law enforcement and mainstream media sources consistently reported that the offender was believed to be implicated in four or more deaths. Clearly this evidence is far from satisfactory, especially where it is based on confessions. Confessions might be a major source in some cases, but there are many factors that could lead a suspect to portray his or her criminal activity as either more or less serious than it truly was. It is also likely that media and police estimates are sometimes exaggerated or simply wrong, but such a reputational approach is perhaps the only means of proceeding in such a contentious area.

Cases were compiled from three major sources. The first involved three well-indexed and authoritative newspapers, the *New York Times, Los Angeles Times*, and *Chicago Tribune*. This material was supplemented from a variety of secondary sources on serial murder (Brian, 1986; Gaute & Odell, 1979; Wilson & Pitman, 1984; Wilson & Seaman, 1983), which have been fully listed in two earlier articles (Jenkins, 1988, 1989). Finally, a number of references were acquired from Michael Newton's recent "encyclopaedia" of serial murder, *Hunting Humans* (1990; compare Newton, 1988), an important source that requires discussion. Unfortunately, the book lacks a scholarly apparatus, and sources are cited only very generally, but the author's use of those sources is cautious and scholarly.

Hunting Humans is by far the most comprehensive available listing of serial murder cases, incorporating the vast majority of references that were found in the search of media and secondary sources. In fact, one of the major criticisms that can be levied against the book is that it is overcomprehensive, including many cases with only two or three reported victims. Although there are omissions—including some spectacular cases such as that of Stephen Nash—Newton has provided an excellent basis for the analysis of trends in American serial murder. (Less confidence can be placed in the book's reliability for other nations.) Combined with the evidence of newspapers and secondary sources, Newton's work permits the compilation of a thorough list of the reported serial murder cases of the last half-century.

● Changes in Reporting Practice

It thus becomes crucial to ask whether the rate of reporting was fairly constant over time. If a study of media sources in the 1940s or 1950s produces far fewer cases than can be found in the 1980s, can it be safely assumed that this reflects a change in the frequency of the offense, or might it simply reflect changes in the practices and interests of the mass media? There is some evidence that metropolitan papers such as the *New York Times* and *Los Angeles Times* did expand their coverage of regional news from the 1950s onwards. This arose not from changes in the marketing or journalistic practices of those particular papers but from wider changes in the newspaper industry as a whole.[1]

From the 1950s, local newspapers were increasingly likely to form part of large chains or corporate groupings, and those chains themselves grew from statewide or regional concerns to national status. About 29 percent of American newspapers were owned by chains in 1960, compared to 63 percent in 1988 (Gaziano, 1989). In the same period, the proportion of chains that were national in scope rose from 11 percent to 33 percent. One consequence of this was that stories that were of any sensational value were less likely to be confined to a purely local market and more likely to be disseminated throughout the chain. Stories would thus reach a national audience and would be picked up (or at least referred to) by other major journals such as the *New York Times*. As the trend towards chain ownership was most marked in the late 1960s, it is possible that the increased reporting of serial murder might, in part, reflect a growing "nationalization" of news.

On the other hand, this would not in itself be a sufficient explanation for any perceived changes. Throughout the century, major serial murder cases have usually been viewed as stories of great journalistic interest, and between about 1900 and 1940 the *New York Times* reported extensively and enthusiastically on serial murder cases as far afield as Colorado, Iowa, Alaska, and South Dakota. There is no reason to believe that media practices or public taste changed suddenly during the 1940s. Even so, the danger of overlooking cases prior to the 1960s is reduced by using Newton's *Hunting Humans*, which draws on regional and local newspaper files from no fewer than 25 states: papers such as the *Eagle-Beacon* of Wichita, Kansas; the *Daily News* of Anchorage, Alaska; and the *Clarion-Ledger* of Jackson, Mississippi. Even a search as wide as this apparently failed to find a large number of midcentury cases that escaped the attention of the major metropolitan press.

Also, newspapers, magazines, and books in midcentury all devoted abundant attention to spectacular crimes such as multiple homicide when they did occur, and this suggests that public interest remained high throughout the period. Magazines on the lines of *True Crime* and *True Detective* were popular. Moreover, cases that might seem comparatively minor or commonplace today would have received enormous attention in terms of column inches in the newspapers or in numbers of published books. Some of the most celebrated and widely discussed cases of these years involved three or four victims, as with Harvey Glatman, William Heirens, and Charles Howard Schmid, whereas modern studies tend to focus on extreme serial cases that claim 10 or 20 casualties. The suggestion is that, if more cases had occurred in earlier years, they would have been reported at length. If a case like that of Ted Bundy had occurred in, say, the early 1950s, it is hard to believe that its sensationalistic potential would have been overlooked.

It might also be suggested that cases were as likely to be reported in midcentury but that police agencies interpreted crimes differently before announcing their conclusions to the media. One possible hypothesis would be that a police agency arresting a suspect in the late 1940s might be slow to investigate his involvement in a series of crimes over many years in a number of states, whereas the agency's modern counterparts would be more familiar with patterns of serial homicide and would thus tend to speculate with greater freedom. Modern agencies also have superior recordkeeping techniques and more experience of interagency cooperation, enhancing the likelihood that a suspect could be linked to a large number of earlier offenses.

This view is superficially attractive, but the contrast with earlier eras is too sharply drawn. Between 1900 and 1940, American police agencies often demonstrated their familiarity with the concept of serial murder and pursued investigations accordingly, so that such offenders were frequently detected and apprehended. Investigators traced the earlier movements of suspects and attempted to link them with crimes in other jurisdictions as a matter of course. There is no evidence that police agencies at midcentury were any less aware of these issues and problems, especially in the aftermath of widely publicized affairs such as the Cleveland torso murders of the

1930s (Nickel, 1989). In 1941, police from several states interrogated the newly arrested multiple murderer Jarvis Catoe in an attempt to link him with crimes in their jurisdictions (Newton, 1990). Moreover, the attention that focused on the "sex maniac" in the 1950s ensured that police and media were continually aware of the possibility that a sexually motivated attack might well be one of a lengthy series.

The reported cases analyzed below can only represent a portion of the real total, but apparent changes over time do not simply reflect differences in police or media reactions to homicide. A significant growth in the number of reported incidents is likely to reflect a real change in the frequency of the behavior itself.

❂ The Frequency of Serial Homicide 1940–1990

On first impressions, it seems that serial murder in the 1940s and 1950s followed patterns that are quite familiar from more recent years. The actions of a multiple homicide such as Melvin D. Rees, for example, closely resemble those of sex-killers of the 1980s, especially those who operated on or near college campuses. Rees raped and killed a Maryland woman in 1957 and massacred a family of four in Virginia in 1959. He was also believed to have carried out four other "sex-slayings" near the University of Maryland. Equally "modern" in character was the case of Jake Bird, a drifter who killed two women in Washington state in 1947. When arrested, Bird confessed to more than 40 homicides in the previous decade, with confirmed offenses recorded in Illinois, Kentucky, Nebraska, South Dakota, Ohio, Florida, and Wisconsin. The reconstruction of his travels and crimes bears obvious resemblances to the investigations of more recent itinerant killers such as Henry Lee Lucas and Gerald Stano, and Stephen Nash of California resembles homosexual killers of later years.

And yet these resemblances can be misleading. There were serial killers of this sort, but they were far fewer than in more recent years. Between 1940 and 1969, there were a maximum of 49 serial murder cases recorded in the United States, and the real number might be smaller. Between 1970 and 1990, there was an absolute minimum of 187. An acceleration of activity is therefore indicated, and the change can be dated with some precision. The figures can be broken down into three periods: the age of very low serial murder rates between 1940 and 1964; a transitional period between 1965 and 1969; and the "murder wave" since 1970.

For the era between 1940 and 1964, Newton cites about 50 American cases of serial murder. This total is substantially reduced when cases with fewer than four victims are excluded. Several of the remainder should also be dismissed because of the clear profit motive underlying the offenses, which brings the crimes into the realm of organized fraud or professional criminal activity; examples include the cases of Alfred Cline, Louise Peete, Martha Beck, and Raymond Fernandez, as well as the medical rackets of Roland E. Clark.

According to these criteria, there remain about 30 cases for the whole 25-year period (see Table 1). Of that total, 7 are believed to be "extreme" cases involving eight or more victims. (These offenders were Jake Bird, Albert DeSalvo, Jarvis Catoe, Nannie Doss, Stephen Nash, Melvin Rees, and Charlie Starkweather.) This is assuredly not a comprehensive list of cases, even of those cases that came to the notice of the media or the authorities, but the sources consulted would have recorded any case that attained even limited or short-lived notoriety. The list of extreme cases is more likely to be valid, as these phenomena were especially likely to draw regional or national attention.

This is not a large number of incidents for a 25-year period, and a list of even this length can be achieved only by bending the criteria somewhat. It is by no means certain that Ed Gein killed as many as four people, although some sources have estimated far higher figures, and Gary Krist's inclusion here is particularly tenuous. Several of the cases also involved at least partial motives of profit and property crime and thus might be excluded. In terms of motivation, these 30 cases can be classified according to the following typologies:

1. *Lust murders,* that is, murders clearly associated with rape, sexual abuse, or perversion: 11 cases (Catoe, DeSalvo, Edwards, Floyd, Gein, Hill, the Illinois child murders, the "Moonlight Murderer," Morse, Nash, Rees).

2. *Irrational or "berserk" murders,* where one or more individuals embark on a killing spree without apparent motive. Property crime might be tangentially involved, but the violence used is wholly disproportionate to the encounter: 9 cases (Bird, Cook, Delage, Krist, McManus, Searl, the "Sidney Sniper," Starkweather, York and Latham).

TABLE 1 *Serial Murder Cases 1940–1964*

Name	Dates active
Clarence Hill	1938–1941
Jarvis Catoe	1939–1941
Nannie Doss	1920s–1954
Jake Bird	1942–1947
Charles Floyd	1942–1949
James Waybern Hall	1945
Monroe Hickson	1946
the "Moonlight Murderer"	1946
Kenneth Dudley and Irene Gwyn	1946–1961
Rhonda B. Martin	1940s–1950s
William Dale Archerd	1947–1966
William Cook	1950–1951
Joseph Taborsky and Arthur Culombe	1951–1956
Frederick E. McManus	1953
Mack Ray Edwards	1953–1970
Anjette Donovan Lyles	1950s
Ed Gein	1954–1957
the Illinois child murders	1955–1957
Melvin D. Rees	1956–1959
Stephen Nash	1950s
Charlie Starkweather and Caril Ann Fugate	1958
George York and James Latham	1959
Hugh Bion Morse	1959
Dennis Whitney	1960
Richard Delage	1960–1975
Charles N. Brown and Charles E. Kelly	1961
Gary S. Krist	1961–1964
Albert DeSalvo	1962–1964
the "Sidney Sniper"	early 1960s
Ralph Ray Searl	1964

3. Murders predominantly associated with *property crimes* such as robbery and burglary: 5 cases (Brown and Kelly, Hall, Hickson, Taborsky, Whitney).

4. *Poison murders,* committed at least partly for financial motive: 4 cases (Archerd, Doss, Lyles, Martin).

5. *Other cases:* 1. (From this group, the Dudley and Gwyn case defies classification. This involved a couple killing six of their children over a prolonged period by a combination of abuse, violence, and conscious neglect.)

These categories cannot be regarded as hard and fast, and other observers might find little to distinguish between the cases in groups 2 and 3. On the other hand, this confirms once again that serial murder as such was uncommon in these years, and "pure" serial murder—lust murder or "berserk" and irrational crime—was especially rare. The limited number of cases makes it extremely difficult to discuss multiple homicide rates, except to say that this type of offense represented a tiny fraction of all murders. The relative lack of cases in midcentury contrasts dramatically with the experience of more recent years. Between 1970 and 1990, there was a minimum of 187 cases, 94 of which were "extreme" in the sense of involving eight or more victims. This number could easily be expanded by including other cases with strong links to robbery or professional crime.

In summary, between 1940 and 1964 a serial murder case was recorded every 10 months or so on average, and an "extreme" case every 43 months. Between 1971 and 1990 a serial case could be expected to emerge in the media every 39 days, and an extreme case every 77 days. By this coarse measure, serial murder cases overall can be seen to have been 8 times as likely in the later period as in the earlier, and extreme cases were reported more than 16 times as frequently. The conclusion seems inescapable: Serial murder has become far more frequent in recent years, and offenders tend to kill larger numbers of victims.

● Serial Homicide in the Literature

The relative scarcity of serial murder in midcentury is confirmed by an examination of the contemporary literature on homicide and violent crime. The dominant intellectual trend of this period within criminology was psychiatric and psychoanalytic, and there was considerable interest in the life histories of strange or bizarre offenders who might illustrate unusual aspects of the human mind (Cassity, 1941; Catton, 1940). In addition, public concern about sex offenders and "sex psychopaths" led to widespread legislative action. In 1955, Tappan suggested that in popular mythology "tens of thousands of homicidal sex fiends stalk the land" (quoted in Cohen, 1980, p. 669). Collections of case studies were published by highly reputable scholars who devoted great attention to psychopathy (Abrahamsen, 1944; Bromberg, 1948; Karpman, 1954). There were numerous accounts of serial homicide and lust murder, and the important distinction between "mass" and "series" murder was beginning to enter the literature (Banay, 1956; Galvin & MacDonald, 1959; MacDonald, 1961).

Many offenders were described, but the overwhelming majority were drawn from countries other than the United States. The classic case studies were mainly of German murderers of the 1920s and 1930s, such as Fritz Haarman, Karl Denke, and Peter Kürten, each of whom claimed 10 or 20 victims in circumstances of extreme brutality and sexual perversion (MacDonald, 1961; Von Hentig, 1948; Wertham, 1949). A similar emphasis on European cases is also to be found in the sensationalistic literature, which recounted gruesome homicide cases in prurient terms (Masters & Lea, 1963). When the Cleveland torso murders became notorious, the affair was seized on by Nazi propagandists anxious to show that the Western nations also had crimes like those that had become so firmly linked to German cities like Hanover and Berlin (Nickel, 1989).

Modern accounts of multiple homicide would probably draw all their examples from American cases, but domestic examples did not then exist in anything like comparable numbers. In a sentence that today seems quite remarkable, Bromberg could write in 1948 that "the paucity of lust-murders in modern criminologic experience makes an analysis of the basic psychopathology difficult" (p. 146). There were "few actual cases" to compare with "Jack the Ripper or other legendary sex-fiends," and the author had to return to 1913 to find an American parallel (compare Karpman, 1954; Neustatter, 1957; and Wertham, 1966).

This is not to suggest that no American cases attracted interest, but the same small group of incidents was described repeatedly. Albert Fish occupied a central place in the literature for many years after his execution in 1936, due in large part to the detailed analysis of the case published by Fredric Wertham in 1949. Kittrie (1971) has suggested that it was this case in particular that helped to form the public perception of the sex offender as a multiple child killer (compare Schechter, 1990). In later years, Ed Gein, Charlie Starkweather, and Albert DeSalvo all earned a like celebrity, and a spate of books and articles began to stimulate renewed interest in multiple homicide (Allen, 1976; Chapman, 1982; DeFord, 1965; Frank, 1967;

37

Galvin & MacDonald, 1959; Gollmar, 1981; MacDonald, 1961; Menninger, 1968; Reinhardt, 1960). The most comprehensive study of specifically American offenders was that of Reinhardt (1962), who described Starkweather, Melvin Rees, Dudley and Gwyn, Brown and Kelly, and Nannie Doss. In addition, writers on extreme violence often referred to the cases of William Heirens and Caryl Chessman, neither of whom falls within our definition (Chessman, 1960; Freeman, 1955; Kennedy, Hoffman, & Haines, 1947).

One remarkable point about such a list is that it omits some of the most spectacular killers, who bore the closest resemblance to the "classic" German cases. One searches in vain for extensive discussion of Jarvis Catoe, Jake Bird, or Clarence Hill, and this lacuna may suggest a political element in the selection of case studies. All three men were black, and in the context of these years it might well have been thought inappropriate or tasteless to focus on their acts. If unduly publicized, these events could have given ammunition to racists and segregationists anxious to justify their opinions about black violence and criminality. Whatever the reason, the consequence was to limit the range of cases available to contemporary criminologists.

The lack of concern about serial murder as a major American problem can be illustrated in a number of ways, but one of the most striking involves the numerous official reports and investigations published in the 1960s on the topics of violence and criminality. In the aftermath of political assassinations and racial disturbances, and against a background of rising crime rates, it became common to express concern about the prevalence of violence in the United States. There were several major investigations into different aspects of the perceived crisis, the most comprehensive undertaken by the National Commission on the Causes and Prevention of Violence from 1968 to 1969, which examined many aspects of violence, political and otherwise, but discussion of mass and serial homicide was conspicuous by its near absence. Some cases were mentioned in the context of different theories of the causation of crime, but the subject of multiple homicide occupied nothing like the role that it might be expected to play in a contemporary discussion. It is not even mentioned in the commission's influential final report (U.S. Government, 1969–1970; see especially volumes 11–13).

● The Evidence of Popular Culture

Also suggestive here is the relative absence of multiple homicide as a theme in American popular culture in midcentury. The celebrated serial cases of the 1920s were recalled in early 1940s films like *Stranger on the Third Floor* and even *Arsenic and Old Lace,* but later treatments rarely referred to contemporary cases (McCarty, 1986). *The Sniper* (1952) was one powerful exception that appeared in the next decade. It addressed the topic of serial murder with a sophisticated and sympathetic awareness of contemporary psychoanalytic and criminological theories, but the main real-life example chosen to illustrate the phenomenon, after so many years, was still Albert Fish. The compulsive nature of the "sniper's" violence also bears an explicit resemblance to the Heirens case, which formed the basis of *While the City Sleeps* (1956).

Only in the 1960s did real-life events once more attract attention, with films based on the careers of Ed Gein (*Psycho*, 1960), Albert DeSalvo (*The Strangler,* 1964, and *The Boston Strangler,* 1968), and Charlie Starkweather (*Badlands,* 1973); *Dirty Harry* (1971) freely synthesized the stories of Gary Krist and "Zodiac." Authentic incidents of mass murder similarly inspired *In Cold Blood* (1967) and *Targets* (1968). The resurgence of interest in multiple homicide was fueled by the steadily increasing reports of actual cases, and "Ripper" or "mad slasher" films have been a profitable, if controversial, genre during the last two decades. The recent vogue provides a dramatic contrast to the apparent absence of notable American cases in the 1940s and 1950s.

● The Years of Transition: 1965-1969

In the mid-1950s the United States enjoyed very low rates of serial homicide. Two decades later the country would be in the midst of an apparent "murder wave," and the transition between the two stages can be dated with fair precision to the mid-1960s. The increase of extreme and seemingly irrational homicide was frequently remarked during these years, and many writers focused on a short period during 1966. In July of that year Richard Speck killed 8 nurses in a Chicago hostel, in an act that may have been the culmination of an already lengthy career of murder, and in August Charles

Whitman killed 16 people during a shooting spree in Texas. Less celebrated were the murder sprees perpetrated later that same year by Robert B. Smith in Arizona and by Kelbach and Lance in Utah.

The media enjoy finding such symbolic events that can be claimed as the harbingers of wider social trends, but there seems to be little doubt that these events were indeed significant. Newton offers a total of 23 cases of serial murder that occurred between 1965 and 1969. Several of these cases that involved fewer than four victims should be removed from consideration, applying the same criteria that were applied to the earlier list, and several other incidents can be added from other sources. Finally, one can identify 19 serial murder cases that were reported during these five years, or an average of one every 96 days (see Table 2).

Although this was below the rates of the 1970s, it was a sharp increase over conditions of the previous two decades, and, as the rate of serial murder intensified, so its nature changed. The new cases included fewer marginal or debatable incidents than had been reported in earlier years. There was an

TABLE 2 *Serial Murder Cases 1965–1969*

Name	Dates active
Jerry Brudos	1968–1969
John Norman Collins	1967–1969
Antone Costa	1969
Janie Gibbs	1968
Walter Kelbach and Myron Lance	1966
Posteal Laskey	1965–1966
Charles Manson and followers	1969
John Meadows	1968–1971
Thomas Lee Penn and William Penn	1966
George Howard "Buster" Putt	1969
Mark Alan Smith	late 1960s
Richard Speck	1966
Leroy Snyder	1969
Richard Steeves	1960s–1980s
Richard Lee Tingler	1968–1969
Clarence Walker	1965
"Zodiac"	1968ff
the New Jersey hospital murders	1966
the New Jersey unsolved murders	1965–1966

especially sharp rise in the number of "Ripper" crimes or "lust murders," of the sort that had been dismissed as so rare in the 1940s but that would become so commonplace after 1970. Between 1940 and 1964, only 11 cases could be classified as lust murders, but another 11 could be so categorized between 1965 and 1969 alone. These were the years of notorious offenders such as John Norman Collins (Keyes, 1977), Jerry Brudos (Rule, 1983a), Antone Costa (Damore, 1990), "Zodiac" (Graysmith, 1987), and others (Hilberry, 1987; Moser & Cohen, 1967). The picture was actually even worse than it appears, because several offenders now began careers of "lust murder" and serial homicide that would not be detected until the 1970s or later.

The frequency of serial homicide was accelerating at the end of the 1960s, but still more cases came to light in the following years (see Table 3). To take the single year of 1973, there were at least 10 arrests of serial killers as well as two incidents that remain unsolved, and the cases in this year

TABLE 3 *Growth of Serial Murder Cases 1970–1980**

Year	Serial killers arrested	Unsolved serial cases terminated	Total
1970	2	—	2
1971	5	—	5
1972	3	2	5
1973	10	2	12
1974	5	2	7
1975	7	5	12
1976	8	—	8
1977	4	4	8
1978	9	2	11
1979	6	2	8
1980	12	3	15
Totals	71	22	93

*This table must be regarded as especially tentative, as it combines two essentially different phenomena. However, this is the only way to suggest the changing scale of repeat homicide. The dates describe serial murder cases that were completed in a particular year, that is, (a) serial killers arrested in that year and (b) unsolved serial murder cases that apparently terminated in that year. The question of when an unsolved series of murders concludes is all but impossible to answer, and this part of the table frequently relies on estimates and opinions of law enforcement authorities.

included several extreme offenders such as Dean Corll, Herbert Mullin, Edmund Kemper, and Girard Schaefer.

A constructionist approach to the problem of serial murder might seek to emphasize the continuity in activity from the 1940s onwards and then attempt to understand the moral and political pressures that led commentators to describe an artificial "upsurge" from the late 1960s. By contrast, this case study supports the "objectivist" view that a genuine phenomenon was occurring and that no creative stereotyping was required to define the problem (compare Goode, 1989). Of course, a constructionist argument might still stress that the real scale of the problem was blown out of proportion or that the debate was shaped to benefit certain interests or ideologies; but new problem there certainly was. There simply were more serial killers, more of whom could be categorized as lust murderers. A new problem was identified because a new problem had come into being.

❧ Social Dimensions

We must therefore address the social factors that gave rise to this change. It is a commonplace that the mid-1960s marked a dramatic transition in many aspects of American life, and any attempt at explaining the growth of serial homicide must deal with an embarrassing surfeit of possible reasons. It would be rash to dismiss the status frustration postulated by Leyton, though additional factors can be suggested. It is often difficult to isolate any one type of causation, as the various elements so often intertwined. Fundamental was the changing demographic composition of the United States and the relative growth of the segment of the population consisting of people in their teens and twenties. This in itself contributed to a sharp rise in overall violence rates, and it may be asked whether the increase in serial homicide was merely a facet of the general growth in crime.

Almost certainly this was not the case. United States homicide rates did rise between the 1940s and the 1980s, but over the whole period they may only have doubled. From 1945 to 1966, the rate per 100,000 population fluctuated between about 4.5 and 6.0; it then began a rapid rise, from 6.0 in 1968 to 8.8 in 1974–1975, and by 1981 it exceeded 10.0. It then fell below 8.0 by the mid-1980s (Riedel & Zahn, 1985). There were particular regions and cities with far higher growth rates in homicide, but few could match the eightfold or tenfold increases that have been suggested for reported serial homicide (Block, 1987).

Simple demographics may have contributed a little to the upsurge in serial murder after 1965, but additional explanations are required. Some can be found in aspects of the distinctive youth counterculture evolved by the "baby boom" generation. Though avowedly pledged to peace and nonviolence, this culture may inadvertently have promoted overtly aggressive behavior, especially with sexual motivations. Only a small number of people might have been affected in this way, but the number of multiple homicide offenders is only in the hundreds nationwide. A vast increase in the availability and consumption of a wide range of drugs presumably had effects that are still difficult to quantify, which would have been especially severe in individuals already prone to violent or disinhibited behavior. From the mid-1960s there was also a rapid increase in the availability of sexually stimulating imagery, both through the media and in everyday life.

It is plausible that greater access to pornography or extremely violent visual material might have shaped the fantasies and consequent actions of some offenders, but neither drugs nor pornography would in itself be an adequate explanation of the changes observed. As has been argued elsewhere, the act of homicide may arise from any number of circumstances peculiar to the offender, but serial murder also presupposes social conditions that permit the creation of a victim population (Jenkins, in press). Such a population is accessible to the offender, and several victims can disappear or be found dead before the authorities become seriously concerned. The nature of responses by police and other justice agencies plays an important role in shaping such opportunities for victimization.

In this view, the vital changes in the 1960s might have been the greater independence of the younger generation and changes in their sexual behavior and attitudes. This greatly enhanced the opportunities for a potential offender to find himself or herself in intimate circumstances with a victim, and the increased physical mobility of these years made it less likely that a young person's disappearance would be immediately noticed. Similarly, the range of acceptable deviancy was greatly expanded in these years. Changes in mores increased a willingness to experiment with alternative belief systems and life styles and made many people less prepared to reject or suspect individuals who might appear strange or deviant. The sum total of these changes was to facilitate encounters between strangers that might have been far more difficult only a few years previously. At the same time, the political fragmentation of the late 1960s discouraged young people from invoking police assistance in what might have been seen as suspicious circumstances.

◉ The Mental Health System

Other possible factors do not directly involve the "baby boom" generation but would nevertheless have similarly encouraged a growth in both potential offenders and their victims. In the forefront were changes in the mental health system. The 1960s were marked by a reluctance to institutionalize deviants and the mentally ill for long periods, and it became difficult to commit a person on the strength of his or her outrageous or threatening acts. The average number of individuals incarcerated in state mental hospitals on any given day fell from 550,000 in 1955 to 200,000 in 1974, a decline of 65 percent (and in proportion to the overall population the fall was still greater). Despite the generally laudable intentions of the movement, the effects of decarceration have often been disastrous, and one tragic effect was to release onto the streets some genuinely dangerous offenders who would hitherto have been maintained in secure institutions (compare Isaac & Armat, 1990; and Johnson, 1990). This was also an incidental effect of the shortening of prison sentences and actual time served and the new emphasis on community care facilities.

Decarceration was part of a more general attack on therapeutic responses to crime and violence reflecting great skepticism about the possibility of predicting and preventing future acts. The assault was seen most clearly in the area of "sexual psychopath" laws, which faced increasingly successful courtroom challenges (Cohen, 1980; Katenbach, 1984; Scull, 1977). In discussing this movement, Kittrie (1971) even writes of the notion of "the illusive psychopath," almost suggesting that the condition itself was mythical. It is ironic that this new legal environment coincided with a probable increase in the number of seriously disturbed offenders in the aftermath of the rapid growth of drug abuse.

The notorious serial killers of the decade following 1965 included many individuals who had been committed or incarcerated periodically for acts of extreme violence but were released with what proved to be too little regard for public safety. To take a specific case, it is difficult to believe that a flamboyantly psychotic offender like Richard Trenton Chase would have escaped lengthy incarceration had he lived in the 1940s. However, the mental health system he encountered was that of 1970s California, where compulsory commitment was much more difficult, and he remained at liberty until the 1978 murder spree that earned him the title of the "Vampire of Sacramento" (Markman & Bosco, 1989).

In one of the most tragic examples of this sort, Carroll E. Cole, who was also from California, made repeated attempts to warn doctors and law enforcement authorities of his sadistic and violent impulses towards women, and he was committed to mental institutions sporadically in the 1960s and early 1970s. However, he remained at large, and he carried out the first of his 13 murders in 1970 (Newton, 1990). Chase and Cole may have represented extreme failures on the part of the courts and the medical profession, but very serious mistakes were also made in the cases of killers such as Jerry Brudos, "Buster" Putt, Herbert Mullin, Ed Kemper, Charlie Hatcher, John Wayne Gacy, and many others (Ganey, 1989; Lunde, 1976; Rule, 1983a, 1983b). All had been diagnosed at some stage as showing strong tendencies to future violence, yet all had been released from youth institutions or from psychiatric custody, often on several occasions. Attempts at predicting violent behavior have a long and controversial history, but it appears that in the 1960s even the most extreme warning signs failed to cause official intervention.

◉ Conclusion

It would be tempting to draw facile political conclusions. If the upsurge in multiple murder from the mid-1960s was in a sense an outgrowth of the political and social liberalism that characterized that era, then one conceivable policy response would be to limit or reverse those trends, to emphasize traditional moral views on issues such as drug use and sexuality. Against this view it is important to stress the limited scale of the multiple homicide problem within the broad spectrum of violent crime and to avoid overemphasizing the purely negative changes associated with the 1960s. In addition, it remains uncertain how far any government could successfully shape moral attitudes and beliefs if the attempt ran against existing social currents. Similarly, it would be misleading to concentrate entirely on the bad effects of changes in the mental health system such as the decline of compulsory commitment laws. Most would agree that due process values were long overdue in the area of psychiatric confinement and treatment, even if the actual process of decarceration left a great deal to be desired.

Perhaps the most important lesson concerns the state of academic research in the area of multiple homicide. It appears that social, legal, and environmental factors play a major role in determining the prevalence of this crime, but the scholarly emphasis continues to focus on the individual offender. If the rate of serial murder is to be reduced, these underlying factors must be understood, and this can be achieved only if the killer is seen not merely as a disturbed individual but as an actor within a changing social context.

Serial killers appear to fall into several distinct psychiatric categories, with paranoid schizophrenics and sexual psychopaths both being frequently recorded, and some authorities would emphasize the role of biological factors no less than the role of psychological factors in causing acts of extreme violence (compare Norris, 1988). It may be that conditions that give rise to irrational violence occur to a similar degree in all human societies, or that social and developmental factors may make this behavior much more common in some societies than in others. In the 1950s, for example, psychiatrists would strongly have emphasized the role of factors such as child-rearing practices, which would be peculiar to a particular society at a given time. In this view, changes in family structure or in attitudes to children could account for variations in extremely violent behavior, as could changes in media depictions of violence or sexuality. It is quite possible that the frequency of aggressive behavior might indeed vary between societies, but that is a different matter from the specific phenomenon of serial homicide. An individualistic approach might account for how one person came to kill, but it cannot explain how he or she found the opportunities to evade detection until several murders had been committed, and it is this latter circumstance that makes an aggressive offender into a serial killer.

If the average number of victims claimed by serial killers rises or falls in a particular era or society, this is less a comment on the changing dynamics of the individual offenders themselves than a function of the social, moral, and bureaucratic context in which they all operate. It would be impossible to understand the murders of the medieval baron Gilles de Rais, "Bluebeard," without discussing the society in which he existed and the means by which he was able to entrap and murder so many innocent victims; it should be equally unthinkable to omit the social context of a modern case in Seattle or Houston. There is thus a crying need for scholarly studies, not merely of single offenders, but of all the cases of a particular region or decade, including discussion of how the killers exploited the opportunities in their particular situations or milieux.

In summary, an effective strategy against multiple homicide must draw on research from both social and individual perspectives. The social perspective will explore the broad victim environment while psychological analysis will aid investigators by profiling offenders and seeking more sophisticated means of predicting future violence. Both approaches must be used if serial homicide is to be reduced.

Endnote

[1] I am grateful to Dr. Daniel W. Pfaff of the School of Communications at Pennsylvania State University for discussions about the changing nature of regional press coverage in recent decades.

References

Abrahamsen, D. (1944). *Crime and the human mind.* New York, NY: Columbia University Press.

Allen, W. (1976). *Starkweather: The story of a mass murderer.* Boston, MA: Houghton Mifflin.

Banay, R. S. (1956). Psychology of a mass murderer. *Journal of Forensic Psychology, 1,* 1.

Best, J. (Ed.). (1989). *Images of issues.* New York, NY: Aldine de Gruyter.

Best, J. (1990). *Threatened children: Rhetoric and concern about child victims.* Chicago, IL: University of Chicago Press.

Block, C. R. (1987). *Homicide in Chicago.* Chicago, IL: Center for Urban Policy, Loyola University of Chicago.

Brian, D. (1986). *Murderers die.* New York, NY: St. Martin's Press.

Bromberg, W. (1948). *Crime and the mind: An outline of psychiatric criminology.* Philadelphia, PA: J. B. Lippincott.

Capote, T. (1965). *In cold blood.* New York, NY: Random House.

Cassity, J. H. (1941). Personality study of 200 murderers. *Journal of Criminal Psychopathology, 2,* 296–304.

Catton, J. (1940). *Behind the scenes of murder.* New York, NY: Norton.

Chapman, I. (1982). *Private Eddie Leonski: The Brownout Strangler.* Sydney, Australia: Hale and Iremonger.

Chessman, C. (1960). *Cell 2455, death row.* Englewood Cliffs, NJ: Prentice-Hall.

Cohen. F. (1980). *The law of deprivation of liberty.* St. Paul, MN: West Publishing.

Damore, L. (1990). *In his garden.* New York, NY: Dell.

DeFord, M. A. (1965). *Murderers sane and mad.* New York, NY: Abelard Schuman.

Egger, S. A. (Ed.). (1990). *Serial murder: An elusive phenomenon.* New York, NY: Praeger.

Experts say mass murders are rare but on the rise. (1988, January 3). *New York Times,* p. A3.

Frank, G. (1967). *The Boston Strangler.* London, England: Jonathan Cape.

Freeman, L. (1955). *Before I kill more.* New York, NY: Crown.

Galvin, J. A. V., & MacDonald, J. M. (1959). Psychiatric study of a mass murderer. *American Journal of Psychiatry, 115,* 1057.

Ganey, T. (1989). *St. Joseph's children: A true story of terror and justice.* Lyle Stuart/Carol.

Gaute, J. H. H., & Odell, R. (1979). *The murderers' Who's Who.* London, England: Harrap.

Gaziano, C. (1989). Chain newspaper homogeneity and presidential endorsements. *Journalism Quarterly, 66*(4), 836–845.

Gollmar, R. H. (1981). *Edward Gein: America's most bizarre murderer.* New York, NY: Pinnacle.

Goode, E. (1989). The American drug panic of the 1980s. *Violence-Aggression-Terrorism, 3*(4), 327–348.

Graysmith, R. (1987). *Zodiac.* New York, NY: Berkeley.

Hilberry, C. (1987). *Luke Karamazov.* Detroit, MI: Wayne State University Press.

Holmes, R. M., & DeBurger J. (1988). *Serial murder.* Beverly Hills, CA: Sage.

Isaac, R. J., & Armat, V. C. (1990). *Madness in the streets: How psychiatry and the law abandoned the mentally ill.* New York, NY: The Free Press.

Jenkins, P. (1988). Myth and murder: The serial murder panic of 1983–1985. *Criminal Justice Research Bulletin, 3*(11), 107.

Jenkins, P. (1989). Serial murder in the USA 1900–1940: A historical perspective. *Journal of Criminal Justice, 17,* 377–392.

Jenkins, P. (in press). Chance or choice: The selection of serial murder victims. In A. Wilson (Ed.), *Dynamics of the victim-offender interaction.* Cincinnati, OH: Anderson.

Johnson, A. B. (1990). *Out of bedlam: The truth about deinstitutionalization.* New York, NY: Basic Books.

Karpman, B. (1954). *The sexual offender and his offenses.* New York, NY: Julian Press.

Katenbach, J. (1984). First born. New York, NY: Atheneum.

Kennedy, F., Hoffman, H. R., & Haines, W. H. (1947). A study of William Heirens. American Journal of Psychiatry, 104, 113.

Keyes, E. (1977). The Michigan murders. London, England: New English Library.

Kittrie, N. N. (1971). The right to be different. Baltimore, MD: Johns Hopkins Press.

Levin, J., & Fox, J. A. (1985). Mass murder: America's growing menace. New York, NY: Plenum.

Leyton, E. (1986). Compulsive killers. New York, NY: New York University Press.

Lindsey, R. (1984, January 22). Officials cite a rise in killers who roam U.S. for victims. New York Times, p. A1.

Lunde, D. T. (1976). Murder and madness. New York, NY: W. W. Norton.

MacDonald, J. M. (1961). The murderer and his victim. Springfield, IL: Charles C Thomas.

Markman, R., & Bosco, D. (1989). Alone with the devil. New York, NY: Doubleday.

Masters, R. E. L., & Lea, E. (1963). Perverse crimes in history. New York, NY: Julian Press.

McCarty, J. (1986). Psychos. New York, NY: St. Martin's Press.

Menninger, K. (1968). The crime of punishment. New York, NY: Viking.

Moser, D., & Cohen, J. (1967). The Pied Piper of Tucson. New York, NY: New American Library.

Nettler, G. (1982). Killing one another. Cincinnati, OH: Anderson.

Neustatter, W. (1957). The mind of the murderer. New York, NY: Philosophical Library.

Newton, M. (1988). Mass murder: An annotated bibliography. New York, NY: Garland Reference Library of Social Science.

Newton, M. (1990). Hunting humans. Port Washington, WA: Loompanics.

Nickel, S. (1989). Torso. Winston-Salem, NC: John F. Blair.

Norris, J. (1988). Serial killers. New York, NY: Dolphin.

Reinhardt, J. M. (1960). The murderous trail of Charlie Starkweather. Springfield, IL: Charles C. Thomas.

Reinhardt, J. M. (1962). The psychology of strange killers. Springfield, IL: Charles C Thomas.

Riedel, M., & Zahn, M. (1985). The nature and patterns of American homicide. Washington, DC: Justice Department, NIJ.

Rule, A. (1983a). Lust killer. New York, NY: Signet.

Rule, A. (1983b). *Want-ad killer.* New York, NY: New American Library.

Schechter, H. (1990). *Deranged.* New York, NY: Pocket.

Scull, A. (1977). *Decarceration.* Englewood Cliffs, NJ: Prentice-Hall.

U.S. Government. (1969–1970). *Report of the National Commission on the Causes and Prevention of Violence* (Vols. 1–13). Washington, DC: Government Printing Office.

Von Hentig, H. (1948). *The criminal and his victim.* New Haven, CT: Yale University Press.

Wertham, F. (1947). *Dark legend.* Garden City, NJ: Doubleday.

Wertham, F. (1949). *The show of violence.* Garden City, NJ: Doubleday.

Wertham, F. (1966). *A sign for Cain: An exploration of human violence.* New York, NY: Macmillan.

Wilson, C., & Pitman, P. (1984). *Encyclopaedia of murder.* London, England: Pan.

Wilson, C., & Seaman, D. (1983). *Encyclopaedia of modern murder.* New York, NY: Perigee.

⚫ ⚫ ⚫

Questions

1. How would a "constructivist" perspective explain the increase in serial murders starting in the 1960s?

2. How would an "objectivist" perspective explain it?

3. Do you believe Jenkins's conclusion? Why or why not?

4. Which types of crime are most difficult to measure accurately? Which are easiest to measure?

5. What other type of crimes fade in and out of the public's awareness? What explains this pattern?

The Execution of the Innocent

Michael L. Radelet and Hugo Adam Bedau

This article explores the use of the death penalty in the United States, and it focuses on the question of whether innocent people are executed. It begins with a discussion of innocence as a legal concept, and it identifies a number of dimensions to innocence that make it a rather broad concept. It then reviews various cases in which evidence suggests that, in fact, innocent people are routinely executed. It concludes with discussion of why various groups in society, such as the courts, lawmakers, and the general public, tend to ignore the execution of the innocent.

No matter how careful courts are, the possibility of perjured testimony, mistaken honest testimony, and human error remain all too real. We have no way of judging how many innocent persons have been executed, but we can be certain that there were some.

Thurgood Marshall[1]

☻ I: Introduction

In February 1997, the (usually conservative) House of Delegates of the American Bar Association ("ABA") overwhelmingly adopted a report from its section on Individual Rights and Responsibilities and went on record as being formally opposed to America's current system of capital jurisprudence, calling for an immediate moratorium on executions.[2] The motion was supported by twenty former presidents of the ABA (some who counted themselves as supporters of the death penalty), and passed in the House of Delegates by a two-thirds margin. Among the issues of concern to the ABA were the lack of competent counsel in death penalty cases, restricted access to appellate courts even when new evidence of innocence is present, and

---

"The Execution of the Innocent," by Michael L. Radelet and Hugo Adam Bedau, reprinted from *Law and Contemporary Problems*, vol. 61, no. 4, 1998, pp. 105–124. Copyright © 1998 by Law and Contemporary Problems.

racial disparities in the administration of capital punishment.[3] In this article, we focus on one of the problems that gave rise to the ABA resolution: the continuing and regular incidence of American trial courts sentencing innocent defendants to death.

Elsewhere, we have published accounts of more than four hundred cases where persons were wrongfully convicted in capital (or potentially capital) cases and described several dozen of these cases in detail.[4] Our discussion in this article falls into three parts. First, we explore the conceptualization of the term "innocence." (Without a precise concept, we have no suitable criterion for deciding who should and should not be considered innocent despite a criminal homicide conviction.) Second, we review the kinds of evidence we have relied on previously to support our conclusion that some defendants sentenced to death and executed were actually innocent. Finally, we consider how government officials and the general public are currently reacting to the issue of possible executions of the innocent and what role this issue plays in contemporary death penalty debates.

❧ II: Conceptualizing the Problem of Innocence

If we are to study how often innocent people are convicted of murder, sentenced to death, and/or executed, special care must be taken in determining when a given convicted defendant can and cannot be judged to be innocent. Previous work on this problem[5] touches what is probably only the tip of an iceberg. Undoubtedly, there are many more cases in which innocent persons have been convicted of homicide that have yet to be thoroughly documented and acknowledged by government officials, much less publicized in a way that will allow those who care to learn lessons from them.

In our initial research on this problem, we included in our inventory of exonerated defendants only those who were totally uninvolved in the capital offense of which they were convicted, or who were convicted of a capital crime that never occurred (for example, consensual sexual relations tried in court as capital rape),[6] or a criminal homicide in which the victim was later discovered alive, which happened, most recently, to our knowledge, in 1974 in California.[7] Such narrow inclusion criteria yield an extremely conservative set of cases. Almost any other plausible conceptualization of innocence would yield a much larger set.

Of course, including only cases where government officials admitted error would result in an even more conservative estimate. To be sure, in some ninety percent of the cases described in our previous publications, there is some acknowledgment by public officials in one or more branches of government that the trial court's judgment of guilt was incorrect. But our investigations failed to disclose a single case in the twentieth century where a government official in this country admitted that an execution carried out under his authority, or to his knowledge in his jurisdiction, took the life of an innocent defendant.[3] By itself, however, that is hardly reason to believe that innocent defendants have not been executed.

Although the conceptualization of innocence could be broadened in several different ways from the conservative definition we have used in our research, we have made no attempt to do so or to investigate the new types of cases that would, as a result, need to be included in our inventory. The task is simply overwhelming. However, we can cite examples of cases that illustrate these alternative ways to broaden the conceptualizations of innocence.

A. Acquittal After Appellate Reversal

One way to broaden the definition is to include all those cases in which the case against the defendant was ultimately dismissed or the defendant was acquitted at retrial. To be sure, in our research, we treat a dismissal of charges after reversal of a defendant's conviction, or a verdict of acquittal at retrial, as evidence of innocence, but we do not regard it as either a necessary or sufficient condition of innocence.[4] Prosecutors sometimes fail to retry the defendant after a reversal not because of doubt about the accused's guilt, much less because of belief that the defendant is innocent or that the defendant is not guilty "beyond a reasonable doubt," but for reasons wholly unrelated to guilt or innocence (for example, the prosecution's chief witnesses may have died or disappeared). Such cases could be included among those we count as miscarriages of justice, on the rationale that, if a trial court conviction is to be treated as conclusive evidence of (legal) guilt, then by parity of reasoning *nolle prosequi* after a reversal could reasonably be treated as evidence of (legal) innocence. Other reasonable observers have included such cases, notably the authors of a 1993 House Subcommittee Staff Report on innocence and the death penalty. They collapse the distinction between being acquitted of charges and being innocent, arguing that "[u]nder the law, there is no distinction between the definitely innocent and those found innocent [that is, acquitted] after a trial but about whom there may remain a lingering doubt."[10]

Other ways to expand the concept of innocence would permit us to include cases where a capital crime was indeed committed but by accident, in self-defense,[11] or by an offender who is certifiably mentally ill. Yet another class of cases consists of defendants who are guilty of criminal homicide, but not of first-degree murder, and who—for any of several reasons—are erroneously convicted of capital murder nevertheless.

B. Accidental Killings

There are many cases in which a defendant, after being convicted of homicide and even sentenced to death, wins a retrial and is acquitted after persuading the jury that the homicide was accidental. Legally, such a defendant is innocent of murder and always was: the original conviction of criminal homicide was a miscarriage of justice.

In this context, consider the Florida case of Clifford Hallman, sentenced to death for killing a waitress in a barroom brawl in Tampa in 1973. Hallman's death sentence was eventually commuted to life imprisonment after it was shown that with proper medical care, the victim would not have died (indeed, the victim's family successfully sued Tampa General Hospital for malpractice). Hallman unquestionably cut the victim during the brawl, but almost certainly did not intend for her to die. Despite being guilty only of accidentally causing death, he remains imprisoned a quarter of a century later.[12]

C. Homicides in Self-Defense

Depending on what theory of legal excuse and legal justification one accepts, homicide in self-defense is either excusable or justifiable and thus not criminal. Yet, persons have been sentenced to death for killing others in self-defense. In 1979 in California, Patrick "Hooty" Croy was sentenced to death for killing a police officer, but at retrial in 1990 he was acquitted when he was able to show his jury that the killing had been done in self-defense.[13] In South Carolina in 1979, Michael Linder was sentenced to death for killing a highway patrol officer, but he was acquitted two years later at retrial when ballistics evidence supported Linder's self-defense claims.[14]

D. Homicide by the Mentally Ill

In another class of cases, the defendant does cause the death of another person but lacks the requisite *mens rea* to be held responsible for the crime. Nevertheless, the trial court convicts the defendant and sentences him to death. Why? Because of the incompetence of his attorney, or the absence or incompetence of expert psychiatric witnesses, or the jury's refusal to believe defense experts, or for other reasons.[15] The result in any case is the same: Innocent defendants (that is, defendants not properly held responsible for their acts) are convicted and sometimes sentenced to death.

A classic example of this type of error involves Erwin Charles Simants, sentenced to death in 1976 for killing six members of a Nebraska family.[16] At retrial in 1979, he was found not guilty by reason of insanity.[17] Not so lucky was Varnall Weeks. On May 13, 1995, readers of *The New York Times* learned that "Varnall Weeks, a convicted killer described by psychiatric experts as a paranoid schizophrenic who believed he would come back to life as a giant flying tortoise that would rule the world, was put to death . . . in Alabama's electric chair."[18] At trial, Weeks's inexperienced court-appointed attorney never raised the issue of the defendant's insanity. As the *Times* editorialized a few days before the execution, "if Alabama is allowed to take this sorry life, it will . . . expose just how barbaric and bloodthirsty this nation has become in its attempt to see justice done."[19] No one knows how many mentally ill convicts there are on America's death rows who do not deserve to be punished, but the number is unquestionably significant.[20]

These three categories of cases are familiar and have been discussed before by others, notably Charles Black; all illustrate what he rightly called the "caprice and mistake" in the criminal justice system where the death penalty is used.[21] But three other categories of innocence that have received less recognition also deserve attention.

E. Noncapital Murderers

Not all convicted murderers are candidates for the executioner. Death penalty abolitionists and retentionists alike agree that capital punishment is not supposed to apply to all murderers; it is to be applied only to the worst among the bad. David Baldus and his colleagues have estimated that "death-eligible" murder cases number at present around 2,000–5,000, or ten to twenty-five percent of all murders and nonnegligent manslaughters in the nation.[22] Data on death sentencing practices in Florida suggest the number of death-eligible defendants may be even smaller; in any case, the system transforms only a few of these defendants into death row prisoners. In Florida, there are about a thousand homicides per year. Yet, despite the popularity of the death penalty, only about three dozen defendants, 3.6%, are actually convicted of first-degree murder and sentenced to death.[23] If we arrange Florida's thousand murders per year on a scale from the most aggravated (perhaps a multiple rape-murder) to the least aggravated (perhaps a mercy killing), we can define "capital murder" (based on the verdicts and sentences of the trial courts themselves) as the crimes committed by the worst three or four percent.

However, some of those three to four percent are not sentenced to death, while some of the others are. Ted Bundy, for example, qualifies in the judgment of most people as one of the nation's worst murderers. Yet he was offered a plea bargain in both of his Florida murder trials.[24] Had he wished to do so, he could have escaped a death sentence by pleading guilty to noncapital murder. His case is not unique. It is common for defendants accused of some of the worst murders to escape the death penalty through plea bargaining. Often the prosecution has little choice: either accept a plea bargain or risk not getting a conviction because of lack of convincing evidence. As the O.J. Simpson case showed, prosecutors may quickly decide not to seek the death penalty—even for those they believe are multiple murderers—when they learn the defendant is able to employ top-notch attorneys.[25]

Other defendants are not so lucky. If measured by statutory "aggravating" circumstances, their crimes do not place them among Florida's worst three to four percent, yet they end up on death row nonetheless. Many examples could be cited here, but consider only the case of Ernest Dobbert, executed in Florida on September 7, 1984. He had been convicted of killing his nine-year-old daughter. His Jacksonville jury, obviously troubled, recommended life imprisonment by a vote of ten to two; Florida's unusual death sentencing law allows the trial judge to reject the jury's recommendation, and the judge sentenced Dobbert to death. The key witness at trial was Dobbert's thirteen-year-old son, who testified that he saw his father kick his daughter.[26] In a dissent from the Supreme Court's denial of *certiorari* written just hours before Dobbert's execution, Justice Thurgood Marshall argued that while there was no question that Dobbert abused his children, there was substantial doubt about his premeditation, necessary to sustain his conviction of first-degree murder. "That may well make Dobbert guilty of second-degree murder in Florida, but it cannot make him guilty of first-degree murder there. Nor can it subject him to the death penalty in that state."[27] If Justice

Marshall's assessment was correct, then Dobbert was not guilty of a capital offense, and—in this qualified sense—Florida executed an innocent man.

Although defendants like Dobbert may be unquestionably guilty of some form of criminal homicide, they are arguably not guilty of capital murder. They do not belong among the death-eligible defendants. We rarely think about this category when discussing innocence and the death penalty, but it is relevant and extremely important. The problem has been with us for at least two centuries, ever since the invention of the distinction between first-degree (capital) murder and second-degree (noncapital) murder and the inclusion of felony murder (in other words, any homicide committed in the course of committing a felony, such as rape or robbery) within first-degree murder. Proper administration of the death penalty requires us to draw careful lines in several different dimensions simultaneously, but a substantial amount of evidence shows we are doing a poor job distinguishing between those who do and those who do not deserve—in a strict legal sense—to be found guilty of capital murder and sentenced to death.[28]

Some of those who are guilty of criminal homicide but factually innocent of capital murder end up on death row because of a politically ambitious prosecutor, a lazy or angry jury, incompetent or over-worked defense counsel, or just bad luck.[29] Others are on death row not out of arbitrariness, but because of systematic bias and discrimination. In Florida[30] and in several other states,[31] taking into account all the relevant facts, those who kill whites are between three and four times more likely to end up on death row as are those who kill blacks.[32] In short, the race of the victim is a strong predictor of which defendants end up on death row, and explains why some who are innocent of capital murder are nonetheless sentenced to death.

Sentencing defendants to death who are innocent of capital murder—or innocent of any homicide—is especially risky in states where the trial judge has the authority to disregard the jury's sentence recommendation, as in Alabama, Delaware, Florida, and Indiana. After interviewing fifty-four jurors from a dozen Florida capital juries (including the jury that judged Ernest Dobbert), William Geimer and Jonathan Amsterdam concluded, "The existence of some degree of doubt about the guilt of the accused was the most often recurring explanatory factor in the life [imprisonment] recommendation cases studied."[33] Clearly, even when jurors believe that certain defendants are "guilty beyond a reasonable doubt," lingering doubts often remain about whether the defendant is guilty of a capital crime, and those doubts understandably make the jurors reluctant to recommend the extreme penalty.

7. Innocent Victims in the Death Row Inmate's Family

No discussion of innocence and the death penalty can be complete without considering how the death penalty affects the inmate's family.

Consider for a moment why some Americans want the death penalty rather than life imprisonment. They argue that the inmate does not suffer enough if punished only by life imprisonment. What is it about the death penalty that makes the inmate suffer more than if he had been sentenced instead to a long term of imprisonment? In many cases, the primary pain felt by men facing execution is seeing what their plight and their anticipated execution does to their families. Life in prison is a miserable life; the inmate knows that even if he were to leave death row via commutation of his sentence, he would be resentenced to life without possibility of parole and would die in prison. Given the widespread availability of life-without-parole sentences, almost all of those sentenced to death, absent the death penalty, will still die in prison. Being executed would end the pain of imprisonment sooner rather than later.

But the pain felt by the inmate anticipating execution is often overshadowed by the pain that innocent family members experience in anticipating the death of their loved one. Their pain arises out of their helplessness, the scorn directed at them, and what they endure immediately prior to, during, and after the execution itself.[34] Families of death row inmates are often indigent and almost always powerless to resist public and political outcries aimed at their incarcerated loved one. While the inmate's suffering is terminated at the instant of death, that of the family members goes on, from the moment they learn the death sentence has been carried out through the years of living with the memories and second-guesses. Arguably, the only thing worse than being executed is to see a member of your family executed.

Sentimental though this may seem to some, we make this point in the context of discussing the execution of the innocent for the following reason. Today, the main rationale generally given for retaining the death penalty is retribution.[35] Retribution gives us the simplest and most direct argument for the death penalty: Execute murderers because they deserve it. However, the death penalty inflicts its harm not with a laser but with a shotgun, injuring the guilty and the innocent alike. In ways very unlike prison sentences, the death penalty creates an ever-widening circle of victims. And many of those caught in the circle as it widens do not deserve it. Obviously, families of

homicide victims do not deserve their pain either. but the discussion about
the death penalty is foremost a discussion of how much misery society
should deliberately inflict in the future. not about the misery that has already
been inflicted in the past (and is therefore unretractable) by the offender.

● III: Have Innocent Defendants Really Been Executed?

In 1985. when we released the first draft of our research on erroneous convictions in capital cases,[35] the reaction by the Reagan Administration took us
by surprise. Then-Attorney General Edwin Meese III. who in California in
1967 (with then-Governor Ronald Reagan) presided over the next to last pre-
Furman[37] execution in America,[38] ordered the Justice Department to prepare
an immediate response.[39] We had evidently hit a sore spot in the Administration's support of the death penalty: neither before nor since has the
Attorney General's office taken such an interest in academic research on the
death penalty.[40] The government's response was not. as one might naively
have hoped. to confirm or disconfirm our findings by throwing its resources
behind a more comprehensive study of the problem. We carried out our initial research over four years on a budget of $9,000; it is anyone's guess what
could have been discovered if the vast resources of the Justice Department
had been available for more extensive research into the 350 cases we studied. much less any of the thousands of cases still waiting to be reexamined.
Instead. the Attorney General's Office designed its response solely to discredit
our work and by implication to insulate the death penalty from the charge
that even in our society. with all the legal protections afforded the accused or
convicted or sentenced capital defendant. there is still an undeniable risk of
executing the innocent. As events would prove. the government's hostile reaction to our work was far different from that of other informed observers.[41]

The Justice Department's response focused on ten of the twenty-three cases
about which we declared our belief that the executed defendant was innocent.
Our critics did little more than rehash the case for the prosecution. because
they thought. or wanted their readers to believe. that we had denied or forgotten that these defendants had been found guilty in court "beyond a reasonable
doubt." Our judgment to the contrary was explained as the result of our care-
less methodology and excessive anti-death penalty zeal. As recently as 1994,
the conservative magazine *National Review* recycled the views of our critics.[42]

Some of the nation's leading judges have given our work more positive attention. For example, Supreme Court Justice Harry Blackmun used our research to support (in part) his decision to abandon any further tinkering with "the machinery of death," as he called it, in the futile hope to make the administration of the death penalty in our society fair and efficient.[43] And, in 1998, the Chief Justice of the Florida Supreme Court, Gerald Kogan, pointed to our work as one reason why he had decided to urge Florida lawmakers to abandon the death penalty.[44]

We should mention in passing that despite not having demonstrated any lack of integrity or reliability in our research, the Justice Department's critique of that work has been very effective. The critique is frequently cited by those who support executions, though they give no evidence of having actually read the critique, much less of having read our law review article, our reply to our critics, or our book. Perhaps this is another example of the complacency that surrounds the public's attitude toward the death penalty and issues of fact on which that attitude ought to depend.

Again and again, our critics point out that no responsible official in any of the nation's capital jurisdictions has ever admitted to executing an innocent person in this century, a point we were the first to make on the basis of our extensive research into the question.[45] Obviously, the government's failure or refusal to acknowledge that an innocent defendant has been executed is hardly evidence that none has been executed.

Getting the state to concede that it has convicted (let alone executed) an innocent defendant is clearly no easy matter. Once an innocent person is convicted, it is almost impossible to get that conviction reversed on grounds of the accused's innocence.[46] Even when prisoners do get released, usually the prosecutor or some other state official will continue to insist publicly that they really are guilty. The Jacobs-Tafero case powerfully and painfully illustrates this point.

In May 1990, Jesse Tafero was executed in Florida. His case gained notoriety because the electric chair malfunctioned and his head caught on fire before he died.[47] Two years later, Jesse's co-defendant, Sonia Jacobs, who had been convicted and sentenced to death on exactly the same evidence that sent Tafero to his death, was released after a U.S. Court of Appeals concluded that her conviction was based on prosecutorial suppression of exculpatory evidence and perjury by a prosecution witness (who was the real killer).[48] Jacobs now lives in Los Angeles, and in early 1996, a television movie of her case was aired.[49] But Tafero is dead. Had he been alive, the evidence that led to Jacobs's release would have led to his release, too.

Did Jacobs's vindication and release cause any Florida official to admit the error in convicting Tafero, much less to apologize on behalf of the state, or even to express second thoughts about Tafero's execution? No. To be sure, a few newspaper articles pointed out the error,[50] but no politician, prosecutor, judge, or ex-juror involved in the case has so far made any public comment on Tafero's fate in light of Jacobs's vindication. Tafero's mother, living impoverished in Pennsylvania, does not have the resources to mount a campaign to clear her son's name. His attorneys have long since moved on to other cases.

So, given that we cannot point to admission of erroneous executions by government officials involved in the cases we have studied, on what grounds can we confidently infer that innocent defendants have been executed? Apart from rare cases like Tafero-Jacobs (where one codefendant is executed before the other codefendant is exonerated), there are at least three kinds of evidence that we believe ought to convince any reasonable person that innocent defendants have been executed: close calls, calculation of the odds, and the role of "Lady Luck."[51]

A. *Close Calls*

Between 1972 and the end of 1996, sixty-eight death row inmates in the nation were released because of doubts about their guilt.[52] These releases do not prove that the system works, as some defenders of the death penalty would argue. Representative Bill McCollum, for example, one of our executioners' best friends in Congress, was "encouraged" by the findings, claiming that the sixty-eight errors in twenty-five years "shows that the system is working quite well."[53] Contrary to such political spin, however, our research indicates that if "the system worked," the defendants would be dead. In virtually all of these cases, the defendants were released only after an expensive and exhausting uphill struggle, unsupported by public funds or public officials, and almost always fiercely resisted by the prosecution and ignored by those with the power to commute a death sentence.

Some of these prisoners, now free, came within a few days of being executed. Randall Adams, sentenced to death in Texas, in 1977 and exonerated in 1989, came to within one week of his execution.[54] Andrew Mitchell, sentenced to death in Texas in 1981, came within five days of death by lethal injection before being vindicated in 1993.[55] Two half-brothers in Florida, William Jent and Ernest Miller, came within sixteen hours of being executed before they were released from prison in 1988.[56] More such cases have been cited elsewhere.[57]

Today, there are more than three thousand prisoners on America's death rows.[55] As things stand, it would be preposterous to believe that all the innocent death row defendants have been identified and exonerated. If the history of the last twenty years is any guide to the future, an average of three death row inmates per year will continue to be vindicated and released. How many equally innocent death row inmates will be unsuccessful in obtaining relief is impossible to know, but the number most certainly is not zero.

B. Calculation of the Odds

Assume we execute two death row inmates, each of whom we believe is guilty "beyond a reasonable doubt" on the evidence. Let belief in guilt "beyond a reasonable doubt" mean that we are ninety percent confident of guilt, and that our belief in both these cases is correct. Nevertheless we are not (and rarely could be) 100% certain, and so, on these assumptions, we are implicitly accepting a ten percent error rate even when we are ninety percent confident. However, because the odds of error are multiplicative, the probability that any two death row prisoners chosen at random are guilty is not ninety percent (0.9), but only eighty-one percent (0.9 × 0.9). Thus, the probability that all 3,000 death row inmates today are guilty, even if we are ninety percent confident of guilt in each case, is minuscule.

To put this another way, if we executed 100 inmates and we were ninety-five percent certain of guilt in each case, we would be implicitly accepting a five percent error rate; in being willing to execute all 100, we are in effect willing to execute five out of the hundred who might be innocent (even though, of course, we do not know which five are innocent, or whether more or any are). If our perceptions on the odds of error are accurate reflections of the real occurrences of error, the number of innocent persons legally executed is quite high—and much higher than our admittedly selective and incomplete research into identifiable cases suggests.

C. The Role of "Lady Luck"

In the heat of their attack on our claim that some two dozen of the several hundred cases we studied involved the execution of the innocent, the Justice Department simply ignored the vast majority of cases where we claim an innocent person was convicted of a capital offense but was not executed.[59] In effect, their silence tacitly concedes that our judgment is correct in more than ninety percent of all the cases and wrong in fewer than ten percent. Why these critics think that small percent matters they have yet to explain. What they conveniently overlook are scores of cases in which they do not—and could not reasonably—dispute our claims, namely, that innocent persons have been convicted and sentenced to death, and that innocent prisoners who were not executed would have been, or might have been, executed except for extraordinary good fortune.

Consider some of the ways good fortune smiled on the innocent death row prisoner. Some of the cases we cite involve a defendant whose release was owing to the timely discovery of a hitherto unknown eyewitness (for example, the case of Jerry Banks[60]). What if that witness had not stepped forward? In other cases we cite, the true culprit confessed in time to save the innocent prisoner (for example, the case of James Foster[61]). What if the true culprit had kept silent about his involvement? In still other cases, vindication depended on a dedicated journalist who took up the cause and established that the convicted defendant is really innocent (for example, the case of Freddie Pitts and Wilbert Lee[62]). What if no journalist had developed a timely interest in the case? In 1993, Kirk Bloodsworth was freed from death row in Maryland when technology not widely available at the time of his trial (DNA testing) proved his innocence.[63] What if this technology had not been developed for another decade, or semen on the body of the victim had not been preserved, or the victim had not been raped as well as murdered? Under any of these conditions, Bloodsworth would not have been exonerated.

In one way or another, virtually every case in which death row inmates are able to prove their innocence is a story of exceptional luck. Only when we realize how lucky the exonerated death row defendants have been can we realize how easy it is for fatal mistakes to go undetected. The more such cases are discovered the greater the likelihood there are other cases so far undetected—and that some of these cases involve the execution of the innocent. Just because boats filled with illegal drugs are regularly intercepted by the police near our shores, it does not follow that all boats carrying such drugs have been intercepted.

❧ IV: Actual and Possible Remedies

The fact that innocent persons (in one or another sense of "innocence") are executed seems to have had little if any real impact on opinion toward the death penalty. Four deaf audiences can be identified: the appellate courts, clemency boards, legislatures, and the general public.

A. Appellate Courts

The Supreme Court has in effect said that appellate courts need not listen to postconviction evidence of a defendant's innocence, unless the circumstances are truly exceptional, as when the inmate has a videotape supporting his alibi that he was not at the scene of the murder. The Court issued a ruling of this very sort in 1995 in the case of Lloyd Schlup.[64] While incarcerated at the Missouri State Penitentiary, Schlup was accused of, and eventually sentenced to death for, the murder of a fellow inmate. Scheduled to be executed in 1993, he came to within nine hours of his death before Governor Mel Carnahan granted a stay and appointed a panel to reinvestigate the case.[65] In addition to the videotape, Schlup had affidavits from twenty other prisoners and a former guard stating that he was not the killer.[66] Schlup's demand for a full hearing on his innocence prevailed in the Supreme Court by the narrowest of margins—one vote.[67] In this case, the Court continued its unremitting effort to reduce access to appellate review via federal habeas corpus by raising the threshold for relief. It ruled that before an inmate could present evidence of his innocence in federal courts in search of a hearing to reopen the case, he must show that "a constitutional violation has probably resulted in the conviction of one who is actually innocent."[68] By "probably," the Court seems to have meant "More likely than not." Prior to *Schlup*, the defendant seeking habeas corpus relief in federal courts had to show by "clear and convincing evidence" that "no reasonable juror would have found him guilty except for a constitutional error at his trial." Although this was a victory for Schlup (a victory that, thanks to Congress, other inmates will not be able to secure; see our discussion below), it demonstrates how reluctant the appellate courts are to hear evidence of innocence. Had there been no videotapes to present to the courts, Schlup would have been executed.

B. Clemency Boards

Government officials with the power to commute death sentences to terms of imprisonment have not been receptive to arguments of the condemned defendant's innocence.[69] In the twenty year period from 1973 to 1992, only twenty-nine death sentences were commuted to prison terms for humanitarian reasons by executive clemency;[ ] doubt about the defendant's guilt was a factor in nine of these cases.[ ] Only one of these commutations came from Texas or California, states with the largest death row populations; in Florida, the only other state with more than three hundred prisoners on death row, there has not been a commutation of a death sentence in more than a dozen years.[72] A defendant's possible innocence has begun to seem almost like an argument against clemency: No one, least of all members of clemency boards, wants to embarrass the state officials who worked to get the prisoner convicted, sentenced, and executed.

C. *L*egislatures

Worry that the innocent might be executed has not persuaded state legislatures to create tighter standards for death sentencing, much less to repeal the death penalty. In 1994, Kansas reenacted the death penalty;[73] New York's legislature did so in 1995,[74] and Massachusetts came within one vote of following suit in 1997,[75] despite evidence of wrongful capital convictions in each of these states,[76] evidence virtually placed in the hands of every member of these state legislatures prior to their votes. In New York, extensive protections demanded by concerned legislators were built into the new death penalty law,[77] with what effect remains to be seen. But the history of wrongful convictions in capital cases did not in the end persuade the majority to vote against reenacting the death penalty. Nor is there any reason to believe that if Governor Pataki in New York (elected in part for his vigorous pro-death penalty stance[78]) were confronted with a plea for clemency from a death row prisoner, he would follow the lead of his predecessors, Alfred E. Smith (1923–28), and Herbert H. Lehman (1933–42). When Smith and Lehman served as New York's governors, death sentences were routinely commuted every time one or more Court of Appeals judges dissented from a ruling that affirmed a conviction.[79]

In recent years, Congress, like the courts, has made it easier to execute the innocent. In 1995, federal funding for attorneys serving indigent death row inmates was severely cut, resulting in the closure of "Resource Centers" in twenty states that provided legal services for condemned inmates.[80] Congress has also restricted the ability of federal courts to hear claims of innocence. Several new barriers to obtaining habeas corpus relief are contained in the Anti-Terrorism and Death Penalty Act signed into law on April

24, 1996.[51] For example, the Act includes a provision that requires "clear and convincing" evidence of innocence rather than simply evidence of "probable" innocence.[52] This supersedes the broader standard articulated by the Supreme Court in the *Schlup* case discussed above. Under the provisions of this legislation, even with his videotapes, Schlup would have been executed.

D. General Public

The risk of executing the innocent has turned out to be a rather weak anti-death penalty card in the current public debates over the death penalty. In a 1985 Gallup Poll, fifteen percent of those who opposed the death penalty justified their position by saying "persons my be wrongly convicted."[53] By 1991, this figure had fallen to eleven percent.[54] Further, the public is increasingly turning a deaf ear to cases in which death row convicts have made a plea of innocence.[55] Apparently so many inmates and their supporters have claimed innocence, legitimately or not, that officials and the general public dismiss such claims, including the valid ones, with the cynical reply that abolitionists claim innocence "all the time." Thus, it has become clear that abolitionists gain nothing from inflated claims of innocence; here as elsewhere, crying "Wolf!" distorts the true situation. There are dozens of cases in which it can be said the defendant might be innocent, and death penalty opponents are absolutely right to point that out and stress the risk involved, but journalists and their audiences appear to tire quickly, signing off on the issue with an attitude that amounts to a "Ho hum, another 'innocent' death row inmate."

In the end, arguing that the death penalty should be abolished because it will eventually kill the innocent is not the best kind of argument to make, just as it is not the best argument against torture to point out that some false confessions will result. Protesting the execution of the innocent does not make one a death penalty abolitionist; the true test is whether one opposes it for the guilty. The innocence argument is important because it undermines the justification of capital punishment on the ground of retributive justice.

As things stand now, we have little or no knowledge about the effect of information about wrongful convictions of capital defendants on the public's support for the death penalty. Here as elsewhere, the Marshall hypothesis (that the public is ignorant of the basic facts about the death penalty but that if it were informed, there would be a tendency to oppose the death penalty)[56] remains untested in recent years.[57] In the decade since our research on miscarriages of justice in capital cases was first published, we have some vivid anecdotal evidence from various conversations and courtroom testimony showing that jurors in capital trials who learn about our work find themselves rethinking their support for the death penalty.[58] However, more systematic research is needed before we can gauge the effect of such knowledge on various constituencies.

It is here that the ABA's call for a moratorium on death sentencing might have its strongest impact.[59] The ABA's call has now been joined by a similar call by the Pennsylvania Bar Association and the Philadelphia Bar Association,[60] and it is likely that other professional associations in the legal profession will follow suit. There are also signs that the religious community is increasingly taking a stand against the death penalty: in October 1997, for example, the twenty-one Catholic Bishops in Texas issued a plea for an end to the death penalty.[61] While such declarations might not turn many of those who strongly support the death penalty into abolitionists, the call for a moratorium can increase the public's ambivalence on the topic.[62] This, in turn, promises to lower the volume on calls for vengeance and to make opposition to the death penalty in general (by the public) or in a specific case (by a troubled juror) more tolerable, leading to fewer death sentences.

Nonetheless, for the immediate future it appears that most Americans will either ignore the risk of executing the innocent or simply accept its inevitability. A recent letter to the *Houston Post* by Rex L. Carter is all too typical.[63] In November 1994, we wrote to the newspaper, pointing out the inevitability of executing the innocent and mentioning the case of Gary Graham.[64] Graham had admitted to a string of armed robberies but denied he was guilty of the murder that sent him to Texas's death row. And, indeed, much of the evidence of his guilt of that crime was suspect.[65] Here is Mr. Carter's response:

> Hugo Bedau had best come in out of the heat. As a defender of the death penalty, I have no problem in admitting innocent people can be executed and couldn't care less what happens to Gary Graham. He should have been executed for what he confessed to. There is a war going on in our own country—against crime and thugs like Graham. It is sad that innocent people get killed in war, but that is the way it is. Ask any wartime veteran. Try 'em, give 'em 90 days for appeal and then hang 'em slowly at noon on the courthouse lawn. Just maybe killers-to-be will get the message, just as Japan did when we dropped the A-bomb.[66]

Mr. Carter's rhetorical flourishes get in the way of his logic, but we have no doubt his sentiments coincide with the feelings of many citizens.

Dale Volker, the state senator from New York whose ten-year quest to reinstate the death penalty in the Empire State finally succeeded in 1995, had this to say about executing the innocent: "I would never think it's impossible. You would hope that it would never happen, but the mere fact that you might fail does not argue that you shouldn't do it."[97]

Or consider the comments of Paul D. Kamenar, executive director of the Washington Legal Foundation, who early in 1995 was quoted in *The New York Times* saying, "I would gladly give them a couple of questionable cases that they are harping about in return for their agreeing to recognize that in the vast majority of cases, there is no question of the guilt of those being executed."[98] This trade we would happily accept; few abolitionists would deny that most of those now on death row are guilty. We doubt, however, that most retentionists would be willing to agree that the vast majority of murderers on death row are not genocidal maniacs, psychopathic serial or multiple murderers, recidivist killers, and thus that they are not the worst among the bad and so do not belong there.

Finally, consider the comments of Florida State University criminologist Larry Wollan. Although a supporter of the death penalty, Wollan realizes that the risk of executing the innocent is undeniable, and he phrases the argument in a responsible way: "Innocent people have been executed," he concedes, but "[t]he value of the death penalty is its rightness vis-à-vis the wrongness of the crime, and that is so valuable that the possibility of the conviction of the innocent, though rare, has to be accepted."[99] Elsewhere, Ernest van den Haag made the same point when he says that our documentation of twenty-three erroneous executions in this century in America "[does] not tell us anything unexpected,"[100] and this liability to grave error does not outweigh the deterrent and moral benefits of the death penalty. Since, in our judgment, those benefits are entirely illusory[101]—we gain nothing in public safety or moral rectitude by the practice of the death penalty—the constant and unavoidable risk of executing the innocent cannot be so complacently tolerated.

❧ V: Conclusion

We close on an ironic note. One of the amazing things that has happened in the decade since our research was first released to the public is that those who defend the death penalty now concede the inevitability of executing the innocent, even though they challenge individual cases that we and others have identified as probably involving the execution of an innocent person. It is a major concession. We know of no defender of the death penalty who, prior to 1985, was willing to make such a public concession. Moreover, this concession has the effect of forcing responsible defenders of capital punishment to rethink their argument in two important respects. First, as retributivists, they must acknowledge that convicting and executing the innocent—those who do not deserve to die—is a terrible wrong, and avoiding it is no less important on retributive grounds than convicting and punishing the guilty. Second, they must explain in convincing detail how a cost/benefit argument, on which they rely, shows that the benefits from the death penalty outweigh the admitted cost of executing the innocent. Elsewhere, we have shown why we believe these arguments must fail.[102]

We are left to ponder how future generations, when they look back, will evaluate America's current love for the executioner.

Endnotes

[1] Furman v. Georgia, 408 U.S. 238, 367–68 (1972) (Marshall, J., concurring) (footnote omitted).

[2] See American Bar Ass'n, *Whatever You Think About the Death Penalty, A System That Will Take Life Must First Give Justice: A Report from the IR&R Death Penalty Committee*, 24 W.T.R. HUM. RTS. 22 (1997).

[3] See id. at 22–24.

[4] See MICHAEL L. RADELET ET AL., IN SPITE OF INNOCENCE (1992) [hereinafter RADELET ET AL., INNOCENCE]; Hugo Adam Bedau & Michael L. Radelet, *Miscarriages of Justice in Potentially Capital Cases*, 40 STAN. L. REV. 21 (1987); Michael L. Radelet et al., *Prisoners Released from Death Rows Since 1970 Because of Doubts About Their Guilt*, 13 T.M. COOLEY L. REV. 907 (1996) [hereinafter Radelet et al., *Doubts*].

[5] See, e.g., C. RONALD HUFF ET AL., CONVICTED BUT INNOCENT: WRONGFUL CONVICTION AND PUBLIC POLICY (1996); RADELET ET AL., INNOCENCE, *supra* note 4; Bedau & Radelet, *supra* note 4; Radelet et al., *Doubts*, *supra* note 4.

[6] For example, see the case of William Henry Anderson, in RADELET ET AL., INNOCENCE, *supra* note 4, at 282. In a five-month period in 1945 in Ft. Lauderdale, Anderson, who was black, was arrested for rape, tried, found guilty, sentenced to death, and executed. Much evidence indicates that the relationship between Anderson and the "victim," who was white, was consensual.

[7] See RADELET ET AL., INNOCENCE, *supra* note 4, at 269–70.

[8] As far as we know, the last execution that was later officially acknowledged to have been in error occurred in Illinois in 1887, when four Haymarket defendants were hanged in Illinois. A fifth defendant took his own life on the eve of the

scheduled executions. Six years later, Governor John Altgeld pardoned the three surviving codefendants because all eight "had been wrongfully convicted and were innocent of the crime. . . ." PAUL AVRICH, THE HAYMARKET TRAGEDY 423 (1984). On August 21, 1993, Governor Walter D. Miller formally apologized for the wrongful hanging of Thomas Egan in 1882. *See generally* C. JONH EGAN, JR., DROP HIM TIL HE DIES (1994).

[9]"Defendants are acquitted for many reasons, the least likely being innocence." Louis B. Schwartz, *"Innocence"—A Dialogue with Professor Sundby*, 41 HASTINGS L.J. 153, 154 (1989).

[10]1 STAFF OF THE SUBCOMM. ON CIV. AND CONST. RIGHTS, OF THE HOUSE COMM. ON THE JUDICIARY, 103D CONG., REPORT ON INNOCENCE AND THE DEATH PENALTY: ASSESSING THE DANGER OF MISTAKEN EXECUTIONS 13 (Subcomm. Print 1993).

[11]Our most recent work extends those parameters slightly by including three cases in which the defendant, initially sentenced to death, was later able to show that the homicide was committed in self-defense. *See* Radelet et al., *Doubts, supra* note 4, at 912.

[12]See Michael L. Radelet & Barbara A. Zsembik, *Executive Clemency in Post*-Furman *Capital Cases*, 27 U. RICH. L. REV. 289, 309 (1993).

[13]See Radelet et al., *Doubts, supra* note 4, at 933–34.

[14]See *id* at 948.

[15]See, e.g., Stephen B. Bright, *Counsel for the Poor: The Death Sentence Not for the Worst Crime but for the Worst Lawyer*, 103 YALE L.J. 1835 (1994) [hereinafter Bright 1994]; Stephen B. Bright, *In Defense of Life: Enforcing the Bill of Rights on Behalf of Poor, Minority and Disadvantaged Persons Facing the Death Penalty*, 57 MO. L. REV. 949 (1992) [hereinafter Bright 1992]; Stephen B. Bright, *The Politics of Crime and the Death Penalty: Not "Soft on Crime," but Hard on the Bill of Rights*, 39 ST. LOUIS U. L.J. 479 (1995) [hereinafter Bright 1995].

[16]See Fred W. Friendly, *A Crime and Its Aftershock*, N.Y. TIMES MAG., Mar. 21, 1976, at 16.

[17]See *Man Guilty of Oklahoma Murders; Defendant in Nebraska Acquitted*, N.Y. TIMES, Oct. 18, 1979, at 16.

[18]Rick Bragg, *A Killer Racked by Delusions Dies in Alabama's Electric Chair*, N.Y. TIMES, May 13, 1995, at A7.

[19]Andrew L. Shapira, *An Insane Execution*, N.Y. TIMES, May 11, 1995, at A29.

[20]See KENT S. MILLER & MICHAEL L. RADELET, EXECUTING THE MENTALLY ILL (1993); Dorothy Otnow Lewis et al., *Psychiatric, Neurological, and Psychoeducational Characteristics of 15 Death Row Inmates in the United States*, 143 AM. J. PSYCHIATRY 838 (1986).

[21]CHARLES L. BLACK, JR., CAPITAL PUNISHMENT: THE INEVITABILITY OF CAPRICE AND MISTAKE 17–18 (2d ed. 1981).

[22]See DAVID C. BALDUS ET AL., EQUAL JUSTICE AND THE DEATH PENALTY: A LEGAL AND EMPIRICAL ANALYSIS 22 & n.* (1990).

[23]See Michael L. Radelet & Glenn L. Pierce, Choosing Those Who Will Die: Race and the Death Penalty in Florida, 43 FLA. L. REV. 1, 20 (1991).

[24]See Michael Mello, On Metaphors, Mirrors, and Murders: Theodore Bundy and the Rule of Law, 18 N.Y.U. REV. L. & SOC. CHANGE 887, 900 (1990–91).

[25]See Kenneth B. Noble, Prosecutor in Simpson Case Won't Seek Death Penalty, N.Y. TIMES, Sept. 10, 1994, at A6.

[26]He later recanted and said his sister had actually died from choking on food.

[27]Dobbert v. Wainwright, 468 U.S. 1231, 1246 (1984).

[28]See GEN. GOV'T DIV., U.S. GEN. ACCOUNTING OFFICE, REP GGD-90-57, DEATH PENALTY SENTENCING: RESEARCH INDICATES PATTERN OF RACIAL DISPARITIES (FEB. 26, 1990); AMNESTY INTERNATIONAL U.S.A. THE MACHINERY OF DEATH: A SHOCKING INDICTMENT OF CAPITAL PUNISHMENT IN THE UNITED STATES (1995); BALDUS ET AL., supra note 22; HUGO ADAM BEDAU, THE CASE AGAINST THE DEATH PENALTY 11–16 (1997); INTERNATIONAL COMMISSION OF JURISTS, ADMINISTRATION OF THE DEATH PENALTY IN THE UNITED STATES: REPORT OF A MISSION (1996); David C. Baldus & George Woodworth, Race Discrimination and the Death Penalty: An Empirical and Legal Overview, in AMERICA'S EXPERIMENT WITH CAPITAL PUNISHMENT: REFLECTIONS ON THE PAST, PRESENT, AND FUTURE OF THE ULTIMATE PENAL SANCTION 385 (James R. Acker et al. eds., 1998); Bright 1994, supra note 15.

[29]See generally Bright 1995, supra note 15; Bright 1994, supra note 15; Bright 1992, supra note 15.

[30]See Radelet & Pierce, supra note 23, at 21.

[31]See BALDUS ET AL., supra note 22; SAMUEL R. GROSS & ROBERT MAURO, DEATH AND DISCRIMINATION: RACIAL DISPARITIES IN CAPITAL SENTENCING (1989).

[32]See Radelet & Pierce, supra note 23, at 28.

[33]William S. Geimer & Jonathan Amsterdam, Why Jurors Vote Life or Death: Operative Factors in Ten Florida Death Penalty Cases, 15 AM. J. CRIM. L. 1, 28 (1987–88).

[34]See Michael L. Radelet et al., Families, Prisons, and Men with Death Sentences: The Human Impact of Structured Uncertainty, 4 J. FAM. ISSUES 593 (1983); Margaret Vandiver, The Impact of the Death Penalty on the Families of Homicide Victims and of Condemned Prisoners, in AMERICA'S EXPERIMENT WITH CAPITAL PUNISHMENT, supra note 28, at 477.

[35]*See* Phoebe C. Ellsworth & Samuel R. Gross. *Hardening of the Attitudes: Americans' Views on the Death Penalty*, 50 J. Soc. Issues 19 (1994), *reprinted in* The Death Penalty in America: Current Controversies 90, 95–98 (Hugo Adam Bedau ed., 1997).

[36]*See* David Margolick, *25 Wrongfully Executed in U.S., Study Finds*, N.Y. Times, Nov. 14, 1985, at A19.

[37]In the 1972 case of *Furman v. Georgia*, 408 U.S. 238, the Supreme Court (in effect) invalidated all existing death penalty statutes in the United States. Thereafter, states drew up new capital laws and procedures, making *Furman* the demarcation of the "modern" era of the death penalty in the United States.

[38]*See* Carl J. Seneker, *Governor Reagan and Executive Clemency*, 55 Cal. L. Rev. 412 (1967).

[39]*See* Stephen J. Markman & Paul G. Cassell, *Protecting the Innocent: A Response to the Bedau-Radelet Study*, 41 Stan. L. Rev. 121 (1988); *see also* Hugo Adam Bedau & Michael L. Radelet, *The Myth of Infallibility: A Reply to Markman and Cassell*, 41 Stan. L. Rev. 161 (1988).

[40]Two other similar distortions of academic scholarship on the death penalty deserve mention. In 1975, when Solicitor General Robert Bork submitted an *amicus* brief in *Fowler v. North Carolina*, 428 U.S. 904 (1976), he asserted that all research that concluded the death penalty had no deterrent effect was severely flawed, and that the research of Isaac Ehrlich, which found that each execution deterred seven murders, provided "a reliable basis for judging whether the death penalty has a deterrent effect." David C. Baldus & James W.L. Cole, *A Comparison of the Work of Thorsten Sellin and Isaac Ehrlich on the Deterrent Effect of Capital Punishment*, 85 Yale L.J. 170 (1975). The inadequacies and inconclusiveness of Ehrlich's research have been extensively demonstrated. *See, eg.,* William C. Bailey & Ruth D. Peterson, *Murder, Capital Punishment, and Deterrence: A Review of the Literature, in* The Death Penalty in America, *supra* note 35, at 135, 141–43; Ruth D. Peterson & William C. Bailey, *Is Capital Punishment an Effective Deterrent for Murder? An Examination of Social Science Research, in* America's Experiment with Capital Punishment, *supra* note 28, at 157, 165–66. In 1972, Henry Peterson, an assistant attorney general in the Nixon Administration, testified before Congress to the effect that a "study" by the ABA showed that the death penalty was an effective deterrent. No such ABA study existed. *See* Hugo Adam Bedau, *The Nixon Administration and the Deterrent Effect of the Death Penalty*, 34 U. Pitt. L. Rev. 557 (1973).

[41]*See, e.g.,* Wendy Kammer, *The Wrong Men*, Atlantic, Dec. 1992, at 147; Lawrence C. Marshall, *Book Review*, 85 J. Crim. L. & Criminology 261 (1994).

[42]*See* Stephen J. Markman, *Innocents on Death Row?*, NAT'L REV., Sept. 12, 1994, at 72.

[43]Callins v. Collins, 510 U.S. 1141, 1145 (1994) (Blackmun, J., dissenting from denial of *certiorari* to Callins v. Collins, 998 F.2d 269 (5th Cir. 1993)).

[44]*See* Jenny Staletovich, *Justice Raising Voice to Bury Death Penalty*, PALM BEACH POST, Jan. 19, 1998, at A1, A8. Kogan is the former chief of the capital crimes unit for the Dade County state Attorney's Office.

[45]"[W]e have found no instance in which the government has officially acknowledged that an execution carried out under lawful authority was in error." Bedau & Radelet, *supra* note 4, at 25.

[46]In an extremely important article, Professor Samuel Gross argued that both the probability of erroneous conviction and the odds of erroneous convictions being ignored by appellate courts and clemency officials are higher in capital than in noncapital cases. *See* Samuel R. Gross, *The Risks of Death: Why Erroneous Convictions Are Common in Capital Cases*, 44 BUFF. L. REV. 469 (1996).

[47]*See* Ellen McGarrahan, *3 Jolts Used to Execute Killer*, MIAMI HERALD, May 5, 1990, at A1.

[48]*See* Jacobs v. Singletary, 952 F.2d 1282 (11th Cir. 1992).

[49]The made-for-television show was entitled *In the Blink of an Eye*, and aired in the spring of 1996.

[50]*See, eg.*, Cynthia Barnett, *New Evidence Might Have Spared Killer*, GAINESVILLE SUN (Fla.), Nov. 21, 1992, at A1.

[51]For an excellent discussion of why American criminal procedures do not protect the innocent from erroneous conviction, see Daniel Givelber, *Meaningless Acquittals, Meaningful Convictions: Do We Reliably Acquit the Innocent?*, 49 RUTGERS L. REV. 1317, 1358–93 (1997).

[52]Radelet et al., *Doubts, supra* note 4. A later report based on our research was issued by the Death Penalty Information Center. *See* DEATH PENALTY INFORMATION CENTER, INNOCENCE AND THE DEATH PENALTY: THE INCREASING DANGER OF EXECUTING THE INNOCENT (1997). This report received extensive national and international publicity. *See, eg.*, Terry Carter, *Numbers Tell the Story*, 83 A.B.A.J. 20 (Oct. 1997).

[53]*See* Carter, *supra* note 52, at 20.

[54]*See* RADELET ET AL., INNOCENCE, *supra* note 4, at 67–69.

[55]*See* Radelet et al., *Doubts, supra* note 4, at 950–51.

[56]*See* RADELET ET AL., INNOCENCE, *supra* note 4, at 318.

[57]For two dozen cases in which innocent prisoners came to within 72 hours of executions, see *id.* at 276; Bedau & Radelet, *supra* note 4, at 72.

⁴⁸On July 1, 1998, the exact number of prisoners on America's death rows stood at 3,474. See NAACP LEGAL DEFENSE & EDUCATIONAL FUND, DEATH ROW, U.S.A., Summer 1998, at 1.

⁴⁹See generally Markman & Cassell, supra note 39.

⁵⁰See RADELET ET AL., INNOCENCE, supra note 4, at 176–88.

⁵¹See id. at 23–39.

⁵²See id. at 326.

⁵³See Radelet et al., Doubts, supra note 4, at 926–27.

⁵⁴See Schlup v. Delo, 513 U.S. 298 (1995).

⁵⁵See id. at 313 n.27.

⁵⁶See Don Terry, Despite New Evidence, A Prisoner Faces Death, N.Y. TIMES, Nov. 15, 1993, at A12.

⁵⁷See Schlup, 513 U.S. at 298.

⁵⁸Id.

⁵⁹For a recent discussion of executive clemency in capital cases, see Daniel T. Kobil, The Evolving Role of Clemency in Capital Cases, in AMERICA'S EXPERIMENT WITH CAPITAL PUNISHMENT, supra note 28, at 531.

⁷⁰See Radelet & Zsembik, supra note 12, at 297–99; cf. Hugo Adam Bedau, The Decline of Executive Clemency in Capital Cases, 18 N.Y.U. REV. L. & SOC. CHANGE 255, 263 (1990–91). These two sources cite different commutation totals for the years in question because Bedau relied upon adjusted Bureau of Justice Statistics (which include some appellate court-ordered resentencing), whereas Radelet and Zsembik's more accurate figures were derived from examining records of all death sentences imposed in the United States since 1972 (primarily in the files of the NAACP Legal Defense Fund).

⁷¹See Radelet & Zsembik, supra note 12, at 300. Since this research was published, four more death row inmates have had their sentences commuted to life imprisonment because of doubts about guilt: Earl Washington, Jr. (Virginia, Jan. 15, 1994), Don Paradis (Idaho, May 24, 1996), Joseph Payne (Virginia, Nov. 7, 1996), and Henry Lee Lucas (Texas, June 26, 1998).

⁷²See id. at 313.

⁷³See John Dvorak, Kansas Approves Death Penalty After 22 Years; Governor Says She Won't Fight Law, TIMES-PICAYUNE (New Orleans), April 9, 1994, at A15.

⁷⁴See James Dao, Death Penalty in New York Reinstated After 18 Years; Pataki Sees Justice Served, N.Y. TIMES, Mar. 8, 1995, at A1.

⁷⁵See Adrian Walker & Doris Sue Wong, No Death Penalty, by One Vote, BOSTON GLOBE, Nov. 7, 1997, at 1.

[76]*See generally* Radelet et al., Innocence. *supra* note 4, at 282–358; Marty I. Rosenbaum, *Inevitable Error: Wrongful New York State Homicide Convictions, 1965–1988,* 18 N.Y.U. Rev. L. & Soc. Change 807 (1990–91).

[77]*See* N.Y. Correct. Law §§ 650–662 (McKinney Supp. 1997).

[78]*See* Ian Fisher, *The 1994 Campaign: Clamor over Death Penalty Dominates Debate on Crime,* N.Y. Times, Oct. 9, 1994, at A45.

[79]*See* Elkan Abramowitz & David Paget, *Executive Clemency in Capital Cases,* 39 N.Y.U. L. Rev. 136, 170 (1964).

[80]*See* Lis Wiehl, *A Program for Death-Row Appeals Is Facing Elimination,* N.Y. Times, Aug. 11, 1995, at B16.

[81]Pub. L. No. 104–132, §§ 101–08, 110 Stat. 1214, 1217–26 (codified at 28 U.S.C. §§ 2244–2266 (Supp. II 1996)).

[82]*See* Marcia Coyle, *Law: Innocent Dead Men Walking?,* Nat'l L.J., May 20, 1996, at 1; Ronald I. Tabak, *Habeas Corpus as a Crucial Protector of Constitutional Rights: A Tribute Which May Also Be a Eulogy,* 26 Seton Hall L. Rev. 1477 (1996); Ronald J. Tabak, *Panel Discussion: Capital Punishment, Is There Any Habeas Left in This Corpus?,* 27 Loy. U. Chi. L.J. 523, 538 n.119 (1996); Panel Discussion, *Dead Man Walking Without Due Process? A Discussion of the Anti-Terrorism and Effective Death Penalty Act of 1996,* 23 N.Y.U. Rev. L. & Soc. Change 163 (1997) (remarks of Ronald J. Tabak, moderator).

[83]Alex Gallup & Frank Newport, *Death Penalty Support Remains Strong,* 309 Gallup Poll Monthly 40,42 (June 1991).

[84]*See id.*

[85]Among those executed in recent years despite doubts about their guilt are James Adams (Florida, May 10, 1984), Edward Earl Johnson (Mississippi, May 20, 1987), Jimmy Wingo (Louisiana, June 16, 1987), Willie Darden (Florida, Mar. 15, 1999), Roger Keith Coleman (Virginia, May 20, 1992), Leonel Herrera (Texas, May 12, 1993), Jesse DeWayne Jacobs (Texas, Jan. 4, 1995), and David Wayne Spence (Texas, Apr. 3, 1997).

[86]*See* Furman v. Georgia, 408 U.S. 238, 360–63 (1972) (Marshall, J., concurring).

[87]*But see* Robert M. Bohm, *American Death Penalty Opinion: Past, Present, and Future in* America's Experiment with Capital Punishment, *supra* note 28, at 25, 31–41; Robert M. Bohm et al., *Knowledge and Death Penalty Opinion: A Test of the Marshall Hypothesis,* 28 J. Res. Crime & Delinq. 360 (1991); Austin Sarat & Neil Vidmar, *Public Opinion, the Death Penalty, and the Eighth Amendment: Testing the Marshall Hypothesis,* 1976 Wis. L. Rev. 171.

[88]*See* Michael L. Radelet, *Sociologists as Expert Witnesses in Capital Cases: A Case Study,* in Expert Witnesses: Criminologists in the Courtroom 119, 127–31 (Patrick R. Anderson & L. Thomas Winfree, Jr., eds., 1987).

89See generally American Bar Ass'n, supra note 2.

90See Michael A. Riccardi, Philadelphia Bar Calls for Execution Moratorium, LEGAL INTELLIGENCER, Dec. 1, 1997, at 1. The motion was passed after strong support from Clifford E. Haines, the former Chief of the Homicide Unit for the Philadelphia prosecutor's office. See id. Haines told the Board of Governors about a case in which he had asked for three death sentences, one of which was ultimately imposed. See id. He later regretted his action because shortly after the death sentence was imposed, the defense attorney in the case lost his license to practice law because of a drug conviction. See id.

91See Cecile S. Holmes, Texas Catholic Bishops Urge End to Death Penalty, HOUS. CHRON., Oct. 21, 1997, at A17.

92For a discussion of America's ambivalence about the death penalty, see Franklin E. Zimring, Ambivalence in State Capital Punishment Policy: An Empirical Sounding, 18 N.Y.U. REV. L. & SOC. CHANGE 729 (1990–91).

93See Rex L. Carter, Letter to the Editor, HOUSTON POST, Nov. 13, 1994, at C2.

94See Ex parte Gary Graham, 853 S.W.2d 565 (Tex. Crim. App. 1993).

95See Susan Blaustein, The Executioner's Wrong: Texas Will Execute Gary Graham for a Murder He Almost Certainly Didn't Commit, WASH. POST, Aug. 1, 1993, at C1.

96Carter, supra note 93.

97We are reminded of the scene in Dr. Strangelove, in which Joint Chief of Staff Chairman General Buck Turgidson (played by George C. Scott) tells the President (Peter Sellars) that a 40-megaton nuclear bomb is about to be dropped in error on a target in Russia:

> The President: General Turgidson, when you instituted the human reliability tests you assured me there was no possibility of such a thing ever occurring.
>
> General Turgidson: Well, ahh, I don't think it's quite fair to condemn the whole program because of a single slipup.
>
> Dr. Strangelove or: How I Learned to Stop Worrying and Love the Bomb (Columbia 1964).

98See Sam Howe Verhovek, When Justice Shows Its Darker Side, N.Y. TIMES, Jan. 8, 1995, at D6.

99See id.

100Ernest van den Haag, Why Capital Punishment?, 54 ALBANY L. REV. 501, 512 (1990).

101See generally THE DEATH PENALTY IN AMERICA, supra note 35, at 95–98; BEDAU, supra note 28.

102See Radelet et al., Doubts, supra note 4, at 271–81.

◉ ◉ ◉

Questions

1. What are the various ways of conceptualizing "innocence" reviewed in this article?

2. How does placing an inmate on death row affect their family?

3. What kinds of evidence suggest that innocent defendants have been executed?

4. The authors claim that the general public has turned a deaf ear to the possibility of executing the innocent. Do you think this is true? If so, why has it happened?

5. Has this article changed your thinking about the death penalty in any way? How?

Becoming a Marihuana User

Howard S. Becker

In this classic work, Howard Becker attempts to frame the theoretical explanations for deviant behavior. In doing so, he moves away from psychologically based explanations and toward a more sociological framework. He explains how social setting, or context, plays a large role in whether individuals become marijuana users (as well as why they continue to use the drug). Even though this article was first published in 1953, the dynamics of marijuana use that Becker detailed are still widely recognized in U.S. society today (especially among young people).

The use of marihuana is and has been the focus of a good deal of attention on the part of both scientists and laymen. One of the major problems students of the practice have addressed themselves to has been the identification of those individual psychological traits which differentiate marihuana users from nonusers and which are assumed to account for the use of the drug. That approach, common in the study of behavior categorized as deviant, is based on the premise that the presence of a given kind of behavior in an individual can best be explained as the result of some trait which predisposes or motivates him to engage in the behavior.[1]

This study is likewise concerned with accounting for the presence or absence of marihuana use in an individual's behavior. It starts, however, from a different premise: that the presence of a given kind of behavior is the result of a sequence of social experiences during which the person acquires a conception of the meaning of the behavior, and perceptions and judgments of objects and situations, all of which make the activity possible and desirable. Thus, the motivation or disposition to engage in the activity is built up in the course of learning to engage in it and does not antedate this learning process. For such a view it is not necessary to identify those "traits" which "cause" the behavior. Instead, the problem becomes one of describing

"Becoming a Marihuana User," by Howard S. Becker, reprinted from *American Journal of Sociology*, vol. 59, 1953, pp. 235–242.

the set of changes in the person's conception of the activity and of the experience it provides for him.[2]

This paper seeks to describe the sequence of changes in attitude and experience which lead to *the use of marihuana for pleasure*. Marihuana does not produce addiction, as do alcohol and the opiate drugs; there is no withdrawal sickness and no ineradicable craving for the drug.[3] The most frequent pattern of use might be termed "recreational." The drug is used occasionally for the pleasure the user finds in it, a relatively casual kind of behavior in comparison with that connected with the use of addicting drugs. The term "use for pleasure" is meant to emphasize the noncompulsive and casual character of the behavior. It is also meant to eliminate from consideration here those few cases in which marihuana is used for its prestige value only, as a symbol that one is a certain kind of person, with no pleasure at all being derived from its use.

The analysis presented here is conceived of as demonstrating the greater explanatory usefulness of the kind of theory outlined above as opposed to the predispositional theories now current. This may be seen in two ways: (1) predispositional theories cannot account for that group of users (whose existence is admitted)[4] who do not exhibit the trait or traits considered to cause the behavior and (2) such theories cannot account for the great variability over time of a given individual's behavior with reference to the drug. The same person will at one stage be unable to use the drug for pleasure, at a later stage be able and willing to do so, and, still later, again be unable to use it in this way. These changes, difficult to explain from a predispositional or motivational theory, are readily understandable in terms of changes in the individual's conception of the drug as is the existence of "normal" users.

The study attempted to arrive at a general statement of the sequence of changes in individual attitude and experience which have always occurred when the individual has become willing and able to use marihuana for pleasure and which have not occurred or not been permanently maintained when this is not the case. This generalization is stated in universal terms in order that negative cases may be discovered and used to revise the explanatory hypothesis.[5]

Fifty interviews with marihuana users from a variety of social backgrounds and present positions in society constitute the data from which the generalization was constructed and against which it was tested.[6] The interviews focused on the history of the person's experience with the drug, seeking major changes in his attitude toward it and in his actual use of it and the reasons for these changes. The final generalization is a statement of that sequence of changes in attitude which occurred in every case known to me in which the person come to use marihuana for pleasure. Until a negative case is found, it may be considered as an explanation of all cases of marihuana use for pleasure. In addition, changes from use to nonuse are shown to be related to similar changes in conception, and in each case it is possible to explain variations in the individual's behavior in these terms.

This paper covers only a portion of the natural history of an individual's use of marihuana,[7] starting with the person having arrived at the point of willingness to try marihuana. He knows that others use it to "get high," but he does not know what this means in concrete terms. He is curious about the experience, ignorant of what it may turn out to be, and afraid that it may be more than he has bargained for. The steps outlined below, if he undergoes them all and maintains the attitudes developed in them, leave him willing and able to use the drug for pleasure when the opportunity presents itself.

● Proper Technique

The novice does not ordinarily get high the first time he smokes marihuana, and several attempts are usually necessary to induce this state. One explanation of this may be that the drug is not smoked "properly," that is, in a way that insures sufficient dosage to produce real symptoms of intoxication. Most users agree that it cannot be smoked like tobacco if one is to get high:

> Take in a lot of air, you know, and . . . . I don't know how to describe it, you don't smoke it like a cigarette, you draw in a lot of air and get it deep down in your system and then keep it there. Keep it there as long as you can.

Without the use of some such technique[8] the drug will produce no effects, and the user will be unable to get high:

> The trouble with people like that [who are not able to get high] is that they're just not smoking it right, that's all there is to it. Either they're not holding it down long enough, or they're getting too much air and not enough smoke, or the other way around or something like that. A lot of people just don't smoke it right, so naturally nothing's gonna happen.

If nothing happens, it is manifestly impossible for the user to develop a conception of the drug as an object which can be used for pleasure, and use will therefore not continue. The first step in the sequence of events that must occur if the person is to become a user is that he must learn to use the proper smoking technique in order that his use of the drug will produce some effects in terms of which his conception of it can change.

Such a change is, as might be expected, a result of the individual's participation in groups in which marihuana is used. In them the individual learns the proper way to smoke the drug. This may occur through direct teaching:

> I was smoking like I did an ordinary cigarette. He said, "No, don't do it like that." He said, "Suck it, you know, draw in and hold it in your lungs till you . . . for a period of time."
>
> I said, "Is there any limit of time to hold it?"
>
> He said, "No, just till you feel that you want to let it out, let it out." So I did that three or four times.

Many new users are ashamed to admit ignorance and, pretending to know already, must learn through the more indirect means of observation and limitation:

> I came on like I had turned on [smoked marihuana] many times before, you know. I didn't want to seem like a punk to this cat. See, like I didn't know the first thing about it—how to smoke it, or what was going to happen, or what. I just watched him like a hawk—I didn't take my eyes off him for a second, because I wanted to do everything just as he did it. I watched how he held it, how he smoked it, and everything. Then when he gave it to me I just came on cool, as though I knew exactly what the score was. I held it like he did and took a poke just the way he did.

No person continued marihuana use for pleasure without learning a technique that supplied sufficient dosage for the effects of the drug to appear. Only when this was learned was it possible for a conception of the drug as an object which could be used for pleasure to emerge. Without such a conception marihuana use was considered meaningless and did not continue.

❧ Perceived Effects

Even after he learns the proper smoking technique, the new user may not get high and thus not form a conception of the drug as something which can be used for pleasure. A remark made by a user suggested the reason for this difficulty in getting high and point to the next necessary step on the road to being a user:

> I was told during an interview, "As a matter of fact, I've seen a guy who was high out of his mind and didn't know it."
>
> I expressed disbelief: "How can that be, man?"
>
> The interviewee said, "Well, it's pretty strange, I'll grant you that, but I've seen it. This guy got on with me, claiming that he'd never got high, one of those guys, and he got completely stoned. And he kept insisting that he wasn't high. So I had to prove to him that he was."

What does this mean? It suggests that being high consists of two elements: the presence of symptoms caused by marihuana use and the recognition of these symptoms and their connection by the user with his use of the drug. It is not enough, that is, that the effects be present; they alone do not automatically provide the experience of being high. The user must be able to point them out to himself and consciously connect them with his having smoked marihuana before he can have this experience. Otherwise, regardless of the actual effects produced, he considers that the drug has had no effect on him: "I figured it either had no effect on me or other people were exaggerating its effect on them, you know. I thought it was probably psychological, see." Such persons believe that the whole thing is an illusion and that the wish to be high leads the user to deceive himself into believing that something is happening when, in fact, nothing is. They do not continue marihuana use, feeling that "it does nothing" for them.

Typically, however, the novice has faith (developed from his observation of users who do get high) that the drug actually will produce some new experience and continues to experiment with it until it does. His failure to get high worries him, and he is likely to ask more experienced users or provoke comments from them about it. In such conversations he is made aware of specific details of his experience which he may not have noticed or may have noticed but failed to identify as symptoms of being high.

> I didn't get high the first time. . . . I don't think I held it long enough. I probably let it out, you, know, you're a little afraid. The second time I wasn't sure, and he [smoking companion] told me, like I asked him for some of the symptoms or something, how would I know, you know . . . so he told me to sit on a stool. I sat on—I think I sat on a bar stool—and he

said, "Let your feet hang," and then when I got down my feet were real cold, you know.

And I started feeling it, you know. That was the first time. And then about a week after that, sometime pretty close to it, I really got on. That was the first time I got on a big laughing kick, you know. Then I really knew I was on.

One symptom of being high is an intense hunger. In the next case the novice becomes aware of this and gets high for the first time:

They were just laughing the hell out of me because like I was eating so much. I just scoffed [ate] so much food, and they were just laughing at me, you know. Sometimes I'd be looking at them, you know, wondering why they're laughing, you know, not knowing what I was doing. [Well, did they tell you why they were laughing eventually?] Yeah, yeah. I come back, "Hey, man, what's happening?" and all of a sudden I feel weird, you know. "Man, you're on, you know. You're on pot [high on marihuana]." I said, "No, am I?" Like I don't know what's happening.

The learning may occur in more indirect ways:

I heard little remarks that were made by other people. Somebody said, "My legs are rubbery," and I can't remember all the remarks that were made because I was very attentively listening for all these cues for what I was supposed to feel like.

The novice, then, eager to have this feeling, picks up from other users some concrete referents of the term "high" and applies these notions to his own experience. The new concepts make it possible for him to locate these symptoms among his own sensations and to point out to himself a "something different" in his experience that he connects with drug use. It is only when he can do this that he is high. In the next case, the contrast between two successive experiences of a user makes clear the crucial importance of the awareness of the symptoms in being high and re-emphasizes the important role of interaction with other users in acquiring the concepts that make this awareness possible:

[Did you get high the first time you turned on?] Yeah, sure. Although, come to think of it, I guess I really didn't. I mean, like that first time it was more or less of a mild drunk. I was happy, I guess, you know what I mean. But I didn't really know I was high, you know what I mean. It was only after the second time I got high that I realized I was high the first time. Then I knew that something different was happening.

[How did you know that?] How did I know? If what happened to me that night would of happened to you, you would've known, believe me. We played the first tune for almost two hours—one tune! Imagine, man! We got on the stand and played this one tune, we started at nine o'clock. When we got finished I looked at my watch, it's a quarter to eleven. Almost two hours on one tune. And it didn't seem like anything.

I mean, you know, it does that to you. It's like you have much more time or something. Anyway, when I saw that, man, it was too much. I knew I must really be high or something if anything like that could happen. See, and then they explained to me that that's what it did to you, you had a different sense of time and everything. So I realized that that's what it was. I knew then. Like the first time, I probably felt that way, you know, but I didn't know what's happening.

It is only when the novice becomes able to get high in this sense that he will continue to use marihuana for pleasure. In every case in which use continued, the user had acquired the necessary concepts with which to express to himself, the fact that he was experiencing new sensations caused by the drug. That is, for use to continue, it is necessary not only to use the drug so as to produce effects but also to learn to perceive these effects when they occur. In this way marihuana acquires meaning for the user as an object which can be used for pleasure.

With increasing experience the user develops a greater appreciation of the drug's effects; he continues to learn to get high. He examines succeeding experiences closely, looking for new effects, making sure the old ones are still there. Out of this there grows a stable set of categories for experiencing the drug's effects whose presence enables the user to get high with ease.

The ability to perceive the drug's effects must be maintained if use is to continue; if it is lost, marihuana use ceases. Two kinds of evidence support this statement. First, people who become heavy users of alcohol, barbiturates, or opiates do not continue to smoke marihuana, largely because they lose the ability to distinguish between its effects and those of the other drugs.[9] They no longer know whether the marihuana gets them high. Second, in those few cases in which an individual uses marihuana in such quantities that he is always high, he is apt to get this same feeling that the drug has no effect on him, since the essential element of a noticeable difference between feeling high and feeling normal is missing. In such a situation, use is likely to be given up completely, but temporarily, in order that the user may one again be able to perceive the difference.

◉ *Learn to Enjoy Effects*

One more step is necessary if a user who has now learned to get high is to continue use. He must learn to enjoy the effects he has just learned to experience. Marihuana-produced sensations are not automatically or necessarily pleasurable. The taste for such experience is a socially acquired one, not different in kind from acquired tastes for oysters or dry martinis. The user feels dizzy, thirsty; his scalp tingles; he misjudges time and distances; and so on. Are these things pleasurable? He isn't sure. If he is to continue marihuana use, he must decide that they are. Otherwise, getting high, while a real enough experience, will be an unpleasant one he would rather avoid.

The effects of the drug, when first perceived, may be physically unpleasant or at least ambiguous:

> It started taking effect, and I didn't know what was happening, you know, what it was, and I was very sick. I walked around the room, walking around the room trying to get off, you know; it just scared me at first, you know. I wasn't used to that kind of feeling.

In addition, the novice's naive interpretation of what is happening to him may further confuse and frighten him, particularly if he decides, as many do, that he is going insane:

> I felt I was insane, you know. Everything people done to me just wigged me. I couldn't hold a conversation, and my mind would be wandering, and I was always thinking, oh, I don't know, weird things, like hearing music different. . . . I get the feeling that I can't talk to anyone. I'll goof completely.

Given these typically frightening and unpleasant first experiences, the beginner will not continue use unless he learns to redefine the sensations as pleasurable:

> It was offered to me, and I tried it. I'll tell you one thing. I never did enjoy it at all. I mean it was just nothing that I could enjoy. [Well, did you get high when you turned on?] Oh, yeah, I got definite feelings from it. But I didn't enjoy them. I mean I got plenty of reactions, but they were mostly reactions of fear. [You were frightened?] Yes. I didn't enjoy it. I couldn't seem to relax with it, you know. If you can't relax with a thing, you can't enjoy it, I don't think.

In other cases the first experiences were also definitely unpleasant, but the person did become a marihuana user. This occurred, however, only after a later experience enabled him to redefine the sensations as pleasurable:

[This man's first experience was extremely unpleasant, involving distortion of spatial relationships and sounds, violent thirst, and panic produced by these symptoms.] After the first time I didn't turn on for about, I'd say, ten months to a year. . . . It wasn't a moral thing; it was because I'd gotten so frightened, bein' so high. An' I didn't want to go through that again. I mean, my reaction was, "Well, if this is what they call bein' high, I don't dig [like] it." . . . So I didn't turn on for a year almost, accounta that. . . .

Well, my friends started, an' consequently I started again. But I didn't have any more, I didn't have that same initial reaction, after I started turning on again.

[In interaction with his friends he became able to find pleasure in the effects of the drug and eventually became a regular user.]

In no case will use continue without such a redefinition of the effects as enjoyable.

This redefinition occurs, typically, in interaction with more experienced users who, in a number of ways, teach the novice to find pleasure in this experience which is at first so frightening.[10] They may reassure him as to the temporary character of the unpleasant sensations and minimize their seriousness, at the same time calling attention to the more enjoyable aspects. An experienced user describes how he handles new comers to marihuana use:

Well, they get pretty high sometimes. The average person isn't ready for that, and it is a little frightening to them sometimes. I mean, they've been high on lush [alcohol], and they get higher that way than they've ever been before, and they don't know what's happening to them. Because they think they're going to keep going up, up, up till they lose their minds or begin doing weird things or something. You have to like reassure them, explain to them that they're not really flipping or anything, that they're gonna be all right. You have to just talk them out of being afraid. Keep talking to them, reassuring, telling them it's all right. And come on with your own story, you know: "The same thing happened to me. You'll get to like that after awhile." Keep coming on like that; pretty soon you talk them out of being scared. And besides they see you doing it and nothing horrible is happening to you, so that gives them more confidence.

The more experienced user may also teach the novice to regulate the amount he smokes more carefully, so as to avoid any severely uncomfortable symptoms while retaining the pleasant ones. Finally, he teaches the new user that he can "get to like it after awhile." He teaches him to regard those ambiguous experiences formerly defined as unpleasant as enjoyable. The older user in the following incident is a person whose tastes have shifted in this way, and his remarks have the effect of helping others to make a similar redefinition:

> A new user had her first experience of the effects of marihuana and became frightened and hysterical. She "felt like she was half in and half out of the room" and experienced a number of alarming physical symptoms of the more experienced users present said, "She's dragged because she's high like that. I'd give anything to get that high myself. I haven't been that high in years."

In short, what was once frightening and distasteful becomes, after a taste for it is built up, pleasant, desired, and sought after. Enjoyment is introduced by the favorable definition of the experience that one acquires from others. Without this, use will not continue, for marihuana will not be for the user an object he can use for pleasure.

In addition to being a necessary step in becoming a user, this represents an important condition for continued use. It is quite common for experienced users suddenly to have an unpleasant or frightening experience, which they cannot define as pleasurable, either because they have used a larger amount of marihuana than usual or because it turns out to be a higher-quality marihuana than they expected. The user has sensations which go beyond any conception he has of what being high is and is in much the same situation as the novice, uncomfortable and frightened. He may blame it on an overdose and simply be more careful in the future. But he may make this the occasion for the rethinking of his attitude toward the drug and decide that it no longer can give him pleasure. When this occurs and is not followed by a redefinition of the drug as capable of producing pleasure, use will cease.

The likelihood of such a redefinition occurring depends on the degree of the individual's participation with other users. Where this participation is intensive, the individual is quickly talked out of his feeling against marihuana use. In the next case, on the other hand, the experience was very disturbing, and the aftermath of the incident cut the person's participation with other users to almost zero. Use stopped for three years and began again only when a combination of circumstances, important among which was a resumption of ties with others, made possible a redefinition of the nature of the drug:

It was too much, like I only made about four pokes, and I couldn't even get it out of my mouth. I was so high, and I got real flipped. In the basement, you know, I just couldn't stay in there anymore. My heart was pounding real hard, you know, and I was going out of my mind; I thought I was losing my mind completely. So I cut out of this basement, and this other guy, he's out of his mind, told me, "Don't, don't leave me, man. Stay here." And I couldn't.

I walked outside, and it was five below zero, and I thought I was dying, and I had my coat open; I was sweating, I was perspiring. My whole insides were all . . . . and I walked about two blocks away, and I fainted behind a bush. I don't know how long I laid there. I woke up, and I was feeling the worst. I can't describe it at all, so I made it to a bowling alley, man, and I was trying to act normal. I was trying to shoot pool, you know, trying to act real normal, and I couldn't lay and I couldn't stand up and I couldn't sit down, and I went up and laid down where some guys that spot pins lay down, and that didn't help me, and I went down to a doctor's office. I was going to go in there and tell the doctor to put me out of my misery . . . because my heart was pounding so hard, you know. . . . So then all week end I started flipping, seeing things there and going through hell, you know, all kinds of abnormal things. . . . I just quit for a long time then.

[He went to a doctor who defined the symptoms for him as those of a nervous breakdown caused by "nerves" and "worries." Although he was no longer using marihuana, he had some recurrences of the symptoms which led him to suspect that "it was all his nerves."] So I just stopped worrying, you know; so it was about thirty-six months later I started making it again. I'd just take a few pokes, you know. [He first resumed use in the company of the same user-friend with whom he had been involved in the original incident.]

A person, then, cannot begin to use marihuana for pleasure, or continue its use for pleasure, unless he learns to define its effects as enjoyable, unless it becomes and remains an object which he conceives of as capable of producing pleasure.

❧ Conclusion

In summary, an individual will be able to use marihuana for pleasure only when he goes through a process of learning to conceive of it as an object which can be used in this way. No one becomes a user without (1) learning to smoke the drug in a way which will produce real effects; (2) learning to recognize the effects and connect them with drug use (learning, in other words, to get high); and (3) learning to enjoy the sensations he perceives. In the course of this process he develops a disposition or motivation to use marihuana which was not and could not have been present when he began use, for it involves and depends on conceptions of the drug which could only grow out of the kind of actual experience detailed above. On completion of this process he is willing and able to use marihuana for pleasure.

He has learned, in short, to answer "Yes" to the question: "Is it fun?" The direction his further use of the drug takes depends on his being able to continue to answer "Yes" to this question and, in addition, on his being able to answer "Yes" to other questions which arise as he becomes aware of the implications of the fact that the society as a whole disapproves of the practice: "Is it expedient?" "Is it moral?" Once he has acquired the ability to get enjoyment out of the drug, use will continue to be possible for him. Considerations of morality and expediency, occasioned by the reactions of society, may interfere and inhibit use, but use continues to be a possibility in terms of his conception of the drug. The act becomes impossible only when the ability to enjoy the experience of being high is lost, through a change in the user's conception of the drug occasioned by certain kinds of experience with it.

In comparing this theory with those which ascribe marihuana use to motives or predispositions rooted deep in individual behavior, the evidence makes it clear that marihuana use for pleasure can occur only when the process described above is undergone and cannot occur without it. This is apparently so without reference to the nature of the individual's personal makeup or psychic problems. Such theories assume that people have stable modes of response which predetermine the way they will act in relation to any particular situation or object and that, when they come in contact with the given object or situation, they act in the way in which their makeup predisposes them.

This analysis of the genesis of marihuana use shows that the individuals who come in contact with a given object may respond to it at first in a great variety of ways. If a stable form of new behavior toward the object is to emerge, a transformation of meanings must occur, in which the person develops a conception of the nature of the object.[11] This happens in a series of communications in which others point out new aspects of his experience to him, present him with new interpretations of events, and help him achieve a new conceptual organization of his world, without which the new behavior is not possible. Persons who do not achieve the proper kind of conceptualization are unable to engage in the given behavior and turn off in the direction of some other relationship to the object or activity.

This suggests that behavior of any kind might fruitfully be studied developmentally, in terms of changes in meanings and concepts, their organization and reorganization, and the way they channel behavior, making some acts possible while excluding others.

Endnotes

[1] See, as examples of this approach, the following: Eli Marcovitz and Henry J. Meyers, "The Marihuana Addict in the Army," *War Medicine*, VI (December, 1944), 382–91: Herbert S. Gaskill, "Marihuana and Intoxicant," *American Journal of Psychiatry*, CII (September, 1945), 202–4: Sol Charen and Luis Perelman, "Personality Studies of Marihuana Addicts," *American Journal of Psychiatry*, CII (March 1, 1946), 674–82.

[2] This approach stems from George Herbert Mead's discussion of objects in *Mind, Self, and Society* (Chicago: University of Chicago Press, 1934), pp. 277–80.

[3] Cf. Roger Adams, "Marihuana," *Bulletin of the New York Academy of Medicine*, XVIII (November, 1942), 705–30.

[4] Cf. Lawrence Kolb, "Marihuana," *Federal Probation*, II (July, 1938), 22–25; and Walter Bromberg, "Marihuana: A Psychiatric Study," *Journal of the American Medical Association*, CXIII (July 1, 1939), 11.

[5] The method used is that described by Alfred R. Lindesmith in his *Opiate Addiction* (Bloomington: Principia Press, 1947), chap. i. I would like also to acknowledge the important role Lindesmith's work played in shaping my thinking about the genesis of marihuana use.

[6] Most of the interviews were done by the author. I am grateful to Solomon Kobrin and Harold Finestone for allowing me to make use of interviews done by them.

[7] I hope to discuss elsewhere other stages in this natural history.

[8] A pharmacologist notes that this ritual is in fact an extremely efficient way of getting the drug into the blood stream (R. P. Walton, *Marihuana: America's New Drug Problem* [Philadelphia: J. B. Lippincott, 1938], p. 48.)

[9] "Smokers have repeatedly stated that the consumption of whiskey while smoking negates the potency of the drug. They find it very difficult to get 'high' while drinking whiskey and because of that smokers will not drink while using the 'weed'" (cf. New York City Mayor's Committee on Marihuana, *The Marihuana*

Problem in the City of New York [Lancaster. Pa.: Jacques Cattell Press. 1944]. p. 13).

[10]Charen and Perelman. *op cit.*, p. 679.

[11]Cf. Anselm Strauss, "The Development and Transformation of Monetary Meanings in the Child," *American Sociological Review*. XVII (June. 1952), 275–86.

❧ ❧ ❧

Questions

1. What three stages must a person progress through to become a regular marijuana user? Are these stages sequential. or can they occur in any order? Explain.

2. What role do peers play in the process of someone's becoming a marijuana user? What would Becker likely say about persons' becoming regular marijuana users in isolation (that is, without peer support)?

3. Given that early marijuana use typically leads to either no effect or negative experiences. why (according to Becker) do some people still become regular users?

4. Becker argues that a person who has successfully gone through all three stages will become a regular marijuana user. Given Becker's view of social learning theory. what sort of dynamic would have to take place for such a person to stop using?

5. How might the process detailed by Becker apply to use of other kinds of drugs today. such as alcohol. tobacco. cocaine. inhalants. etc.? Would you expect any differences in the process between use of legal drugs (such as alcohol and tobacco) and illegal drugs (cocaine. inhalants, etc.)? Explain your thinking.

Choosing the Target

RICHARD T. WRIGHT AND SCOTT H. DECKER

In this excerpt from their book Burglars on the Job, *Richard Wright and Scott Decker explain how residential burglars choose their targets. With data collected from in-depth interviews with active burglars, the authors explore the various aspects of choosing a dwelling to burgle. For example, how do burglars identify target houses? How often do they steal from friends and acquaintances? To what extent do locks deter them?*

*T*he motivation to commit a residential burglary is not itself sufficient to cause offenders to carry out the offense. Obviously, they must pick out a specific dwelling before acting on that motivation. In theory, the supply of residential properties is so vast that finding a target would seem to be a simple matter. In practice, however, potential targets are fairly limited. The offenders, after all, typically are seeking to solve a pressing problem, financial or other, and feel under pressure to act quickly. At the same time, they are reluctant to break in to a place without first determining the potential risks and rewards. As offenders attempt to settle on a target, therefore, they are under the influence of two seemingly conflicting demands: one calling for immediate action, and the other counselling caution. How do they manage to reconcile these demands and select a specific dwelling? That is the question which this [selection] seeks to answer. This issue already has received considerable attention from researchers, especially from those favoring a rational choice explanation of property offending (e.g., Bennett and Wright, 1984; Cromwell et al., 1991). These researchers, however, have failed to place the target selection process into the wider context of the lifestyles and daily activities of offenders.

It is widely assumed that offenders typically make a decision to commit a residential burglary and only then set out to search for a suitable target. Burglary prevention advice admonishing homeowners to create the illusion of occupancy while they are away—by, among other things, using an auto-

"Choosing the Target," by Richard T. Wright and Scott H. Decker, reprinted from *Burglars on the Job: Streetlife and Residential Break-Ins*, 1992, pp. 62–67, 73–74, 77–81, 85–87, 91–92, 94–97, 99–102. Copyright © 1992 by Northeastern Books.

matic timer to switch lights on and off—clearly is founded on this assumption. A great deal of the experimental research on the way in which burglars choose targets also rests on the same paradigm (e.g., Bennett and Wright, 1983; 1984; Logie et al., 1992; Nee and Taylor, 1988; Taylor and Nee, 1988; Wright and Logie, 1988). In reality, offenders often have a potential target in mind when they decide to do a burglary and, therefore, have no need to search for one. Nearly nine out of ten of the subjects in our sample—89 of 100—said that usually they had decided on a specific dwelling *before* setting out to commit the burglary. These subjects were unwilling to break into a residence without knowing something about the people who lived there and the kinds of things it contained.

> I never go into a house where I don't know nothing about it or who's
> [living] there. You got to at least know something. (Andre Neal—No. 059)

Accordingly, when the need for money arose, they would not simply search for a target and commit a spur-of-the-moment offense; they had to have a place already lined up, that is, they needed reliable information regarding its contents and the routine of the residents. In practice, this could be accomplished in one of three ways: (1) through knowing the occupants; (2) through receiving a tip; or (3) through observing a potential target.

● Knowing the Occupants

It is taken for granted among criminologists that crimes of violence often involve a victim who is known to the offender. Research on homicide (e.g., Wolfgang, 1958), rape (e.g., Amir, 1971), and assault (e.g., Vera Institute, 1977) consistently has shown this to be the case. Less well appreciated is the fact that the offender knows the victim in a sizable proportion of certain property crimes (Black, 1983). Shover (1991: 93), based on an examination of National Crime Survey data, concluded that "upward of 42 percent of victims who chance to encounter a burglar in their home may discover the burglar is not a stranger." More than one in five of the offenders we interviewed—21 of 100—reported that typically they chose to break into dwellings where they knew the occupants.

> [N]ine times out of ten, if I am just laying around the house with nothing
> to do [and] I want some fast money, I just try to [choose a target using] the
> people I know and got their phone numbers. "Where you going? What you

93

up to? You gonna leave? Who's at the house now?" . . . I can find out where they be at. (No. 069)

Only a few offenders selected targets belonging to relatives or close friends. Most picked homes occupied by what might be termed casual acquaintances, who often were neighborhood residents encountered by the offenders in the course of their daily rounds (see Walsh, 1986).

> I knew [the burglary victim] before anyway. We was all just on the street getting high and drinking. [The victim] said, "We can go to my house and smoke this shit." That's how I ended up over at his house. . . . He wasn't a friend of mine, just somebody I knew. I was at their house getting high and it was, like, three days later I wanted to get high [again] and I needed some money. I was thinking, "Where can I make some money at?" I said, "I can go over to John's house." (No. 079)

In many cases, the offenders had not become acquainted with the victims in order to burglarize their dwellings. Rather, they tended to select these places on short notice, typically because they wanted money quickly and knew there was something inside worth stealing. Often these decisions resulted from a session of spontaneous partying, with offenders being invited to visit the home of a would-be victim for the purpose of socializing and then noticing something of value. One subject explained the process this way: "Like, say I be over at your house and you might have a motherfucking solid gold lamp on the table. Now I ain't saying that I plan to steal it from you, but we over there. Then tomorrow I wake up and I need some money; I can get about forty dollars for that motherfucker." In such circumstances, the offenders seldom reported selecting their targets by carefully weighing up a variety of possible places to attack; instead, the idea of burglarizing one particular dwelling suddenly popped into their heads as they contemplated ways to get some fast cash.

Quite a few of the offenders targeted residences belonging to acquaintances whom they knew to be drug dealers. In doing a dealer's place, they were able to obtain drugs directly and avoid the problem of converting stolen goods into cash.

> I knew exactly where to go to get what I needed. I didn't want no items. I didn't want to have to sell nothing. I just wanted to get some drugs and some money, so I knew exactly where to go. (No. 069)

These offenses could be carried out more or less on the spur of the moment precisely because the offenders were acquainted with the victims and, at a minimum, knew something about their daily movements. An added benefit of burglarizing dwellings belonging to drug dealers, of course, was that such people were unlikely to report break-ins to the police.

A number of the offenders in our sample cultivated relationships with people with the express purpose of burglarizing their residences. One female offender, for instance, regularly picked up men in bars as a means of locating potential burglary sites. She would strike up a conversation with a man drinking alone, spend the evening in his company surreptitiously gathering information about such things as his work and travel schedule, and eventually agree to accompany him to his place for sex. While at this residence, she would check for any special security devices, note the floor plan, and determine the location of valuables—a task that she found easy: "You know how men are, they always want to show off. So they get out their gun collection or coin collection, stamp collection or whatever. They always do." Several weeks later she would return, often with her boyfriend, to break into the dwelling. Similarly, two other female offenders, working as partners, usually located targets in the course of their prostitution activities. Advertising themselves as "two women for the price of one," they offered their clients, who often were intoxicated elderly men, an in-home service. Once inside a residence, one of the women would distract the man while the other would steal his keys. After two or three days had passed, they would come back and do the burglary. Likewise, one of the male subjects worked hard to establish rapport with local drug dealers so that he could set them up for a burglary.

> My house burglaries are based on dope dealers. The way I do it is watch them, learn them, get up under them—try to get next to them and peep [the house] to find out where the stash is at. I might not hit them that day, or that time, or that month; not until I've learned it. (No. 024)

· · ·

Offenders who had jobs that gave them the chance to enter people's homes legitimately found it particularly easy to locate prospective burglary targets. Several, for instance, were employed by home decorating or remodeling companies. These offenders frequently spent days or weeks working in the same residence; this allowed them to get a good sense of the occupants' daily routine. What is more, they often were left unsupervised by homeowners. This provided ample opportunities to explore dwellings unmolested, checking security arrangements, and determining where valuables were kept.

> In my everyday routine. I can see things. Like, I works for a interior deco-
> rator company, so I travels a lot and I sees a lot. . . . When [the company]
> calls me . . . to go set up paneling or something, I look around. [The occu-
> pants] got money; they buyin' from that company, they got some money.
> (Bob More—No. 012)

• • •

Offenders who worked on the outside of residences (e.g., roofers or
gardeners) also could gather information about potential targets. At a minimum, they could watch occupants come and go and develop some notion
of their daily schedule without attracting suspicion. They often were permitted to enter dwellings to get a drink of water, make a telephone call, or use
the toilet, and thereby were able to learn a good deal more about the inte-
rior. One study subject, a gardener, was given a house key by the owners of
a residence so that he could let himself in when they were not at home. He
worked for these people for some time and did not steal anything from them
as long as he remained in their employ. Shortly before quitting, he had a
duplicate key cut. He continues to use this key to gain entry to the house
from time to time, despite the fact that the residence has changed hands
twice. On each occasion, he is careful to steal just one small item, believing
that with no sign of a forced entry the occupants either will not miss the
piece or will conclude that they have misplaced it. As he put it: "See, they
not expectin' it. If you go taking like a TV or stereo and stuff like that, that's
easy to miss. But by the time they find out that I done took something, I'm
back again and done got somethin' else." He noted that a major advantage
of burglarizing the same place repeatedly was that one developed a fairly
reliable way of predicting when the occupants would be away.

> I always go back [to the same places] because, once you been there, you
> know just about when you been there before and when you can go back.
> And every time I hit a house, it's always on the same day [of the week] I
> done been before cause I know there ain't nobody there. (John Ross—
> No. 051)

This might go some way toward explaining the general process by which
certain dwellings come to be burglarized repeatedly (Forrester et al., 1988).
People are creatures of routine: having established through offending that
the residents of an attractive target were out at a given time of day burglars
can be fairly confident that the dwelling will usually be unoccupied at this
time. Why, then, should they select a brand new target where the presence
of occupants may be more at issue?

· · ·

The finding that a substantial number of the offenders in our sample typically knew the people whose homes they victimized suggests that property crimes may not be all that different from violent ones in terms of the relationship between offender and victim. While some might object that the offenders often had only a very superficial acquaintanceship with their victims, this is true for many violent crimes as well. The important point is that burglars were able to take advantage of a preexisting relationship with potential victims—however brief or casual—to gather intelligence about their daily activities, possessions, and household security. This facilitated the selection of a target when the need to commit the crime arose. As Lofland (1969: 73) has observed: "Built-in vulnerabilities in the standing social arrangements of [o]thers" have a way of becoming particularly obvious at these times.

❧ Receiving a Tip

Where burglary offenders do not select their victims on the basis of personal knowledge, they may rely on "inside" information provided by others as a means of locating targets. Sometimes they receive this information from "tipsters," that is, people who regularly pass on intelligence about good burglary opportunities for a fee or a cut of the take (Shover, 1973). At other times offenders pick up information more informally through friends or criminal associates. This information is valuable to offenders because, as Shover (1973) has noted, it can reduce the risks as well as enhance the rewards of residential burglary considerably. Getting good intelligence about lucrative targets on anything approaching a routine basis requires that offenders have access to a reliable network. Not many do. Just six of the subjects in our sample said that they usually selected their residential targets on the basis of a tip given to them by someone else. What is more, only two of these offenders regularly used information from persons who might be considered tipsters. One of them had an arrangement with an airport employee under which he received information about departing passengers with local addresses.

> [It's summer and] a lot of people are goin' to Hawaii. France, and Rome and stuff like that. Paris. I'm a bee [busy]. (Eric Thompson—No. 047)

· · ·

The remaining subjects who routinely relied on tips as a means of locating targets picked up their information from various sources on the street.

> I know a lot of people and they know my game, so they put me up on certain people: "So and so's leavin' town next week." I don't like nobody in the house. . . . Say, for instance, a friend of theirs might be going out of town and they want something out of the deal, they ain't doing it for nothing. They scared to go do it, so they tell [me] about it. (Robert Johnson—No. 067)

These offenders did not have a formal arrangement for obtaining information about potential burglary targets. Their interest in such information, however, was well-known on the street and people often offered them a "lick," that is, a promising burglary site, in exchange for some part of the proceeds.

While only a few of the offenders regularly used information from others to locate targets, many of them occasionally did so. One offender, for example, took us to a mansion that he recently had burglarized. This offense was triggered by information received from one of the victim's neighbors, a well-to-do businessman who provided the offender with tips from time to time.

> [I didn't] find this house exactly. I went out to do a cable job. So the person I did the cable job for, like I say, he ain't exactly what you call straight up, he just live in a good place . . . and he told me that [the next door neighbors] had certain things that he wanted, so we compromised. I got what I wanted and he got what he wanted. . . . You know; this person called me [later] and told me that [his neighbors] will be back [from vacation] this week and, if I was gonna take care of my business, do it now. (No. 056)

Another offender told us about several lucrative residential burglaries that he had committed with the aid of an insurance agent. The agent, using the files of coworkers as well as his own, was able to identify properties containing insured valuables and to determine any special security precautions. Several other subjects recounted offenses where a person employed as a maid or gardener had let them know that the occupants of a house would not be home at a certain time.

• • •

In summary, while few of the offenders regularly relied on tips as a means of locating targets, many of them occasionally selected a dwelling on the basis of inside knowledge provided by someone else. The people who gave them this information might be thought of as "facilitating others" (Lofland, 1969: 72–81) in at least two senses. First, in assuming that the offenders wanted this information, they reinforced their deviant identity as people who were willing to commit residential burglaries. Perhaps they even conveyed, however subtly, an *expectation* that the offenders should act on the information given to them. Second, and more directly, by identifying a specific target, they handed the offenders an opportunity that could be exploited in a time of need.

❂ Watching the Target

While in many residential burglaries the offenders have inside knowledge about the occupants either through personal acquaintance or by way of a tip provided by someone else, this certainly does not characterize all—or even most—such crimes. Nonetheless, most targets do not appear to be chosen randomly or on the spur of the moment. Oftentimes offenders have been watching a specific dwelling for some time prior to breaking in to it. Indeed, the majority of the subjects in our sample—62 of 100—reported that this typically was the case for them.

> I get about two [houses] a month, somewhere in there. It all depends on how my money is. [Just] because I'm always lookin' out there [for a place], don't make me do it every time. But I be lookin'. Then, if I just happen to be in the vicinity again, I might say, "Damn, this is the house I'm gon' get." Then I might see that house two or three more times 'fore I make up my mind to go in it. . . . I look at a house two or three times before I go in it . . . But the day I go in, I done made my mind up. (James Cook—No. 016)

> If we going shopping, for instance, we'll pick a house; we'll be just walking around and stuff and we pick a house. . . . You see, it's real simple and easy, you know. We watch it for a while, we don't just go jump into it. It's got to be a house we done watched for a while. (Sharon Adams—No. 071)

Through observing residences, the offenders were able to acquire various bits and pieces of information about the occupants, the most important of which was their daily routine. Almost all of the offenders who regularly watched potential targets beforehand, said that they did so to "clock" the comings and goings of the residents.

> I don't just go there and do a burglary. I done already checked it out. I can sit back for about a month and estimate how many people are there. What

time they leave and what time they coming back. Just like the police do; sitting in front of a dope house and watching how many people are coming or going out of there. (Mike Bird—No. 028)

Well, first you have to look at the house. You don't want to go in when the people are there [so] you check it out a day or two and see what they schedule is. See when they go to work, when they get home, where the kids at. (No. 057)

You have to go out and look and see what's the best. What's what and where [the occupants] gonna be, how long they gonna be there. Does the wife work? Husband work? You find them things out. You could see that early in the morning. If two cars are there and both of them are gone between eight and twelve, then you know both of them work. If you see one of them gone and the other one's back at about eight-thirty or nine, you know the wife's usually there. She's just dropped the kids off to school. (No. 035)

Some subjects also kept an eye on places prior to breaking in to them to ascertain whether they contained enough valuable merchandise to make a burglary worthwhile. They inferred this information from the appearance of the occupants, particularly the clothing and jewelry that they wore (see Merry, 1981).

If I spot a easy house or something. I got to really check you out first and see what you got. Cause I ain't gon just go in your house and I don't see you dressin' like nothin' or not wearin' no jewelry. You be wastin' my time. (Bill Anderson—No. 050)

Furthermore, a few offenders attempted to collect additional information such as the timing of police patrols, the daily activities of neighbors, and the presence of any extraordinary security precautions. These offenders, however, were the exception; most simply watched places as a way of reducing the chances of anyone being home when they actually committed the burglary.

The practice of watching possible targets prior to attacking them facilitates the commission of residential burglary in situations where offenders find themselves short of cash. When faced with the need to get money quickly, offenders who have a specific target lined up are liable to be especially open to the possibility of committing burglary. After all, once a place has been located and checked out, much of the groundwork has already been completed.

I wasn't gon to do the house that day, [but] my money got funny. So I had to think of a quick way [of getting some]. So I thought about that one there. (No. 015)

But how do offenders come to be watching these places to begin with? Do they purposely seek them out? Or do they simply stumble on them in the course of their daily rounds? For most of the offenders in our sample who typically watched dwellings before breaking in to them, the answer seemed to fall somewhere between these two extremes. The subjects usually did not go out with the specific intention of looking for potential targets. Nor did they generally just happen upon places when locating prospective burglary sites was the last thing on their minds. Rather they were continually "half looking" for targets. As one put it: "When you out here without a job, you got to keep your eyes and ears open all the time." While not actively seeking targets, these offenders nevertheless remained attuned to their surroundings as they went about their day-to-day, "routine activities" (Felson, 1986: 126).

> You could be just coming from somewhere. I might have some business that I got to do in [a nearby municipality] and I'm on the way back home and I see a house. (Jerome Little—No. 064)

> I don't really look for any kind of area, just, I don't know, I don't really go out looking for a house just, like, if I'll see it and it looks good. (Milo Davis—No. 076)

They were aware that they would need to commit additional burglaries in the future but, not needing to do so at the moment, were not motivated to take the necessary steps to locate targets. Viewed in the context of their lives, lives largely oriented toward keeping the party going, this makes perfect sense. From the perspective of the offenders, actively searching for targets that might not be needed for some time was "too much like hard work" and interrupted enjoyment of the moment. Such enjoyment, of course, often entailed loitering with friends on streetcorners and front porches in the neighborhood and this facilitated the process of discovering potential targets.

Nonetheless, some of the subjects who routinely watched their targets prior to offenses actually sought out these places in a more or less systematic fashion. Even in these cases, however, their efforts were usually lackadaisical.

> I might go to the neighborhood park or something and then I might say, "Well, I'm a go home this way today." Then while I'm walkin' up the street I just be lookin', checkin' it out. (No. 057)

> I'll say, like, "I'm a walk from [one part of the city to another]." And I walk, you know. Then my mind might wander, you know. So I might say, "Let me turn here or there," you know, scopin' . . . as I go. . . . You know, I might say, "It's nice here" and I write that down. . . . Your mind just wanders and you just turn here or turn there and you don't really think about it. (No. 009)

Certainly, none of these subjects searched for potential targets with any marked determination. They went about the task in a casual, unhurried way as befits those who are under no immediate pressure. In this sense, they were not dissimilar from their counterparts who only "half looked" for possible burglary sites. In the end, all of the offenders found dwellings without putting much effort into the process. Indeed, many indicated that promising targets virtually leapt out at them.

> I might get up and just ride the bus. . . . I ain't saying, "Well, I'm going out here to do a burglary." I might just ride to think where I could do a burglary. Then, as I'm riding I say, "Uh oh, there one is!" (No. 018)

But what drew the attention of the offenders to these particular places to begin with? What was it about specific residences that caused the offenders to consider them worth watching?

Almost all of the offenders initially were attracted to residences which, judging from the outside, appeared to them to contain "good stuff" (see Merry, 1981). Conversely, only a few of them were drawn to places simply because they looked easy or safe. This should not be surprising; after all, the offenders made it a practice to watch potential targets for some days before burglarizing them. Thus, they could assess and deal with such matters in the fullness of time. Several externally visible cues suggested to the burglars that a residence contained things worth stealing. These cues, of course, were subjective, being judged both in relation to the poor housing conditions in which a majority of the offenders found themselves living and in light of the realistically available alternatives. The most obvious cue was the size of the structure. Other things being equal, a large house was regarded as promising the biggest payoff.

> If a house is big, it's got some money. A big house, you got to go through all them rooms and you got four or five people stayin' there, so all of them got they own stash; I'm goin' to get it! (No. 009)

Another cue was the condition of the property. Well-maintained dwellings were believed to contain the most desirable goods.

. . .

The type of car parked in the driveway of a residence also influenced some of the subjects. In their view, an expensive car outside meant valuable property inside.

> Here's this big ol' huge house sittin' up there and in the driveway is two BMWs and a Mercedes. This other house might have a van or something like that . . . so I visualize that [the intended target] must have more things than that house. (No. 017)

Several of the offenders said they were attracted to residences specifically by BMWs and Mercedes-Benzs rather than by expensive cars generally. In part this probably reflects the fact that these makes are reputed to be popular with successful drug dealers. As noted earlier, many offenders regard places belonging to drug dealers as ideal targets.

. . .

In short, most of the subjects in our sample usually watched potential targets for some time before committing a burglary. By and large, they were attracted to these targets by external cues suggesting that there were goods worth stealing inside. This finding flies in the face of the results of previous studies indicating that most residential burglars choose targets because they appear to be "safe," that is, well covered and unoccupied (e.g., Bennett and Wright, 1984; Wright and Logie, 1988). Undoubtedly, this difference is due to the fact that these earlier studies contained a large proportion of offenders who searched for targets with the intention of committing an offense there and then. Under such circumstances, offenders *must* be attuned to safety cues; they are not planning to take the time required to assess the risks more fully.

❧ Searching for a Target

Some offenders do not routinely have a potential target available when they decide to do a residential burglary. Ten of the subjects in our sample said that when faced with the pressing need to commit burglary, they usually first had to go out and search for a suitable dwelling to attack.

> Sometime I wake up with a burglary on my mind. I'll wake up thinkin', "Where am I gon get some money from?" . . . I'll wake up early in the morning about five or six in the mornin'; and go out knockin' on doors. I usually find me a house to do. (Howard Ford—No. 014)

> It's nothing like, "Tomorrow we gon sit down here and we gon run in this person's house." We might just be sittin' here like we sittin' now and I'll say, "Let's go to such and such a place." . . . We end up goin' for a ride lookin' for some houses we could get into . . . [And when we find them] we don't just up and say, "Tomorrow we gon get this and that." We just do it [right then]. (William Jones—No. 038)

Virtually all of the offenders said that they occasionally were obliged to locate a vulnerable target and burglarize it immediately. At times, they did not have a potential target lined up or, if they did, it sometimes was unavailable because the occupants were at home. One way around this problem was to search for a dwelling that could be broken in to right then. This solution carried a large element of risk because the offenders knew nothing about the occupants or their daily routine. Accordingly, they approached the selection of such a target with considerable trepidation.

When searching for a residential burglary site, the offenders typically were required to make two basic decisions. First, they had to decide on a suitable area for their search. And second, they had to select a specific target from within this area. What were the factors that underpinned their choices?

In selecting an area, the offenders did not have an infinite supply from which to choose. Both physical and psychological barriers limited their horizons (Brantingham and Brantingham, 1981). Many offenders, for instance, did not have access to a car when the need arose to locate a burglary target. This meant that, for all intents and purposes, they were restricted to areas that were within walking distance. Moreover, this distance could be severely circumscribed, particularly in cases where they hoped to steal heavy or bulky items.

> I ain't gonna go no further than ten blocks; that's a ways to be carryin' stuff . . . Since I'm on foot, I got to keep walkin' back and forth until I get it all. (Howard Davis—No. 020)

> I don't have no car and I don't want to be walking or catching no bus. If I
> go out in [a distant municipality] and do a burglary, how am I going to get
> back with all the stuff? (Tom Bryant—No. 026)

> It's hard as hell gettin' on a bus carrying a big picture or a vase. People will
> look at you like, "Where did he get that from?" or "Where's he going with
> that?" . . . You subject to get caught. So it's really a [lack of] transportation
> thing with me. (No. 040)

And even offenders who did have a car sometimes could not travel very far
because they were out of money and low on gas.

> [I was out of money and] I didn't have that much gas to really be ridin' far
> out the way. (No. 014)

The logistical problems posed by committing burglaries a long way from
home without reliable transportation became very obvious during our
research. On one occasion, an offender was arrested because his car, laden
with stolen goods, broke down a short distance from the house he had just
burglarized. Unable to start the vehicle and many miles from home, he
returned to the target on foot and called for a taxi. When the cab arrived, he
filled it with his booty and asked the driver to take him to a spot near his
own house. The driver complied but, having become suspicious, called the
police immediately after dropping him off. The offender was easily apprehended as he struggled home with the evening's takings.

Beyond the practical constraints, there also were psychological factors
that served to restrict the range of areas available to the offenders. As
Brantingham and Brantingham (1981: 37) have observed, a great deal of the
territory that is objectively accessible to criminals is subjectively out-of-
bounds, being "unknown . . . [and] populated with the terrors of the
unfamiliar." From the offender's perspective, *all* residential burglaries are
committed in an environment alive with hazards. But this is especially true
where the occupants are not known and the target has not been watched
beforehand; there is no reliable way of assessing the risks. Many of the
offenders responded to this hazard by conducting their searches for potential burglary sites only in a location with which they already were intimately
familiar. They knew the layout of the area and felt comfortable or safe there.

> Basically, all [of my burglaries are committed on the south side of the city].
> I guess I know the area. I don't know, I'm comfortable with it I guess. . . .
> I'm basically familiar with it. You know, if it came down to me having to

run and stuff like that. I'd know pretty much where to go. (Bonnie Williams—No. 007)

Perhaps a more important reason, though, was that the offenders had an intuitive understanding of the people who lived in the area. They had a "feel" for what the residents were like. This, they believed, gave them a basis on which to predict the behavior of the local population.

> Whenever I decide to do [a burglary], it's always on the north side . . . because I know the people in general . . ., I know they movements. (No. 040)

These offenders had a vested interest in being able to rely on predictions about the habits of the occupants of an intended target. Absent specific information about the occupants, a general familiarity with the sort of people who resided in the area represented the next best means of making such predictions.

. . .

Interestingly, the white offenders tended to view black neighborhoods as policed more heavily than other places, while the black subjects typically said that white areas received the most intensive patrolling.

. . .

The subjects, then, perceived areas populated predominantly by another racial group in terms of generalizations which suggested to them that offending in these areas was too dangerous. However, they drew much finer distinctions when it came to areas residentially dominated by members of their own race. Within these areas, the subjects had clear ideas about unsafe locations for burglaries; these were micro-level distinctions, sometimes involving just one block of a single street. Many of the burglars wanted to avoid neighborhoods that were heavily patrolled or aggressively policed. As one observed: "You got to stay away from where the police ride real tough." This created an ironic situation in which some offenders were unwilling to hunt for targets in "high crime" areas.

> [I stay away from the neighborhoods like my own because] where I live, I do a burglary and then I get robbed. It's like the police is in my area. Whereas there might be one cop [in another area], there's four in my neighborhood. (No. 019)

In practice, this usually meant staying away from neighborhoods characterized by the open selling of drugs since such areas often are subjected to intense scrutiny by the police. As a member of the sample noted: "You don't want to look in bad neighborhoods where they sellin' dope and all that cause the police ride steady." Police patrols also often are intensified in neighborhoods that have recently experienced a spate of burglaries. Being aware of this, most of the offenders varied the places in which they searched for burglary sites.

> Well, like if I went to [a certain area] today. I wouldn't go tomorrow cause, once the people in [that area] have reported it, [the police] going to be a little bit more on they toes. Not to prevent anything, just to let the people who payin' their salaries to them know that the security is beefed-up. So you have to kind of think like a cop. (No. 019)

. . .

As well as avoiding heavily policed areas, most of the offenders wanted to steer clear of neighborhoods in which the residents appeared to be keeping an eye out for each other.

> [Those neighborhoods] are just a hassle. You walk down the street and the police come get you cause somebody done looked out the window and saw you walking. (No. 016)

They inferred whether this might be the case from a variety of factors including the general condition of the area and the age composition of its population. Other things being equal, well-kept neighborhoods with a high proportion of elderly residents were viewed by the offenders as poor areas from which to select targets. The residents of such neighborhoods were presumed to be especially vigilant and prone to reporting suspicious-looking persons to the police.

> The thing is, if you got a lot of elderly people on one block, that'll get you killed mostly. . . . I wanted to do [a burglary] over here by the bakery shop, but that's a retired area. Almost everybody that live on that block is retired and they constantly lookin' out windows and watchin' [out] for each other. Ain't nothin' you can do about that. (James West—No. 044)

There was considerable disagreement among the offenders about whether a street sign declaring that the residents of an area were participating in a "Neighborhood Watch" scheme indicated that a neighborhood really was being monitored. Certainly, some believed that this was so and avoided offending in these locations.

. . .

In this sense, the decision making of these offenders closely resembled that of the "extremely pragmatic" inner-city robbers described by Murray (1983: 117–18): "Their calculations seemed to be based on a hard-headed appreciation of the facts. Real risk of being observed [and] real risk of someone calling the police or intervening . . . loomed largest in their thinking. . . . [S]ymbolic evidence of the site's cohesiveness, and symbolic increases in the risk of observation and apprehension seemed to be of little deterrence value." The pervasive view among our group of subjects was epitomized by one who commented: "Yeah, I'm worried about [Neighborhood Watch], long as they really watchin'." His tone left little doubt that he believed that this was seldom the case.

The subjects were largely in agreement about the general characteristics of a safe neighborhood in which to commit residential burglaries. Such a place had to be quiet and infrequently patrolled by the police.

> [A safe place is] a quiet neighborhood . . . where the police don't ride around too often up and down the street. (No. 014)

It also had to appear somewhat affluent.

> I wouldn't say [the area had to be] rich, but a neighborhood with money. (No. 014)

> Where I do my thing at [has] pretty houses, they up-to-date. [The houses] look nice. (No. 020)

Obviously, these characteristics are relative and must be viewed from the perspective of offenders who have only a limited range of areas from which to choose. A neighborhood which they judge to be quiet or affluent might well not be regarded as such by others. This fact, however, does not alter the reality of their decision-making calculus.

Having settled on an area, the offenders next needed to locate a specific target. In doing so, they had to find a place that was acceptable to them in terms of probable reward, potential risk, and ease of access. Moreover, their decision had to be made from the sidewalk or street. Once they had stepped from public to private property, their actions became considerably more vulnerable to challenge. Recognizing this, most were reluctant to approach residences without first making certain that they were viable targets. Practically speaking, therefore, the offenders were committed to carrying out an offense *before* they entered the grounds of an intended burglary site. This fact has largely been overlooked in previous research on residential burglary, but carries important implications for crime prevention measures. For example, offenders typically cannot determine from the street the type of locks fitted to a dwelling. Nor can they see window decals stating that the property inside has been engraved with an identification number. And by the time they are close enough to detect such measures, they often have developed a high degree of commitment to going through with the burglary, come what may. Thus, they may disregard or downplay the significance of these situational factors and elect to carry on with the offense.

In searching for a suitable target, the offenders were initially drawn to residences by many of the same factors that attracted those who typically watched places for a time before burglarizing them. In general, they were most tempted by dwellings that were better maintained or more expensively adorned than others in the area, believing that this was a reliable indicator of potential reward.

> It's the way [the residents] keep the yard, keep it nice and trim and have little statues of something out there. You look at that and you say, "Hey, this is a well kept up house." That tells you that a person spends a little on they property. (No. 046)

As these offenders intended to commit an offense immediately upon locating a target, however, factors suggesting that a residence contained valuable goods were insufficient in and of themselves to cause a place to be selected. More importantly, prevailing conditions had to be assessed as being low-risk. The offenders were not willing to break into a dwelling—no matter how lucrative it looked—where they perceived the odds of getting caught to be excessively high.

In assessing risk, the burglars focussed primarily on the issue of occupancy. With few exceptions, they were averse to burglarizing a residence while anyone was inside, and thus were attuned to factors which, in their minds at least, provided some indication of whether the residents were at home. Many situational factors were taken into account by the offenders in making a judgment about occupancy.

> [A car in the driveway might mean someone is in], but if a car is there and you see a lot of leaves piled up [beside it] then the car is not running or these people are not at home. If there's mail in the slot and it's this time of night and you know the mailman ran earlier, either they're not there or they asleep or dead or something. Why else would they not get their mail? (No. 019)

Beyond these factors, however, several offenders mentioned that they simply got "a feeling" about whether or not a place was occupied. The offender quoted above, for instance, added that determining occupancy involved more than rational calculation: "Those are the obvious signs, but there are some other signs that unconsciously come to you. It's basically a feeling you have." Here again, we are encountering a process that the offenders perceived as magical, whereby targets that objectively seemed acceptable took on an added, metaphysical appeal (Katz, 1988).

Burglar alarms and dogs, of course, can function as "occupancy proxies" (Waller, 1979), that is, as substitutes for occupancy by the residents. Therefore, it should come as no surprise that many of the offenders wanted to avoid them.

> If I see an alarm out, like I say, they usually have them outside the house. I'll leave them alone automatically. (No. 046)

> If there's a Rover in [the house], no way we goin' in there. (No. 026)

Alarms, however, seldom are installed on residences containing little of value. Indeed, a few of the offenders regarded the devices not so much as deterrents as indicators of potential reward. Previous experience had convinced them that alarms could be defeated.

> Basically, I look for alarms in certain areas. Like in [an affluent suburb] if they got alarms, then you can look for gold and silver and tea sets. If there's an alarm on the first floor, it probably ain't hooked to the top floor. If it's hooked to the top floor, then it ain't hooked to the attic or it's not hooked to the exhaust system. (No. 019)

In any case, the presence of alarms or dogs often was not easily assessed from the street. This meant that these factors frequently could not enter into the initial target selection process, but rather came into play when the offenders attempted to burglarize the chosen targets.

After occupancy, the subjects generally regarded visibility as the next most important issue in assessing risk. They did not want to be observed while entering or leaving a residence and therefore were drawn to dwellings with access points that could not be seen easily from the street or from surrounding buildings.

> Usually I see how the houses and shit around [the potential target] is. How big the trees are [around the place] and shit like that. (No. 016)

· · ·

Concerns about being seen or heard by neighbors ruled out the possibility of finding targets in apartment buildings or public housing projects for a number of subjects. One offender explained his reasons for avoiding such places: "You got all them doors in the hallway. I might be pryin' one open and somebody comes out of another one. Or somebody might hear me."

. . .

The burglars seemed more unwilling than unable to overcome such obstacles; they just did not want to take the extra time and effort required. Since they were under pressure to act as quickly as possible, this makes sense. Add to this the fact that those who search for burglary sites with the intention of offending "there and then" have no foolproof way to predict the likely payoff, and the aversion to well-protected places is more sensible still. Why should they invest extraordinary energy where the reward cannot be guaranteed?

In summary, while few of the offenders in our sample routinely had to search for a target in order to commit a residential burglary, nearly all of them occasionally had to do so. On these occasions, the search was facilitated by their personal knowledge and beliefs about good and bad areas, as well as by their skill, built up through experience, in reading the cues relating to risks, possible rewards, and ease of access. This combination of knowledge and skill perhaps was what caused the offenders to view the commission of a residential burglary as a feasible means of dealing with a pressing problem in the absence of a preexisting target. They possessed the "know-how" to locate a burglary site on short notice and this allowed them to consider the prospect of breaking in to a dwelling (see Lofland, 1969: 82–84).

● Seizing an Opportunity

In the popular imagination, residential burglars are usually thought of as "opportunistic" offenders. Certainly, this is how they are portrayed in the crime prevention literature produced by police and other organizations. There is no consensus, however, regarding what qualifies a criminal as an opportunist (Bennett and Wright, 1984), though common sense would suggest that such an offender is one who "just happens upon" a vulnerable target and, as a result, commits an offense on the spur of the moment. And by this definition, only one of the offenders in our sample might reasonably be considered opportunistic. Typically his burglaries were committed imme-diately following the chance discovery of an unprotected dwelling.

> Yeah, [I'm an opportunist] cause I find myself walkin' down the street with no intentions on doing a burglary. But I may see somebody leaving the house and, at that time, the idea [to break in] may pop in my head, right at that instant. I may look at the house first and see what kind of house it is. . . . See just how I can get in there. Lot of times I may do it right there on the spot. (No. 013)

. . .

Overall, then, it is misleading to label the subjects we interviewed as opportunists, even though many of them occasionally had exploited oppor-tunities that cropped up in the course of their daily rounds (see Cromwell et al., 1991). Interestingly, all of the opportunistic burglaries described by those in our sample were precipitated by the fortuitous sighting of people leaving a residence. Putting it another way, not one offense was prompted by the discovery of an open door or window. More than anything, this prob-ably reflects the fact that, first and foremost, the majority of offenders are concerned with occupancy; they do not want to attack a dwelling while the residents are inside. Therefore, the sight of people leaving a place can repre-sent a powerful temptation. Conversely, although an open door or window may suggest ease of access, it also may indicate that someone is at home. And few offenders are prepared to gamble in these circumstances.

❧ Summary

When faced with a pressing problem, financial or otherwise, that needed to be resolved quickly, a majority of the offenders typically had a potential resi-dential burglary target already lined up. This involved not merely having a specific dwelling in mind, but also possessing reliable information about such things as the routine of its occupants. In most cases, the target initially had been located during the course of the offender's daily activities and then casually kept under surveillance for a period of time. Sometimes, though, the target was selected because the offender either knew the occupants personally or else had received a tip from someone with inside knowledge of the place. In these cases, there was no need to watch the residence before burglarizing it; the offender already had satisfactory intelligence. Regardless of the way in which the potential target was located, however, its very avail-ability served to facilitate the commission of a residential burglary by making the offense that much more "proximate and performable" (Lofland. 1969: 61).

Only a few of the offenders usually found themselves without a possible residential burglary site when under pressure to act in response to an immediate need. Many of them, however, occasionally were in this position. Even here, though, the offenders almost invariably had a clear idea of how to locate a promising target without undue risk or difficulty. This facilitated the commission of a residential burglary in much the same way as did having a specific target lined up.

That the offenders, at the time of actually contemplating a residential burglary, typically had a target fully assessed and "waiting in the wings," has at least two important implications for attempts to prevent their crimes. First, it suggests that they often had direct knowledge regarding matters such as household security and the daily routine of occupants and, therefore, were somewhat immune to symbolic measures designed to confuse them (e.g., by creating the illusion of occupancy). Second, it indicates that they generally possessed a more realistic basis on which to judge risk than is commonly imagined, evidence that might weaken the case for the inhibiting influence of threatened sanctions. . . .

References

Amire, M. (1971). *Patterns in Forcible Rape*. Chicago: University of Chicago Press.

Bennett, T., and Wright, R. (1983). "Offenders' Perception of Targets." *Home Office Research Bulletin* 15: 18–20. London: Home Office Research and Planning Unit.

——. (1984). *Burglars on Burglary: Prevention and the Offender*. Aldershot: Gower.

Black, D. (1983). "Crime as Social Control." *American Sociological Review* 48: 34–45.

Brantingham, P., and Brantingham, P. (1981). *Environmental Criminology*. Beverly Hills, CA: Sage.

Cromwell, P., Olson, J., and Avary, D. (1991). *Breaking and Entering: An Ethnographic Analysis of Burglary*. Newbury Park, CA: Sage.

Felson, M. (1986). "Linking Criminal Choices: Routine Activities, Informal Control, and Criminal Outcomes." In Cornish, D., and Clarke, R., *The Reasoning Criminal: Rational Choice Perspectives on Offending*. pp. 119–28. New York: Springer-Verlag.

Forrester, D., Chatterton, M., and Pease, K. (1988). *The Kirkholt Burglary Prevention Project*. London: Her Majesty's Stationery Office.

Katz, J. (1988), *Seductions of Crime: Moral and Sensual Attractions in Doing Evil*, New York: Basic Books.

Lofland, J. (1969), *Deviance and Identity*, Englewood Cliffs, NJ: Prentice-Hall.

Logie, R., Wright, R., and Decker, S. (1992), "Recognition Memory Performance and Residential Burglary," *Applied Cognitive Psychology* 6, no. 2: 109–23.

Merry, S. (1981), *Urban Danger: Life in a Neighborhood of Strangers*, Philadelphia: Temple University Press.

Murray, C. (1983), "The Physical Environment and Community Control of Crime." In Wilson, J., *Crime and Public Policy*, pp. 107–22, San Francisco: ICS Press.

Nee, C., and Taylor, M. (1988), "Residential Burglary in the Republic of Ireland: A Situational Perspective," *The Howard Journal* 27, no. 2: 105–16.

Shover, N. (1973), "The Social Organization of Burglary," *Social Problems* 20: 499–514.

_____. (1991), "Burglary," In Tonry, M., *Crime and Justice: A Review of Research*, vol. 14, pp. 73–113, Chicago: University of Chicago Press.

Taylor, M., and Nee, C. (1988), "The Role of Cues in Simulated Residential Burglary: A Preliminary Investigation," *British Journal of Criminology* 28, no. 3: 396–401.

Vera Institute of Justice (1977), *Felony Arrests: Their Prosecution and Disposition in New York City's Courts*, New York.

Waller, I. (1979), "What Reduces Residential Burglary: Action and Research in Seattle and Toronto." Paper presented at the Third International Symposium on Victimology, Muenster.

_____. (1986), "Victim Selection Procedures among Economic Criminals: The Rational Choice Perspective." In Cornish, D., and Clarke, R., *The Reasoning Criminal: Rational Choice Perspectives on Offending*, pp. 40–52, New York: Springer-Verlag.

Wolfgang, M. (1958), *Patterns in Criminal Homicide*, Philadelphia: University of Pennsylvania Press.

Wright, R., and Logie, R. (1988), "How Young House Burglars Choose Targets," *The Howard Journal of Criminal Justice* 27, no. 2: 92–104.

❧ ❧ ❧

Questions

1. What two conflicting demands face burglars when they're choosing a target?

2. Do burglars ever steal from people they know? Why or why not?

3. How often do burglars spontaneously pick a residence to rob, without planning?

4. What is a burglar's main goal in selecting a target house?

5. After reading this article, how would you recommend reducing or preventing burglary?

Why Americans Fear the Wrong Things

BARRY GLASSNER

Americans fear many things, and often fear the wrong things. One of the more recent moral panics in American society was the fear of school violence, particularly school shootings. The media continually told us that we were in the middle of an epidemic of growing proportion, legislators told school districts that they had to develop emergency response protocols, and parents mobilized to more effectively reach at-risk youth. Underlying this moral panic was little knowledge of the facts: at its peak, slightly more than 50 children were killed in school shootings in a given year while more than 50 million children were enrolled in school. The truth was that a child has better odds of being struck by lightning or killed at the hands of a family member in his own home than being the victim of school violence. So why do we fear school violence more than lightning or domestic violence? In this selection, Barry Glassner explores why Americans fear the wrong things.

$\mathcal{W}$hy are so many fears in the air, and so many of them unfounded? Why, as crime rates plunged throughout the 1990s, did two-thirds of Americans believe they were soaring? How did it come about that by mid-decade 62 percent of us described ourselves as "truly desperate" about crime—almost twice as many as in the late 1980s, when crime rates were higher? Why, on a survey in 1997, when the crime rate had already fallen for a half dozen consecutive years, did more than half of us disagree with the statement "This country is finally beginning to make some progress in solving the crime problem"?

In the late 1990s the number of drug users had decreased by half compared to a decade earlier; almost two-thirds of high school seniors had never used any illegal drugs, even marijuana. So why did a majority of adults rank drug abuse as the greatest danger to America's youth? Why did nine out of ten believe the drug problem is out of control, and only one in six believe the country was making progress?[2]

Give us a happy ending and we write a new disaster story. In the late 1990s the unemployment rate was below 5 percent for the first time in a quarter century. People who had been pounding the pavement for years could finally get work. Yet pundits warned of imminent economic disaster. They predicted inflation would take off, just as they had a few years earlier— also erroneously—when the unemployment rate dipped below 6 percent.[3]

We compound our worries beyond all reason. Life expectancy in the United States has doubled during the twentieth century. We are better able to cure and control diseases than any other civilization in history. Yet we hear that phenomenal numbers of us are dreadfully ill. In 1996 Bob Garfield, a magazine writer, reviewed articles about serious diseases published over the course of a year in the *Washington Post*, the *New York Times*, and *USA Today*. He learned that, in addition to 59 million Americans with heart disease, 53 million with migraines, 25 million with osteoporosis, 16 million with obesity, and 3 million with cancer, many Americans suffer from more obscure ailments such as temporomandibular joint disorders (10 million) and brain injuries (2 million). Adding up the estimates, Garfield determined that 543 million Americans are seriously sick—a shocking number in a nation of 266 million inhabitants. "Either as a society we are doomed, or someone is seriously double-dipping," he suggested.[4]

Garfield appears to have underestimated one category of patients: for psychiatric ailments his figure was 53 million. Yet when Jim Windolf, an editor of the *New York Observer*, collated estimates for maladies ranging from borderline personality disorder (10 million) and sex addiction (11 million) to less well-known conditions such as restless leg syndrome (12 million) he came up with a figure of 152 million. "But give the experts a little time," he advised. "With another new quantifiable disorder or two, everybody in the country will be officially nuts."[5]

Indeed, Windolf omitted from his estimates new-fashioned afflictions that have yet to make it into the *Diagnostic and Statistical Manual of Mental Disorders* of the American Psychiatric Association: ailments such as road rage, which afflicts more than half of Americans, according to a psychologist's testimony before a congressional hearing in 1997.[6]

The scope of our health fears seems limitless. Besides worrying disproportionately about legitimate ailments and prematurely about would-be diseases, we continue to fret over already refuted dangers. Some still worry, for instance, about "flesh-eating bacteria," a bug first rammed into our consciousness in 1994 when the U.S. news media picked up on a screamer headline in a British tabloid, "Killer Bug Ate My Face." The bacteria, depicted as more brutal than anything seen in modern times, was said to be spreading faster than the pack of photographers outside the home of its latest victim. In point of fact, however, we were not "terribly vulnerable" to these "superbugs," nor were they "medicine's worst nightmares," as voices in the media warned.

Group A strep, a cyclical strain that has been around for ages, had been dormant for half a century or more before making a comeback. The British pseudoepidemic had resulted in a total of about a dozen deaths in the previous year. Medical experts roundly rebutted the scares by noting that of 20 to 30 million strep infections each year in the United States fewer than 1 in 1,000 involve serious strep A complications, and only 500 to 1,500 people suffer the flesh-eating syndrome, whose proper name is necrotizing fasciitis. Still the fear persisted. Years after the initial scare, horrifying news stories continued to appear, complete with grotesque pictures of victims. A United Press International story in 1998 typical of the genre told of a child in Texas who died of the "deadly strain" of bacteria that the reporter warned "can spread at a rate of up to one inch per hour."

❧ Roosevelt Was Wrong

We had better learn to doubt our inflated fears before they destroy us. Valid fears have their place; they cue us to danger. False and overdrawn fears only cause hardship. . . .

We all pay one of the costs of panics: huge sums of money go to waste. Hysteria over the ritual abuse of children cost billions of dollars in police investigations, trials, and imprisonments. Men and women went to jail for years "on the basis of some of the most fantastic claims ever presented to an American jury," as Dorothy Rabinowitz of the *Wall Street Journal* demonstrated in a series of investigative articles for which she became a Pulitzer Prize finalist in 1996. Across the nation expensive surveillance programs were implemented to protect children from fiends who reside primarily in the imaginations of adults.

The price tag for our panic about overall crime has grown so monumental that even law-and-order zealots find it hard to defend. The criminal justice system costs Americans close to $100 billion a year, most of which goes to police and prisons. In California we spend more on jails than on higher education. Yet increases in the number of police and prison cells do not correlate consistently with reductions in the number of serious crimes committed. Criminologists who study reductions in homicide rates, for instance, find little difference between cities that substantially expand their police forces and prison capacity and others that do not.[9]

The turnabout in domestic public spending over the past quarter century, from child welfare and antipoverty programs to incarceration, did not even produce reductions in *fear* of crime. Increasing the number of cops and jails arguably has the opposite effect: it suggests that the crime problem is all the more out of control.[10]

Panic-driven public spending generates over the long term a pathology akin to one found in drug addicts. The more money and attention we fritter away on our compulsions, the less we have available for our real needs, which consequently grow larger. While fortunes are being spent to protect children from dangers that few ever encounter, approximately 11 million children lack health insurance, 12 million are malnourished, and rates of illiteracy are increasing.[11]

I do not contend, as did President Roosevelt in 1933, that "the only thing we have to fear is fear itself." My point is that we often fear the wrong things. In the 1990s middle-income and poorer Americans should have worried about unemployment insurance, which covered a smaller share of workers than twenty years earlier. Many of us have had friends or family out of work during economic downturns or as a result of corporate restructuring. Living in a nation with one of the largest income gaps of any industrialized country, where the bottom 40 percent of the population is worse off financially than their counterparts two decades earlier, we might also have worried about income inequality. Or poverty. During the mid- and late 1990s 5 million elderly Americans had no food in their homes, more than 20 million people used emergency food programs each year, and one in five children lived in poverty—more than a quarter million of them homeless. All told, a larger proportion of Americans were poor than three decades earlier.[12]

One of the paradoxes of a culture of fear is that serious problems remain widely ignored even though they give rise to precisely the dangers that the populace most abhors. Poverty, for example, correlates strongly with child abuse, crime, and drug abuse. Income inequality is also associated with adverse outcomes for society as a whole. The larger the gap between rich and poor in a society, the higher its overall death rates from heart disease, cancer, and murder.

❧ Two Easy Explanations

In the following discussion I will try to answer two questions: Why are Americans so fearful lately, and why are our fears so often misplaced? To both questions the same two-word answer is commonly given by scholars and journalists: premillennial tensions. The final years of a millennium and the early years of a new millennium provoke mass anxiety and ill reasoning, the argument goes. So momentous does the calendric change seem, the populace cannot keep its wits about it.

Premillennial tensions probably do help explain some of our collective irrationality. Living in a scientific era, most of us grant the arbitrariness of reckoning time in base-ten rather than, say, base-twelve, and from the birth of Christ rather than from the day Muhammad moved from Mecca. Yet even the least superstitious among us cannot quite manage to think of the year 2000 as ordinary. Social psychologists have long recognized a human urge to convert vague uneasiness into definable concerns, real or imagined. In a classic study thirty years ago Alan Kerckhoff and Kurt Back pointed out that "the belief in a tangible threat makes it possible to explain and justify one's sense of discomfort."[13]

Some historical evidence also supports the hypothesis that people panic at the brink of centuries and millennia. Witness the "panic terror" in Europe around the year 1000 and the witch hunts in Salem in the 1690s. As a complete or dependable explanation, though, the millennium hypothesis fails. Historians emphasize that panics of equal or greater intensity occur in odd years, as demonstrated by anti-Indian hysteria in the mid 1700s and McCarthyism in the 1950s. Scholars point out too that calendars cannot account for why certain fears occupy people at certain times (witches then, killer kids now).[14]

Another popular explanation blames the news media. We have so many fears, many of them off-base, the argument goes, because the media bombard us with sensationalistic stories designed to increase ratings. This explanation, sometimes called the media-effects theory, is less simplistic than the millennium hypothesis and contains sizable kernels of truth. When researchers from Emory University computed the levels of coverage of various health dangers in popular magazines and newspapers they discovered an inverse relationship: much less space was devoted to several of the major causes of death than to some uncommon causes. The leading cause of death, heart disease, received approximately the same amount of coverage as the eleventh-ranked cause of death, homicide. They found a similar inverse relationship in coverage of risk factors associated with serious illness and death. The lowest-ranking risk factor, drug use, received nearly as much attention as the second-ranked risk factor, diet and exercise.[15]

Disproportionate coverage in the news media plainly has effects on readers and viewers. When Esther Madriz, a professor at Hunter College, interviewed women in New York City about their fears of crime they frequently responded with the phrase "I saw it in the news." The interviewees identified the news media as both the source of their fears and the reason they believed those fears were valid. Asked in a national poll why they believe the country has a serious crime problem, 76 percent of people cited stories they had seen in the media. Only 22 percent cited personal experience.[16]

When professors Robert Blendon and John Young of Harvard analyzed forty-seven surveys about drug abuse conducted between 1978 and 1997, they too discovered that the news media, rather than personal experience, provide Americans with their predominant fears. Eight out of ten adults say that drug abuse has never caused problems in their family, and the vast majority report relatively little direct experience with problems related to drug abuse. Widespread concern about drug problems emanates, Blendon and Young determined, from scares in the news media, television in particular.[17]

Television news programs survive on scares. On local newscasts, where producers live by the dictum "if it bleeds, it leads," drug, crime, and disaster stories make up most of the news portion of the broadcasts. Evening newscasts on the major networks are somewhat less bloody, but between 1990 and 1998, when the nation's murder rate declined by 20 percent, the number of murder stories on network newscasts increased 600 percent (not counting stories about O.J. Simpson).[18]

After the dinnertime newscasts the networks broadcast newsmagazines, whose guiding principle seems to be that no danger is too small to magnify into a national nightmare. Some of the risks reported by such programs would be merely laughable were they not hyped with so much fanfare: "Don't miss *Dateline* tonight or YOU could be the next victim!" Competing for ratings with drama programs and movies during prime-time evening hours, newsmagazines feature story lines that would make a writer for "Homicide" or "ER" wince.[19]

"It can happen in a flash. Fire breaks out on the operating table. The patient is surrounded by flames," Barbara Walters exclaimed on ABC's "20/20" in 1998. The problem—oxygen from a face mask ignited by a surgical instrument—occurs "more often than you might think," she cautioned in her introduction, even though reporter Arnold Diaz would note later, during the actual report, that out of 27 million surgeries each year the situation arises only about a hundred times. No matter, Diaz effectively nullified the reassuring numbers as soon as they left his mouth. To those who "may say it's too small a risk to worry about" he presented distraught victims: a woman with permanent scars on her face and a man whose son had died.[20]

The gambit is common. Producers of TV newsmagazines routinely let emotional accounts trump objective information. In 1994 medical authorities attempted to cut short the brouhaha over flesh-eating bacteria by publicizing the fact that an American is fifty-five times more likely to be struck by lightning than die of the suddenly celebrated microbe. Yet TV journalists brushed this fact aside with remarks like, "whatever the statistics, it's devastating to the victims" (Catherine Crier on "20/20"), accompanied by stomach-turning videos of disfigured patients.[21]

Sheryl Stolberg, then a medical writer for the *Los Angeles Times*, put her finger on what makes the TV newsmagazines so cavalier: "Killer germs are perfect for prime time," she wrote. "They are invisible, uncontrollable, and, in the case of Group A strep, can invade the body in an unnervingly simple manner, through a cut or scrape." Whereas print journalists only described in words the actions of "billions of bacteria" spreading "like underground fires" throughout a person's body, TV newsmagazines made use of special effects to depict graphically how these "merciless killers" do their damage.[22]

❧ Morality and Marketing

To blame the media is to oversimplify the complex role that journalists play as both proponents and doubters of popular fears. It is also to beg the same key issue that the millennium hypothesis evades: why particular anxieties take hold when they do. Why do news organizations and their audiences find themselves drawn to one hazard rather than another?

The short answer to why Americans harbor so many misbegotten fears is that immense power and money await those who tap into our moral insecurities and supply us with symbolic substitutes.

Endnotes

[1]Crime data here and throughout are from reports of the Bureau of Justice Statistics unless otherwise noted. Fear of crime: Esther Madriz, *Nothing Bad Happens to Good Girls* (Berkeley: University of California Press, 1997), ch. 1; Richard Morin,

"As Crime Rate Falls, Fears Persist," *Washington Post* National Edition, 16 June 1997, p. 35; David Whitman, "Believing the Good News," *U.S. News & World Report*, 5 January 1998, pp. 45–46.

[2] Eva Bertram, Morris Blachman et al., *Drug War Politics* (Berkeley: University of California Press, 1996), p. 10; Mike Males, *Scapegoat Generation* (Monroe, ME: Common Courage Press, 1996), ch. 6; Karen Peterson, "Survey: Teen Drug Use Declines," *USA Today*, 19 June 1998. p. A6; Robert Blendon and John Young, "The Public and the War on Illicit Drugs," *Journal of the American Medical Association* 279 (18 March 1998): 827–32. In presenting these statistics and others I am aware of a seeming paradox: I criticize the abuse of statistics by fear-mongering politicians, journalists, and others but hand down precise-sounding numbers myself. Yet to eschew all estimates because some are used inappropriately or do not withstand scrutiny would be as foolhardy as ignoring all medical advice because some doctors are quacks. Readers can be assured I have interrogated the statistics presented here as factual. As notes throughout the book make clear, I have tried to rely on research that appears in peer-reviewed scholarly journals. Where this was not possible or sufficient, I traced numbers back to their sources, investigated the research methodology utilized to produce them, or conducted searches of the popular and scientific literature for critical commentaries and conflicting findings.

[3] Bob Herbert, "Bogeyman Economics," *New York Times*, 4 April 1997, p. A15; Doug Henwood, "Alarming Drop in Unemployment," *Extra*, September 1994, pp. 16–17; Christopher Shea, "Low Inflation and Low Unemployment Spur Economists to Debate 'Natural Rate' Theory," *Chronicle of Higher Education*, 24 October 1997, p. A13.

[4] Bob Garfield, "Maladies by the Millions," *USA Today*, 16 December 1996, p. A15.

[5] Jim Windolf, "A Nation of Nuts," *Wall Street Journal*, 22 October 1997, p. A22.

[6] Andrew Ferguson, "Road Rage," *Time*, 12 January 1998, pp. 64–68; Joe Sharkey, "You're Not Bad, You're Sick. It's in the Book," *New York Times*, 28 September 1997, pp. N1, 5.

[7] Malcolm Dean, "Flesh-eating Bugs Scare," *Lancet* 343 (June 1994): 1418; "Flesh-eating Bacteria," *Science* 264 (17 June 1994): 1665; David Brown, "The Flesh-eating Bug," *Washington Post* National Edition, 19 December 1994, p. 34; Sarah Richardson, "Tabloid Strep," *Discover* (January 1995): 71; Liz Hunt, "What's Bugging Us," *The Independent*, 28 May 1994, p. 25; Lisa Seachrist, "The Once and Future Scourge," *Science News* 148 (7 October 1995): 234–35. Quotes are from Bernard Dixon, "A Rampant Non-epidemic," *British Medical Journal* 308 (11 June 1994): 1576–77; and Michael Lemonick and Leon Jaroff, "The Killers All Around," *Time*, 12 September 1994, pp. 62–69. More recent coverage: "Strep A Involved in Baby's Death," UPI, 27 February 1998; see also, e.g., Steve Carney, "Miracle Mom," *Los Angeles Times*, 4 March 1998, p. A6; KTLA, "News at Ten," 28 March 1998.

[8]Dorothy Rabinowitz, "A Darkness in Massachusetts," *Wall Street Journal*, 30 January 1995, p. A20 (contains quote); "Back in Wenatchee" (unsigned editorial), *Wall Street Journal,* 20 June 1996, p. A18; Dorothy Rabinowitz, "Justice in Massachusetts," *Wall Street Journal*, 13 May 1997, p. A19. See also Nathan and Snedeker, *Satan's Silence*; James Beaver, "The Myth of Repressed Memory," *Journal of Criminal Law and Criminology* 86 (1996): 596–607; Kathryn Lyon, *Witch Hunt* (New York: Avon, 1998); Pam Belluck, "'Memory' Therapy Leads to a Lawsuit and Big Settlement," *New York Times*, 6 November 1997, pp. A1, 10.

[9]Elliott Currie, *Crime and Punishment in America* (New York: Metropolitan, 1998); Tony Pate et al., *Reducing Fear of Crime in Houston and Newark* (Washington, DC: Police Foundation, 1986); Steven Donziger, *The Real War on Crime* (New York: HarperCollins, 1996); Christina Johns, *Power, Ideology and the War on Drugs* (New York: Praeger, 1992); John Irwin et al., "Fanning the Flames of Fear," *Crime and Delinquency* 44 (1998): 32–48.

[10]Steven Donziger, "Fear, Crime and Punishment in the U.S.," *Tikkun* 12 (1996): 24–27, 77.

[11]Peter Budetti, "Health Insurance for Children," *New England Journal of Medicine* 338 (1998): 541–42; Eileen Smith, "Drugs Top Adult Fears for Kids' Well-being," *USA Today*, 9 December 1997, p. D1. Literacy statistic: Adult Literacy Service.

[12]"The State of America's Children," report by the Children's Defense Fund, Washington, DC, March 1998; "Blocks to Their Future," report by the National Law Center on Homelessness and Poverty, Washington, DC, September 1997; reports released in 1998 from the National Center for Children in Poverty, Columbia University, New York; Douglas Massey, "The Age of Extremes," *Demography* 33 (1996): 395–412; Trudy Lieberman, "Hunger in America," *Nation*, 30 March 1998, pp. 11–16; David Lynch, "Rich Poor World," *USA Today*, 20 September 1996, p. B1; Richard Wolf, "Good Economy Hasn't Helped the Poor," *USA Today*, 10 March 1998, p. A3; Robert Reich, "Broken Faith," *Nation*, 16 February 1998, pp. 11–17.

[13]Alan Kerckhoff and Kurt Back, *The June Bug* (New York: Appleton-Century-Crofts, 1968), see esp. pp. 160–61.

[14]Stephen Jay Gould, *Questioning the Millennium* (New York: Crown, 1997); Todd Gitlin, "Millennial Mumbo Jumbo," *Los Angeles Times Book Review*, 27 April 1997, p. 8.

[15]Karen Frost, Erica Frank et al., "Relative Risk in the News Media," *American Journal of Public Health* 87 (1997): 842–45. Media-effects theory: Nancy Signorielli and Michael Morgan, eds., *Cultivation Analysis* (Newbury Park, CA: Sage, 1990); Jennings Bryant and Dolf Zillman, eds., *Media Effects* (Hillsdale, NJ: Erlbaum, 1994); Ronald Jacobs, "Producing the News, Producing the Crisis," *Media, Culture and Society* 18 (1996): 373–97.

[16]Madriz, *Nothing Bad Happens to Good Girls*, see esp. pp. 111–14; David Whitman and Margaret Loftus, "Things Are Getting Better? Who Knew," *U.S. News & World Report*, 16 December 1996, pp. 30–32.

[17]Blendon and Young, "War on Illicit Drugs." See also Ted Chiricos et al., "Crime, News and Fear of Crime," *Social Problems* 44 (1997): 342–57.

[18]Steven Stark, "Local News: The Biggest Scandal on TV," *Washington Monthly* (June 1997): 38–41; Barbara Bliss Osborn, "If It Bleeds, It Leads," *Extra*, September–October 1994, p. 15; Jenkins, *Pedophiles and Priests*, pp. 68–71; "It's Murder," *USA Today*, 20 April 1998, p. D2; Lawrence Grossman, "Does Local TV News Need a National Nanny?" *Columbia Journalism Review* (May 1998): 33.

[19]Regarding fearmongering by newsmagazines, see also Elizabeth Jensen et al., "Consumer Alert," *Brill's Content* (October 1998): 130–47.

[20]ABC "20/20," 16 March 1998.

[21]Thomas Maugh, "Killer Bacteria a Rarity," *Los Angeles Times*, 3 December 1994, p. A29; Ed Siegel, "Roll Over, Ed Murrow," *Boston Globe*, 21 August 1994, p. 14. Crier quote from ABC's "20/20," 24 June 1994.

[22]Sheryl Stolberg, "'Killer Bug' Perfect for Prime Time," *Los Angeles Times*, 15 June 1994, pp. A1, 30–31. Quotes from Brown, "Flesh-eating Bug"; and Michael Lemonick and Leon Jaroff, "The Killers All Around," *Time*, 12 September 1994, pp. 62–69.

● ● ●

Questions

1. What are some examples of supporting evidence that Americans fear the wrong things?

2. What are some costs of having misplaced fears?

3. Why does Glassner contend Americans fear the wrong things?

4. Now that the "new millennium" has passed, does the construction of fear seem to have subsided or changed in any way? Explain.

5. Provide two examples of things we are supposed to fear right now in American society. How well do these examples fit the explanation(s) provided by Glassner?

Gun Availability and Violent Crime

LISA STOLZENBERG AND STEWART J. D'ALESSIO
Florida International University

More than any other developed country, the United States has a lot of guns. As such, it makes sense to ask how gun availability affects violence and crime. Though some people maintain that a high number of guns fosters violent crime, others argue the reverse, that guns actually deter crime. This study examines the links between gun availability and violent crimes. The authors find that, in fact, some types of guns do alter levels of violent crime.

*T*he effect of gun availability on violent crime rates continues to be a topic of contentious debate among social scientists. Two opposing views currently exist regarding this relationship. One perspective, often termed the objective dangerousness hypothesis, maintains that gun availability increases levels of violence. An alternative viewpoint asserts that gun availability has a negative rather than a positive effect on violence rates because the ownership of guns by law-abiding citizens acts as a deterrent to crime. Furthermore, even if a positive association does exists between gun availability and violent crime, it is plausible that increased violence engenders fear among the general public, which in turn leads to the acquisition of guns for self-defensive purposes.

Although a fairly large and diverse body of empirical research has accumulated that examines the effect of gun availability on violent crime, this research allows few definitive conclusions. Some empirical studies report that gun availability increases violence levels (Blumstein 1995; Cook, Molliconi & Cole 1995; McDowall 1991; Sloan et al. 1990), whereas others evince either a negative (Bordua 1986; Lott 1998; Lott & Mustard 1997) or a weak (KLeck & Patterson 1993; Magaddino & Medoff 1984; McDowall 1986) association. Still others report mixed findings (Dezhbakhsh & Rubin 1998). Based on these inconsistent findings, it appears that further empiri-

"Gun Availability and Violent Crime," by Lisa Stolzenberg and Stewart J. D'Alessio, reprinted from *Social Forces*, vol. 78, no. 4, 2000, pp. 1461–1482.

cal evidence is necessary before a defensible position can be reached regarding the relationship between gun availability and violence. However, as Kleck (1997) points out, "It will take a substantially more complex analysis of considerably more evidence to ascertain what causal links do exist" (23). We agree that it is unlikely that any single study can contribute substantially to the existing literature unless it goes beyond the typical practice of relying on Uniform Crime Reports (UCR) to test the effect of gun availability on violence levels.

In this article, we improve upon previous research by employing data drawn from the National Incident-Based Reporting System (NIBRS) for South Carolina. The use of NIBRS rather than the UCR aids in the investigation of the relationship between gun availability and violent crime in several important respects. First, NIBRS enables the creation of a theoretically relevant measure of illegal gun availability: the number of stolen guns reported to the police. This measure, which has not been used previously by researchers, serves as a suitable indicator of illegal gun availability because stolen guns are often employed by individuals in illegal activities (Sheley & Wright 1995; Wright & Rossi 1986). In addition, it is important that a distinction is made between illegal and legal gun availability because illegal guns may be relevant in increasing violence levels, whereas legitimate guns may be salient in reducing violence levels (Cook 1979).

A second advantage is that NIBRS allows for the creation of a comprehensive measure of gun violence. In contrast to previous research that examined the effect of gun availability on a limited number of crime categories such as armed robbery, assaults, and/or homicides committed with a gun, we have the ability with NIBRS to measure the "total" number of crimes committed with a gun that are reported to the police. For example, if an offender uses a gun in the commission of a rape or a kidnapping, these data are captured by NIBRS. This information is not contained in the UCR.

Finally, NIBRS data can be disaggregated by offender demographic characteristics and weapon usage. For example, a researcher can determine whether a youth was arrested for a crime in which a gun was used. The ability to disaggregate crime data by age and weapon usage is important because of the growing problem of youth gun violence (Greenfeld & Zawitz 1995).

⊚ *G*un *A*vailability and *V*iolent *C*rime

Debate among social scientists persists regarding the effect of gun availability on violent crime. One viewpoint argues that gun availability increases levels of gun violence (Cook 1983; Newton & Zimring 1969). A number of empirical studies find support for this thesis (see Cook 1991 for a comprehensive review). For example, Kleck (1979) examined the effect of gun manufacturing and imports on murder rates in the United States. Using a simultaneous estimation procedure to account for reciprocal causation, he found that increased gun production resulted in higher rates of homicide. In another study, McDowall (1991) examined the relationship between gun availability and homicide rates in Detroit from 1951 to 1986. He measured gun availability as a composite variable comprised of the proportion of robberies and suicides committed with a gun. His time-series analysis indicates that gun density had a strong positive effect on Detroit's homicide rate. Other studies have also reached the conclusion that gun prevalence engenders greater violence (Sloan et al. 1990).

There are strong theoretical expectations for the hypothesis that gun availability increases violent crime rates. Some theorists argue, for example, that a gun may encourage an individual to initiate a crime against others who would otherwise appear too invulnerable to challenge. Adherents to this view maintain that a weapon empowers its possessor to terrify and to coerce a victim into compliance (Luckenbill 1982). Surveys conducted by Wright and Rossi (1986) and Sheley and Wright (1995) indicate that offenders frequently use guns to intimidate and control their victims. A number of empirical studies are also consistent with this logic. Using survey data on 12,000 robbery victims, Cook (1980) found that 55% of the commercial robberies involved guns. Conversely, he observed that a gun was used in only 13% of the noncommercial robberies. He also noted that the relatively few gun robberies of individuals tended to target relatively invulnerable groups such as young adult males, whereas nongun street robberies most often targeted women, children, and elderly victims. He theorized that guns enhanced the power of offenders by affording them the ability to victimize relatively invulnerable targets. In a later study, Cook (1982) found additional support for his theory. Specifically, he observed that guns were more commonly used in homicides in which the attacker was older and presumably weaker and the victim younger and presumably stronger. Sampson and Lauritsen (1994) also report evidence that guns are used to overcome victim invulnerability rather than to fatally injure the victim. Using data drawn from the National Crime Victimization Survey (NCVS), they found that approximately 41% of male victims of violent crimes other than homicide were attacked with a gun. In contrast, only 29% of female victims were attacked by persons with weapons.

There are other ways in which gun availability may increase violence. For example, some have argued that guns facilitate attack by persons too squeamish to come into close contact with their victims (Newton & Zimring 1969). The sight of a gun may also elicit aggression from an angered individual because of the learned association between weapons and aggressive behavior (Berkowitz 1993). Finally, guns may facilitate the element of surprise, since they enable their possessor to attack a victim from a distance greater than normally possible. Given the plausibility of each of these explanations, a strong theoretical rationale exists for expecting that gun availability, at least to some degree, influences violent crime in society.

● Gun Availability and Self-Defense

A number of social scientists remain unconvinced that gun availability increases violent crime. Specifically, they argue that the ownership of guns by citizens, rather than increasing violence levels, actually acts as a deterrent to crime (Loft 1998). For example, citizens who use guns in self-defense are believed to outnumber individuals who use guns to commit criminal acts. Kleck and Gertz (1995) estimate that while 1.1 million violent crimes are committed annually with guns, approximately 2.5 million citizens employ guns each year to defend themselves from criminals.[1] Several empirical studies provide support for this position. In a series of studies using county-level data, Lott (1998) and his associates (Bronars & Lott 1998; Lott & Mustard 1997) found a negative association between concealed-handgun laws and crime rates. This relationship remained robust even when a substantial number of control variables were taken into account. In a survey of 1,900 incarcerated felons, Wright and Rossi (1986) found that 40% of the felons reported that they decided not to commit a crime because they thought that the intended victim might be armed. Additionally, three-fifths of the surveyed felons acknowledged that they were more fearful of confronting an armed victim than a law enforcement officer.

Other studies also report that people who defend themselves with a gun are more likely to avoid injury and prevent completion of the crime (Kleck & DeLone 1993).[2] For example, Kleck (1997) notes that data drawn from the NCVS from 1979 to 1987 show that criminals were successful in only about 14% of burglary attempts at occupied residences in which an individual defended his or her property with a gun. This finding is interesting when one considers that burglaries have a completion rate of 33% overall. Additionally, he points to cross-national data that shows that countries with lower levels of gun ownership than the United States have much higher rates of burglaries of occupied residences (Kleck 1997). The fear of being shot by a gun-wielding homeowner is thought to explain the nonconfrontational nature of burglary in the United States.

Many social scientists also remain skeptical of the objective dangerousness hypothesis because a positive association between gun availability and gun violence is consistent with the view that people, including criminals (Webster, Gainer & Champion 1993; Wright & Rossi 1986), arm themselves for self-defensive purposes (Sheley & Wright 1993). Basically, advocates of this viewpoint maintain that previous analysts interpreted the causal sequence backward: violence is not the consequence of gun ownership, but rather the cause of it. This position is supported by some survey research. For example, in a recent nationally representative telephone survey, Cook and Ludwig (1997) found that 46% of gun owners acquired a gun for protection against crime. Lizotte, Bordua, and White (1981) reported that people who own guns for self-defense reasons were more likely not only to view crime as a serious problem but also to fear criminal victimization. Lizotte and his associates also noted that people in areas with higher crime rates were more likely to report that they owned a gun for personal protection (see also Bjerregaard & Lizotte 1995). In a survey of serious male incarcerated juvenile offenders and a survey of male inner-city high school students, Sheley and Wright (1993) found that the main reason given by juveniles for owning or carrying a gun was self-protection. Other survey research reports similar findings (Lizotte et al. 1994; Smith & Uchida 1988).

Studies undertaken at the macro level also find evidence that violent crime influences gun ownership levels. For example, McDowall and Loftin (1983) observe that the demand for handgun permits in Detroit was related both to the violent crime rate and to police strength. In another study, which analyzed data from a California county, Archer and Erlich-Erfer (1991) report that handgun sales increased substantially after the media reported several murders committed by two serial killers and after the arrest of each of the offenders. Magaddino and Medoff (1984) found that the homicide rate increased handgun ownership levels.

In sum, then, a number of studies have found that gun availability increases levels of violence, whereas others have failed to evince a substantive effect. Several shortcomings in the literature may have engendered these discrepant findings. One problem relates to a general failure among social scientists to recognize the possibility that both illegal and legal gun availability may be important in predicting violence rates, but in different ways. When one examines the extant research on gun violence, it is evident that most studies have used excessively broad measures of gun availability. For example, researchers have employed fatal gun accident rates (Seitz 1972), gun owners license or registration rates (Bordua 1986), gun import and export figures (Kleck 1979; Magaddino & Medoff 1984), and aggravated assaults, robberies, homicides, and/or suicides committed with a gun (Cook 1979; McDowall 1986, 1991) as indicators of gun availability. However, the problem with these measures is that they fail to differentiate between illegal and legal gun prevalence levels (Bordua 1986; Cook 1979; Kleck & Patterson 1993).

There are two salient reasons for making this distinction. First, stolen guns are frequently employed by criminals in gun-related crimes. For example, a survey of prison inmates conducted by Wright and Rossi (1986) found that 47% of the felons had stolen guns in their lives and 320 of the felons who possessed handguns when sent to prison had personally obtained their most recently acquired handgun by theft. In addition, among the handguns most recently acquired by the felons, 46% were regarded by their owners as "definitely stolen" and another 24% as "probably stolen" (Wright & Rossi 1986:196). In a survey of confined juvenile offenders, Sheley and Wright (1993) found that 50% of the respondents had stolen at least one gun in their lives and 24% had stolen their most recently obtained handgun. The findings drawn from these surveys indicate that a majority of the guns in the possession of criminals, and presumably most of those used in gun-related crimes, have been stolen at some time in the past, but not necessarily by their current criminal owner.

Another important consideration relates to policy implications. If a positive relationship is observed between the theft of guns and gun violence, a logical policy initiative would be to educate gun owners as to the most effective ways to secure their weapons. As Sheley and Wright (1993) state, "An effective gun ownership policy, of necessity, must confront the issue of firearms theft" (10). Such a strategy may prove more effective in reducing gun violence than tougher licensing regulations.

A second problem with previous research pertains to the measurement of gun crime. In the UCR, the use of a gun during the commission of a crime is recorded for only a limited number of crime categories. These offense categories include homicide/manslaughter, aggravated assault, robbery, and weapons offenses. No information is provided as to whether an offender in other types of crimes, such as rape or kidnapping, used a gun. Consequently, because all prior studies that relied on UCR data underestimated the actual number of gun-related crimes and because these underestimates may vary over time and across geographical locations, it is possible that measurement error may have contributed to some of the inconsistent findings reported in the literature.

The purpose of this study is to shed additional light on the debate over gun availability and violence. First, we investigate whether illegal and legal gun availability influences violence levels. The importance of distinguishing between illegal and legal gun availability levels cannot be overemphasized, since "it is possible that gun possession among prospective aggressors increases lethal violence, while gun possession among prospective victims reduces it, with no net effect of overall gun ownership levels on violence rates" (Kleck 1997:215). Following this logic, we speculate that illegal gun availability is relevant in increasing violence levels, whereas legitimate gun availability is salient in reducing violence levels.

Second, we evaluate whether gun availability impacts gun crime and youth gun crime. This latter analysis is especially relevant because youth gun violence has increased considerably in recent years (Fox 1996) and because research indicates that young people frequently use stolen guns to commit their crimes (Sheley & Wright 1993).

Finally, we explore the possibility of a weapon substitution effect. That is, an attempt is made to discern empirically whether criminals opt to use knives against their victims when guns become less readily available. Some studies have found evidence of a displacement effect (Sloan et al. 1990), whereas others have not (Loftin et al., 1991). Answers to each of these questions will furnish greater insight into the relationship between gun availability and violent crime as well as determine the utility of policy efforts directed at reducing violence in our society.

❧ Data and Methods

The data used in this study were obtained from the National Incident-Based Reporting System for South Carolina for the years 1991 to 1994. We focus on South Carolina because it was an original test state for the implementation of NIBRS and because it has 100% reporting across the state. The purpose of NIBRS is "to enhance the quantity, quality, and timeliness of crime statistical data collected by the law enforcement community and to improve the methodology used for compiling, analyzing, auditing, and publishing the collected crime data" (U.S. Department of Justice 1988:1). Both the guidelines and the specifications used in the development of NIBRS can be found in the *Blueprint for the Future of the Uniform Crime Reporting Program* (Abt Associates 1985). Because NIBRS is capable of producing more detailed, accurate, and meaningful data than those generated by the traditional UCR, it provides researchers with an indispensable tool for studying crime.[3]

Our data are aggregated at the county level because the county is the smallest geographical unit for which data were made available. Additionally, using county-level data allows us to examine the relationship between gun availability and violent crime across a wide range of social contexts. A number of previous analyses that relied on county-level data found that gun availability was either unrelated or negatively related to violent crime (Bordua 1986; Bronars & Lott 1998; Lott 1998; Lott & Mustard 1997).

❧ Dependent Variables

Four dependent variables are analyzed in this study. The first variable, violent crime rate, is measured as the number of violent felony offenses divided by the county population and multiplied by 100,000. Violent crimes include murder and nonnegligent manslaughter, kidnapping/abduction, forcible rape, forcible sodomy, sexual assault with an object, forcible fondling, robbery, aggravated assault, and extortion/blackmail. The second variable, gun crime rate, is operationalized as the number of violent felony offenses where a gun was used by one or more offenders divided by the county population and multiplied by 100,000. We measure the third dependent variable, youth gun crime rate, as the number of incidences involving one or more violent felony offenses where a gun was used by an arrested youth divided by the county population and multiplied by 100,000. Because it is unlawful in South Carolina for any person under the age of 21 to possess a handgun, we define "youth" as any person who was under 21 at the time of his or her arrest.[4] The final dependent variable, knife crime rate, is measured as the number of violent felony offenses where a knife or other cutting instrument was used by the offender(s) divided by the county population and multiplied by 100,000. Knife/cutting instruments include such objects as axes, ice picks, screwdrivers, and switchblades.

◉ Independent Variables

We measure gun availability in two distinct ways: (1) illegal gun availability and (2) legal gun availability. We measure illegal gun availability as the yearly number of guns in each county reported stolen to the police divided by the county population and multiplied by 100,000. Guns are defined as weapons that fire a shot by force of an explosion (i.e., handguns, rifles, shotguns, and the like, but not BB, pellet, or gas-powered guns). We believe that this measure, which is contained only in NIBRS, is a much better indicator of illegal gun availability than other measures used in previous analyses. For example, after examining a number of gun availability measures, Kleck and Patterson (1993) concluded that the percentage of the dollar value of all stolen property reported to the police that was due to gun thefts was probably the best single indicator of illegal gun availability. However, while Kleck and Patterson's measure is probably superior to other measures of illegal gun availability contained in the UCR, its major limitation is that the price of a weapon is not necessarily related to its effectiveness in a crime.[5] For example, a cheap revolver will serve a criminal equally well in a crime as a high-priced antique pistol. Furthermore, not only do guns such as rifles and shotguns have a higher monetary value than handguns, but they are also less likely than handguns to be used in crimes. As a consequence, it is unclear whether the percentage of the dollar value of all stolen property reported to the police that was due to gun thefts would reveal a positive or a negative effect of illegal gun availability on violent crime.

We measure legal gun availability as the yearly number of concealed weapon permits (CWP) issued to citizens in each county divided by the county population and multiplied by 100,000. Although gun registration data are probably an incomplete measure of legal gun availability because approximately two million guns per year are acquired in off-the-book transactions not involving federally licensed gun dealers (Cook & Ludwig 1997), researchers frequently use concealed weapon permits as a measure of legitimate gun availability. A number of previous empirical studies have found either a positive (McDowall, Loftin & Wiersema 1995) or a negative (Bronars & Lott 1998; Lott 1998; Lott & Mustard 1997) relationship between concealed weapon permits and crime rates. A positive coefficient for the legal gun measure in the equations would be consistent with the argument that, net of other factors expected to impact violence levels, the availability of legal guns engenders violence. On the other hand, a substantive negative coefficient would suggest that legitimate gun availability reduces violent crime.

● Control Variables

Prior research suggests that several contextual variables may influence violent crime rates (see Reiss & Roth 1993). These variables include the divorce rate, Aid to Families with Dependent Children (AFDC), the lagged unemployment rate, the lagged arrest rate, the lagged prison admission rate, the lagged juvenile commitment rate, percentage of high school dropouts, and population density. All these control variables were included in each of the estimated models to avoid basing conclusions on spurious or suppressed relationships. Except for the lagged measures of unemployment$_{(t-1)}$, prison admissions$_{(t-1)}$, juvenile commitments$_{(t-1)}$, and arrests made by police$_{(t-1)}$, all of the control variables in a particular equation are for the same year as for the dependent variable. The means, standard deviations, and definitions for all the variables used in the primary analyses are presented in Table 1.

● Results

Table 2 presents results of violent crime rates, gun crime rates, youth gun crime rates, and knife crime rates on illegal and legal gun availability and the other explanatory variables for our sample of 46 counties observed for a four-year period from 1991 to 1994. We estimated pooled cross-section time-series equations in which all the counties in South Carolina were

TABLE 1 *Means, Standard Deviations, and Definitions for Variables Used in the Analysis*

Variable	Mean	S.D.	Definition
Violent crime rate	985.23	406.69	Number of violent felony offenses divided by the county population and multiplied by 100,000
Gun crime rate	248.72	116.43	Number of violent felony offenses where a gun was used by the offenders) divided by the county population and multiplied by 100,000
Youth gun crime rate	27.57	17.66	Number of incidences involving one or more violent felony offenses where a gun was used by an arrested youth divided by the county population and multiplied by 100,000
Knife crime rate	197.23	91.99	Number of violent felony offenses where a knife or other cutting instrument was used by the offender(s) divided by the county population and multiplied by 100,000
Gun theft rate	229.09	84.23	Number of guns stolen divided by the county population and multiplied by 100,000
CWP rate	29.87	17.96	Number of concealed weapon permits (CWP) issued divided by the county population and multiplied by 100,000
Divorce rate	345.35	83.36	Number of divorces where children were involved divided by the county population and multiplied by 100,000
AFDC percent	4.99	2.43	Percent of the population participating in Aid to Families with Dependent Children (AFDC)

(Continued on next page)

TABLE 1 *Means, Standard Deviations, and Definitions for Variables Used in the Analysis*

Variable	Mean	S.D.	Definition
Dropout percent	3.16	1.28	Percent of students enrolled in high school (grades 9–12) who dropped out prior to graduation or completion of a course of studies without transferring to another school or institution
Population density	110.79	94.97	Population per square mile of land area is calculated by dividing the county population by the land area (square miles) of the county. Land area estimates are based on the April 1. 1990. census.
Arrest rate	5.212.35	1.799.09	Number of persons arrested divided by the county population and multiplied by 100.000
Unemployment rate	8.02	2.54	Percent of persons in the annual average civilian labor force who are unemployed
Prison admission rate	334.20	111.73	Number of inmates admitted to the South Carolina Department of Corrections divided by the county population and multiplied by 100.000
Juvenile commitment rate	92.21	47.90	Number of juvenile offenders committed to institutional programs. including Reception and Evaluation Centers and correctional facilities. divided by the county population and multiplied by 100.000

treated as distinct observations to estimate the effect of illegal and legal gun availability on each of the dependent variables. This type of analytic design is ideally suited for studying both the temporal and spatial patterns of gun availability because it can analyze multiple units across multiple time points. The methodological strategy employed here takes into account both cross-sectional and temporal complications of the data. In contrast, OLS gives inefficient estimates of slopes and negatively biased estimates of standard errors with pooled cross-section time-series data because it fails to take into account the error components common to the same counties in different periods and to different counties in the same periods (Kessler & Greenberg 1981).

We used a two-way fixed-effects model that includes an overall constant as well as a group effect for each unit (i.e., county) and a time effect for each period (i.e., year) to generate parameter estimates (Greene 1998). This model is of the form

$$y_{it} = \alpha_0 + \alpha_i + y_t + \beta' x_{it} + \varepsilon_{it},$$

where α_0 is the constant; α_1 and y_t are the fixed-county and fixed-year effects, respectively; $\beta' x_{it}$ denotes the exogenous variables in county i year t; and ε_{it} is the error term. This model effectively controls for the effects of both measured and unmeasured differences between counties that do not change over time. In addition, the fixed-year effects account for factors that impact the counties equally but that vary over time. We employed this model because a Hausman test, which assessed whether the fixed-effects model and random-effects model produce similar results, indicated that the fixed-effects model was superior (Hausman & Taylor 1981).

Model 1 of Table 2 includes the effects of the independent and control variables on the violent crime rate.[6] The results for this model reveal that illegal gun availability strongly influences violent crime levels. As the stolen gun rate increases, the violent crime rate also rises. Figure 1 graphically illustrates this association. In contrast, the effect of the legitimate gun availability measure is trivial in magnitude and not of substantive importance (see Figure 2). The legal gun availability measure and the control variables are largely insignificant.

Models 2 and 3 estimate the effect of the exogenous variables on the gun crime rate and the youth gun crime rate. The results for these two models are virtually identical to those reported in Model 1. The illegal gun avail-

TABLE 2 *Two-Factor Fixed-Effects Models*

Independent Variable	Model 1 Violent Crime Rate	Model 2 Gun Crime Rate	Model 3 Youth Gun Crime Rate	Model 4 Knife Crime Rate
Gun theft rate	1.056***	.474***	.090***	.102
	(.297)	(.097)	(.024)	(.086)
CWP rate	.317	.079	.009	.200
	(1.022)	(.332)	(.083)	(.295)
Divorce rate	-.037	.014	-.010	-.076
	(.198)	(.064)	(.016)	(.057)
AFDC percent	-25.501	-26.297*	1.130	-3.551
	(39.799)	(12.936)	(3.223)	(11.493)
Dropout percent	-17.836	-5.697	-.061	.897
	(13.676)	(4.445)	(1.108)	(3.949)
Population density	-1.699	.737	-.410	-.431
	(5.218)	(1.696)	(.423)	(1.507)
Arrest rate$_{(t-1)}$	.002	-.002	-.001	.002
	(.008)	(.003)	(.001)	(.002)
Unemployment rate$_{(t-1)}$	.289	-.016	-.006	.060
	(.337)	(.110)	(.027)	(.097)
Prison admission rate$_{(t-1)}$	.078	.055	-.001	-.046
	(.142)	(.046)	(.011)	(.041)
Juvenile commitment rate$_{(t-1)}$	-.487	-.063	.002	-.063
	(.289)	(.094)	(.023)	(.083)
Constant	1,121.450	196.133	51.272	267.040
R^2	.938	.920	.783	.898

Note: Standard errors are in parentheses.

* $p < .05$ *** $p < .001$

ability measure again achieves statistical significance in both equations. The legal gun variable and the control variables are also largely insignificant, although AFDC shows some predictive power in the gun crime rate equation. As the percentage of people on AFDC rises, the violent crime rate declines. Although this finding seems counterintuitive, it is most likely the result of poverty in South Carolina being concentrated in rural counties with low violent crime levels. To illustrate, we ranked the counties in ascending order based on population density for 1991. We then divided the 46 counties into two equal groups. Counties with low population densities not only have lower violent crime levels, but they also have a higher percentage of

FIGURE 1 *Violent Crime Rates by County Gun Theft Rates*

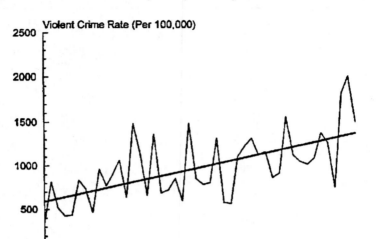

Note: Counties are reported in ascending order according to their gun theft rates. The violent crime rate is then calculated for each county.

their population on AFDC. In contrast, more heavily populated counties have a higher violent crime rate and a lower percentage of their population on AFDC.

Model 4 explores the possibility of whether criminals opt to use knives or other cutting instruments against their victims when illegal guns become less readily available. Research on this issue has been divided. Some studies find a displacement effect, while others do not. In contrast to the previous estimated equations, results show that the stolen gun rate variable is not of substantive importance. This finding suggests that offenders are not substituting knives for guns when illegal guns become scarce. Furthermore, Kleck (1997) has argued that stolen gun rates along with other frequently used measures of firearm availability (i.e., number of aggravated assaults, robberies, and homicides committed with guns) may be correlated positively with violence levels simply because they are all measures of criminal activ-

FIGURE 2 *Violent Crime Rates by County Concealed Weapon Permit Rates*

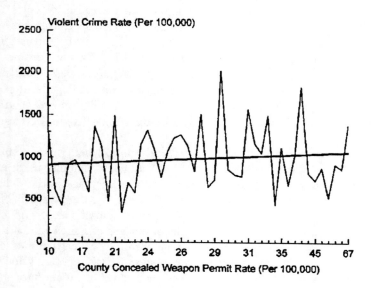

Note: Counties are reported in ascending order according to their concealed weapon permit rates. The violent crime rate is then calculated for each county.

ity. However, our failure to evince a strong positive relationship between stolen guns and violent crimes committed with knives seems to cast some doubt on this argument. None of the effects of the control variables is statistically significant in model 4.[7]

● Supplemental Analyses

We conducted three supplemental analyses to ensure that our original findings remained robust across different specifications. First, our original analyses were based on the assumption that the relationship between gun availability and violence was generated by a unidirectional effect of one variable on the other. We assumed that any association between guns and violence reflected the effect of gun availability on violence rates. However, it is also plausible that high levels of violent crime engender fear and, as a

141

consequence, people for self-defense purposes acquire more guns. If gun availability affects violence levels and if violence levels impact gun availability, our fixed-effects models would be misspecified because we failed to model these simultaneous effects. We used the Hausman specification error test to determine whether there was simultaneity between legitimate gun availability and the violent crime rate (Hausman 1978). This test enables a researcher to determine whether a potentially endogenous regressor variable is correlated with the error term. Results for this test indicated that legitimate gun availability and the violent crime rate were mutually exclusive, and it was therefore appropriate to rely on the unidirectional fixed-effects estimates.[8]

Second, because we felt it prudent to determine whether our results would vary depending on the measure of illegal gun availability used, we estimated an alternative model that included the percentage of the dollar value of all stolen property reported to the police that was due to gun thefts. This measure, which is contained in the UCR, was recommended previously by Kleck and Patterson (1993). The results of this analysis showed that the value of stolen guns had no substantive relationship to violent crime levels (β = -1.720, p = .672). Our failure to find an effect for the reported value of stolen guns is mostly the result of an insufficient range of variation for this measure. To illustrate, the mean and standard deviation scores for this variable were 3.20 and 3.10, respectively. These figures suggest that there probably was not a sufficient amount of variation to expect even modest effects to emerge in the analysis. Since measuring illegal gun availability is a primary concern for researchers, it appears, based on the results reported here, that the actual number of stolen guns reported to police is a much better measure of illegal gun availability than the reported value of stolen guns.

Third, because gun registration data are considered by some to be an incomplete measure of legal firearm availability, we conducted a supplemental analysis using the firearm suicide rate ($\bar{x}$ = 9.05, S.D. = 5.50) as our legitimate gun availability measure (see McDowall 1991). The results for this analysis were nearly identical to those in the other models estimated. While the firearm suicide rate was not of substantive importance (β = .287, p = .886), the effect of the illegal guns remained noteworthy (β = 1.080, p < .001).[9]

● Summary and Conclusions

In this study we investigated the effect of gun availability on violent crime in South Carolina using NIBRS data and a cross-sectional pooled-time series research design. Our study period was from 1991 to 1994. We organized our analysis in terms of two competing hypotheses: the objective danger-ousness hypothesis and the self-defense hypothesis. Previous studies have been unable to adjudicate between these two alternative hypotheses. The most plausible reasons for this situation relate to an inability to distinguish adequately between illegal and legal gun availability and to the continued use of incomplete measures of gun crime.

After estimating several models, with a broad array of outcome meas-ures and independent variables, we found virtually no evidence that legitimate gun availability influenced the violent crime rate or crimes committed with a gun. Although concealed weapon laws have been linked previously to reduced levels of crime in both theoretical arguments and by empirical evidence, our analysis finds no credible evidence for the view that concealed weapon permits are associated with violent crime rates. Such a finding contradicts the self-defense hypothesis, namely, that legitimate gun availability reduces violent crime. Apparently, the fear of possibly confronting an armed victim is not an important factor in deterring a would-be offender. Similarly, we found little support for the position that as the number of legitimate guns in the general population increases, violent crime also rises. Rather, our results show the primary of illegal gun availability in predicting the violent crime rate. Illegal gun availability is the only variable that shows consistent, nontrivial effects across all models estimated. These strong effects persist even after controlling for a variety of potentially rival causal factors.

In addition to demonstrating a strong positive effect of illegal gun avail-ability on the violent crime rate, our results lend credence to the importance of stolen guns in the manifestation of youth gun crime. We argued previ-ously that because youths can only obtain handguns illegally, the number of stolen guns in an area should influence the frequency with which they commit crimes with a gun. Our results bear this prediction out. As the number of guns reported stolen increases, the rate at which youths are arrested for gun-related crimes also rises. In contrast, the effect of legitimate guns on youth gun violence is trivial and not of substantive importance. Finally, our results show no indication of a displacement effect. That is, offenders do not appear to use knives against their victims when guns became less readily available. This finding provides indirect support for the view that a gun somehow enhances the ability of an individual to commit a crime.

The findings generated from our analyses are not surprising when one considers that survey research has consistently shown that both adult and juvenile offenders frequently acquire their guns from thefts (Sheley & Wright 1993; Wright & Rossi 1986). This observation has led some scholars to argue that it is not the total number of guns in circulation that is related to crime levels, but rather the carrying of guns in high-risk places at high-risk times by individuals with a propensity for violence (Wilson 1994). For example, Sherman, Shaw, and Rogan (1995) recently found that while Kansas City had an estimated 100,000 handguns in circulation, the seizure of only 29 guns by police during a six-month police crackdown reduced gun-related crime by 49%. Our results add support to this perspective by showing that rather than responding to the availability of legitimate guns, the violent crime rate was influenced by the number of guns reported stolen by citizens. Thus, it seems that the distribution of guns in society may be more important in predicting violent crime than the overall number of guns in circulation (Polsby 1995).

Our findings have important policy implications. Reducing violent crime while recognizing the right of a citizen to own a gun has always been the central challenge facing gun control advocates. Most gun control efforts have been directed at restricting the acquisition of guns or at employing weapon enhancement statutes to deter individuals from committing crimes with guns. The first approach is based on the logic that by reducing the pool of guns among potential gun offenders, fewer people will be in a position to carry a gun or use it for criminal purposes. The second strategy suggests that individuals are less likely to carry or use a weapon if criminal penalties are severe. Evidence regarding the effectiveness of these two approaches is mixed.

Based on this study, however, it would appear that there are two alternative approaches that could be implemented in order to actualize a substantive reduction in violent crime. One approach is to encourage gun owners to better secure their weapons in their home. It is estimated that slightly more than 50% of all owned guns in this country are stored unlocked (Cook & Ludwig 1997). Encouraging owners to better secure their weapons in their homes, especially when they are away, can be achieved through a variety of avenues, such as educational programs or the use of locked gun cases and safes. Although some may argue that these types of approaches have costs for gun owners' in terms of their individual freedoms and independence, the consequences of such a policy in reference to violent crime reduction are clear.

A second strategy is to focus law enforcement efforts on reducing the theft of firearms. In our data set, approximately 43% of the weapons reported stolen were acquired in burglaries and another 26% were obtained illegally from motor vehicles. When one considers that approximately 74% of gun owners own two or more guns (Cook & Ludwig 1997) and that approximately 35% of the individuals arrested for burglaries in South Carolina where a gun was reported stolen were juveniles, a policy aimed at reducing the theft of firearms seems warranted.

This is not to say that we have satisfactorily resolved all important issues relating to the effect of gun availability on violent crime over time and across geographical units. We view as a significant advance our inclusion of a measure of illegal gun availability as a factor underlying differences over time and across counties in predicting violence levels. However, it is only one of many conceivable measures of illegal gun availability. For example, our measure ignores the effect of weapons obtained from illegal gun markets. Even though some scholars argue that the trade in illegal weapons is relatively small (Cook, Molliconi & Cole 1995; Kleck 1997), and it seems unlikely that a large number of youths are involved in illegal gun markets, one might still want to consider its effect in future research. Other measures such as gun seizures by the police can also be employed, though such measures are invariably confounded with law enforcement practices. Our analysis is also restricted to a single state during a specific historical period.

Because our data spanned only four years, one could make a reasonable argument that a longer period of analysis would enable a more accurate assessment of the relationship between firearm availability and violence. Although it would have been desirable to extend the period of analysis, NIBRS data were available only for the period covered in this study.[10] It remains to be seen how well our findings generalize to other states and to other time periods. We also must acknowledge the need to explain why an individual uses a gun to commit a crime. The aggregate nature of our data precludes identification of microlevel relationships between the rationale of offenders and gun usage. For example, there is simply no way of determining if individuals employ guns to overcome victim invulnerability or to

145

enhance the element of surprise. Future research may wish to uncover the microlevel casual mechanisms responsible for the results generated from our aggregate analyses. Such studies would undoubtedly enhance our understanding of the processes underlying the relationship between guns and violent crime.

Endnotes

[1] However, Cook and Ludwig (1998) argue that self-report surveys overestimate the frequency with which citizens use guns against criminals.

[2] However, the issue of time-order still remains problematic in these studies (Cook 1991).

[3] For a comprehensive discussion of the advantages of using NIBRS to study crime, see Mackenzie, Baunach, and Roberg (1990).

[4] This requirement does not apply to the temporary loan of a handgun for instruction purposes when the minor is under the immediate supervision of a parent or adult instructor.

[5] The value of a stolen gun is estimated by its owner.

[6] We examined the model's correlogram for the presence of serial autocorrelation (Stimson 1985). All autocorrelations of the residuals were within plus or minus two standard errors of zero, and no significant patterns were observed. Additionally, by analyzing spatial units, the possibility exists that the disturbances in our analysis might be correlated because contiguous counties may be similar in regard to socioeconomic characteristics. Although several methods can be employed to test for the presence of spatial autocorrelation, the Moran I test is considered both convenient and effective (Doreian 1980). The results produced from this test revealed no indication of spatial autocorrelation in the data.

[7] Tests for multicollinearity revealed no major problems with any of our models. The highest zero-order correlation among our independent variables was between population density and the percentage of the population participating in AFDC ($r = -.50$). All other correlations were .39 or below. We also computed variance inflation factors to determine the extent to which any independent variable was a linear combination of two or more other independent variables. These analyses indicated that harmful collinearity did not vitiate our results.

[8] Hausman specification tests produced similar results for the other equations. In addition, no simultaneity was observed between illegal gun availability and the violent crime rate.

[9]An anonymous reviewer also suggested that we incorporate additional variables in our original analyses to reduce the problem of specification error. These recommended variables included percent nonwhite ($\bar{x}$ = 38.56, S.D. = 15.94) and median family income ($\bar{x}$ = 31,156.79, S.D. = 4,702.18). However, both percent nonwhite (r = .854, p < .001) and median family income (r = -.817, p < .001) had large bivariate associations with AFDC and with each other (r = -.797, p < .001). As a consequence, we first added percent nonwhite to each of the four models to determine whether this variable modified the effects of the other exogenous variables. We then dropped this variable and added median family income to the models. The measure for AFDC was omitted from all the equations. The results generated from these analyses showed little change in the magnitude of the previously included variables. The impact of each of the variables of interest, or lack thereof, remained stable. The effect of the illegal gun variable remained robust in each of the eight estimated equations. In contrast, neither percent nonwhite nor median family income achieved statistical significance in any of the models. Tables reporting these results are available from the first author.

[10]NIBRS data are extremely difficult to obtain. Because the Federal Bureau of Investigation is unwilling to furnish these data, they must be derived from individual states. Currently, only three states have fully operational NIBRS systems: Alabama, North Dakota, and South Carolina. South Carolina was the only state willing to provide us with its NIBRS data, and even then, it only furnished certain segments of the data.

References

Abt Associates. 1985. *Blueprint for the Future of the Uniform Crime Reporting Program.* Bureau of Justice Statistics.

Archer, Dane, and Lynn Erlich-Erfer. 1991. "Fear and Loading Archival Traces of the Response to Extraordinary Violence." *Social Psychology Quarterly* 54:343–52.

Berkowitz, Leonard. 1993. *Aggression: Its Causes, Consequences, and Control.* Temple University Press.

Bjerregaard, Beth, and Alan J. Lizotte. 1995. "Gun Ownership and Gang Membership." *Journal of Criminal Law and Criminology* 86:37–58.

Blumstein, Alfred. 1995. "Youth Violence, Guns, and the Illicit-Drug Industry." *Journal of Criminal Law and Criminology* 86:10–36.

Bordua, David J. 1986. "Firearms Ownership and Violent Crime: A Comparison of Illinois Counties." Pp. 156–88 in *The Social Ecology of Crime,* edited by James M. Byrne and Robert J. Sampson. Springer-Verlag.

Bronars, Stephen G., and John R. Lott, Jr. 1998. "Criminal Deterrence, Geographic Spillovers, and the Right to Carry Concealed Handguns." *American Economic Review* 88:475–79.

Cook, Philip J. 1979. "The Effect of Gun Availability on Robbery and Robbery Murder: A Cross-Section Study of Fifty Cities." Pp. 743–81 in *Policy Studies Review Annual*. Vol. 3, edited by Robert Haveman and B. Bruce Zellner. Sage.

———. 1980. "Reducing Injury and Death Rates in Robbery." *Policy Analysis* 6:21–45.

———. 1982. "The Role of Firearms in Violent Crime." Pp. 236–91 in *Criminal Violence*, edited by Marvin E. Wolfgang and Neil A. Weiner. Sage.

———. 1983. "The Influence of Gun Availability on Violent Crime Patterns." Pp. 49–89 in *Crime and Justice: An Annual Review of Research*. Vol. 4, edited by Michael Tonry and Norval Morris. University of Chicago Press.

———. 1991. "The Technology of Personal Violence." Pp. 1–71 in *Crime and Justice: A Review of Research*. Vol. 14, edited by Michael H. Tonry. University of Chicago Press.

Cook, Philip J., and Jens Ludwig. 1997. *Guns in America: National Survey on Private Ownership and Use of Firearms*. National Institute of Justice.

———. 1998. "Defensive Gun Uses: New Evidence from a National Survey." *Journal of Quantitative Criminology* 14:111–31.

Cook, Philip J., Stephanie Molliconi, and Thomas B. Cole. 1995. "Regulating Gun Markets." *Journal of Criminal Law and Criminology* 86:59–92.

Dezhbakhsh, Hashem, and Paul H. Rubin. 1998. "Lives Saved or Lives Lost? The Effects of Concealed-Handgun Laws on Crime." *American Economic Review* 88:468–74.

Doreian, Patrick. 1980. "Linear Models with Spatially Distributed Data: Spatial Disturbances or Spatial Effects?" *Sociological Methods and Research* 9:29–60.

Fox, James Alan. 1996. *Trends in Juvenile Violence: A Report to the United States Attorney General on Current and Future Rates of Juvenile Offending*. Bureau of Justice Statistics.

Greene, William H. 1998. *LIMDEP* (7.0). Rev ed. Econometric Software.

Greenfeld, Lawrence A., and Marianne W. Zawitz. 1995. *Weapons Offenses and Offenders*. Bureau of Justice Statistics.

Hausman, J. A. 1978. "Specification Tests in Econometrics." *Econometrica* 46:1251–71.

Hausman, J. A., and W. Taylor. 1981. "Panel Data and Unobservable Individual Effects." *Econometrica* 49:1377–98.

Kessler, Ronald C., and David E Greenberg. 1981. *Linear Panel Analysis*. Academic Press.

Kleck, Gary. 1979. "Capital Punishment, Gun Ownership, and Homicide." *American Journal of Sociology* 84:882–910.

————. 1997. *Targeting Guns: Firearms and Their Control*. Aldine de Gruyter.

Kleck, Gary, and Miriam DeLone. 1993. "Victim Resistance and Offender Weapon Effects in Robbery." *Journal of Quantitative Criminology* 9:55–82.

Kleck, Gary, and Marc Gertz. 1995. "Armed Resistance to Crime: The Prevalence and Nature of Self-Defense with a Gun." *Journal of Criminal Law and Criminology* 86:150–87.

Kleck, Gary, and Britt Patterson. 1993. "The Impact of Gun Control and Gun Ownership Levels on Violence Rates." *Journal of Quantitative Criminology* 9:249–87.

Lizotte, Alan J., David J. Bordua, and Carolyn S. White. 1981. "Firearms Ownership for Sport and Protection: Two Not So Divergent Models." *American Sociological Review* 46:499–503.

Lizotte, Alan J., James M. Tesoriero, Terence P. Thornberry and Marvin D. Krohn. 1994. "Patterns of Adolescent Firearms Ownership and Use." *Justice Quarterly* 11:51–74.

Loftin, Colin, David McDowall, Brian Wiersema, and Talbert J. Cottey. 1991. "Effects of Restrictive Licensing of Handguns." *New England Journal of Medicine* 325:1615–20.

Lott, John R., Jr. 1998. *More Guns, Less Crime*. University of Chicago Press.

Lott, John R., Jr., and David B. M. Mustard. 1997. "Crime, Deterrence and the Right-to-Carry Concealed Handguns." *Journal of Legal Studies* 26:1–68.

Luckenbill, David R. 1982. "Compliance under the Threat of Severe Punishment." *Social Forces* 60:811–25.

Mackenzie, Doris Layton, Phyllis Jo Baunach, and Roy R. Roberg. 1990. *Measuring Crime: Large-Scale, Long-Range Efforts*. SUNY Press.

Magaddino, Joseph E., and Marshall H. Medoff. 1984. "An Empirical Analysis of Federal and State Firearm Control Laws." Pp. 225–58 in *Firearms and Violence: Issues of Public Policy*, edited by Don B. Kates, Jr. Ballinger.

McDowall, David. 1986. "Gun Availability and Robbery Rates: A Panel Study of Large US. Cities, 1974–1978." *Law and Policy* 8:135–48.

————. 1991. "Firearm Availability and Homicide Rates in Detroit, 1951–1986." *Social Forces* 69:1085–1101.

McDowall, David, and Colin Loftin. 1983. "Collective Security and the Demand for Legal Handguns." *American Journal of Sociology* 88:1146–61.

McDowall, David, Colin Loftin, and Brian Wiersema. 1995. "Easing Concealed Firearm Laws: Effects of Homicide in Three States." *Journal of Criminal Law and Criminology* 86:193–204.

Newton, George D., and Franklin E. Zimring. 1969. *Firearms and Violence in American Life: A Staff Report to the National Commission on the Causes and Prevention of Violence.* U.S. Government Printing Office.

Polsby, Daniel D. 1995. "Firearms Costs, Firearms Benefits and the Limits of Knowledge." *Journal of Criminal Law and Criminology* 86:207–37.

Reiss, Albert J., Jr., and Jeffery A. Roth, eds. 1993. *Understanding and Preventing Violence.* National Academy Press.

Sampson, Robert J., and Janet L. Lauritsen. 1994. "Violent Victimization and Offending: Individual-, Situational-, and Community-Level Risk Factors." Pp. 1–114 in *Understanding and Preventing Violence: Social Influences.* Vol. 3, edited by Albert J. Reiss and Jeffrey A. Roth. National Academy Press.

Seitz, Stephen T. 1972. "Firearms, Homicides, and Gun Control Effectiveness." *Law and Society Review* 6:595–614.

Sheley, Joseph F., and James D. Wright. 1993. *Gun Acquisition and Possession in Selected Juvenile Samples.* National Institute of Justice.

Sherman, Lawrence W., James W. Shaw, and Dennis P. Rogan. 1995. *The Kansas City Gun Experiment.* National Institute of Justice.

Sloan, John Henry, Arthur L. Kellermann, Donald T. Reay, James A. Ferris, Thomas Koepsell, Frederick P. Rivara, Charles Rice, Laurel Gray, and James LoGerfo. 1990. "Handgun Regulations, Crime, Assaults, and Homicide." *New England Journal of Medicine* 319:1256–62.

Smith, Douglas A., and Craig D. Uchida. 1988. "The Social Organization of Self-Help: A Study of Defensive Weapon Ownership." *American Sociological Review* 53:94–102.

Stimson, James A. 1985. "Regression in Space and Time: A Statistical Essay." *American Journal of Political Science* 29:914–47.

U.S. Department of Justice. 1988. *National Incident-Based Reporting System: Data Collection Guidelines.* Vol. 1. U.S. Government Printing Office.

Webster, David W., Patricia S. Gainer, and Howard R. Champion. 1993. "Weapon Carrying among Inner-City Junior High School Students: Defensive Behavior vs. Aggressive Delinquency." *American Journal of Public Health* 83:1604–8.

Wilson, James Q. 1994. "Just Take Away Their Guns: Forget about Gun Control." *New York Times*, March 20, 46–47.

Wright, James D., and Peter H. Rossi. 1986. *Armed and Considered Dangerous: A Survey of Felons and Their Weapons*. Aldine de Gruyter.

● ● ●

Questions

1. Explain how *decreased* gun availability might reduce violent crime (the objective-dangerousness hypothesis).

2. Explain how *increased* gun availability might reduce violent crime (the self-defense hypothesis).

3. Describe the data analyzed in this article.

4. According to the authors' analysis, what type of gun ownership increases gun crimes? Why does this make sense?

5. In light of what you have learned from this article, how would you change current gun laws to reduce gun violence?

A Routine Activity Approach

LAWRENCE E. COHEN AND MARCUS FELSON
University of Illinois, Urbana

This article describes an intriguing way to explain crime rates. Instead of emphasizing the characteristics of people who commit crime, as many other theories do, this approach focuses on the circumstances in which crimes, especially predatory offenses, occur. The authors argue that crime takes place when three conditions (which the authors call routine activities) come together: (1) a likely offender, (2) a suitable target, and (3) the absence of a "capable guardian." Increases in any of one of these conditions will increase crime rates.

*I*n its summary report the National Commission on the Causes and Prevention of Violence (1969: xxxvii) presents an important sociological paradox:

Why, we must ask, have urban violent crime rates increased substantially during the past decade when the conditions that are supposed to cause violent crime have not worsened—have, indeed, generally improved?

The Bureau of the Census, in its latest report on trends in social and economic conditions in metropolitan areas, states that most "indicators of well-being point toward progress in the cities since 1960." Thus, for example, the proportion of blacks in cities who completed high school rose from 43 percent in 1960 to 61 percent in 1968; unemployment rates dropped significantly between 1959 and 1967 and the median family income of blacks in cities increased from 61 percent to 68 percent of the median white family income during the same period. Also during the same period the number of persons living below the legally-defined poverty level in cities declined from 11.3 million to 8.3 million.

"A Routine Activity Approach," by Lawrence E. Cohen and Marcus Felson, reprinted from *American Sociological Review*, vol. 44, no. 4, 1979, pp. 588–608.

Despite the general continuation of these trends in social and economic conditions in the United States, the *Uniform Crime Report* (FBI, 1975:49) indicates that between 1960 and 1975 reported rates of robbery, aggravated assault, forcible rape and homicide increased by 263%, 164%, 174%, and 188%, respectively. Similar property crime rate increases reported during this same period[1] (e.g., 200% for burglary rate) suggest that the paradox noted by the Violence Commission applies to nonviolent offenses as well.

In the present paper we consider these paradoxical trends in crime rates in terms of changes in the "routine activities" of everyday life. We believe the structure of such activities influences criminal opportunity and therefore affects trends in a class of crimes we refer to as *direct-contact predatory violations*. Predatory violations are defined here as illegal acts in which "someone definitely and intentionally takes or damages the person or property of another" (Glaser, 1971:4). Further, this analysis is confined to those predatory violations involving direct physical contact between at least one offender and at least one person or object which that offender attempts to take or damage.

We argue that structural changes in routine activity patterns can influence crime rates by affecting the convergence in space and time of the three minimal elements of direct-contact predatory violations: (1) motivated offenders, (2) suitable targets, and (3) the absence of capable guardians against a violation. We further argue that the lack of any one of these elements is sufficient to prevent the successful completion of a direct-contact predatory crime, and that the convergence in time and space of suitable targets and the absence of capable guardians may even lead to large increases in crime rates without necessarily requiring any increase in the structural conditions that motivate individuals to engage in crime. That is, if the proportion of motivated offenders or even suitable targets were to remain stable in a community, changes in routine activities could nonetheless alter the likelihood of their convergence in space and time, thereby creating more opportunities for crimes to occur. Control therefore becomes critical. If controls through routine activities were to decrease, illegal predatory activities could then be likely to increase. In the process of developing this explanation and evaluating its consistency with existing data, we relate our approach to classical human ecological concepts and to several earlier studies.

The Structure of Criminal Activity

Sociological knowledge of how community structure generates illegal acts has made little progress since Shaw and McKay and their colleagues (1929) published their path-breaking work, *Delinquency Areas*. Variations in crime rates over space long have been recognized (e.g., see Guerry, 1833; Quètelet, 1842), and current evidence indicates that the pattern of these relationships within metropolitan communities has persisted (Reiss, 1976). Although most spatial research is quite useful for describing crime rate patterns and providing post hoc explanations, these works seldom consider—conceptually or empirically—the fundamental human ecological character of illegal acts as *events* which occur at specific locations in *space* and *time,* involving specific persons and/or objects. These and related concepts can help us to develop an extension of the human ecological analysis to the problem of explaining changes in crime rates over time. Unlike many criminological inquiries, we do not examine why individuals or groups are inclined criminally, but rather we take criminal inclination as given and examine the manner in which the spatio-temporal organization of social activities helps people to translate their criminal inclinations into action. Criminal violations are treated here as routine activities which share many attributes of, and are interdependent with, other routine activities. This interdependence between the structure of illegal activities and the organization of everyday sustenance activities leads us to consider certain concepts from human ecological literature.

Selected Concepts from Hawley's Human Ecological Theory

While criminologists traditionally have concentrated on the *spatial* analysis of crime rates within metropolitan communities, they seldom have considered the *temporal* interdependence of these acts. In his classic theory of human ecology, Amos Hawley (1950) treats the community not simply as a unit of territory but rather as an organization of symbiotic and commensalistic relationships as human activities are performed over both space and time.

Hawley identified three important temporal components of community structure: (1) *rhythm,* the regular periodicity with which events occur, as with the rhythm of travel activity; (2) *tempo,* the number of events per unit of time, such as the number of criminal violations per day on a given street; and (3) *timing*, the coordination among different activities which are more or less interdependent, such as the coordination of an offender's rhythms with those of a victim (Hawley, 1950:289; the examples are ours). These components of temporal organization, often neglected in criminological research, prove useful in analyzing how illegal tasks are performed—a utility which becomes more apparent after noting the spatio-temporal requirements of illegal activities.

The Minimal Elements of Direct-Contact Predatory Violations

As we previously stated, despite their great diversity, direct-contact predatory violations share some important requirements which facilitate analysis of their structure. Each successfully completed violation minimally requires an *offender* with both criminal inclinations and the ability to carry out those inclinations, a person or object providing a suitable target for the offender, and absence of guardians capable of preventing violations. We emphasize that the lack of any one of these elements normally is sufficient to prevent such violations from occurring.[2] Though guardianship is implicit in everyday life, it usually is marked by the absence of violations; hence it is easy to overlook. While police action is analyzed widely, guardianship by ordinary citizens of one another and of property as they go about routine activities may be one of the most neglected elements in sociological research on crime, especially since it links seemingly unrelated social roles and relationships to the occurrence or absence of illegal acts.

The conjunction of these minimal elements can be used to assess how social structure may affect the tempo of each type of violation. That is, the probability that a violation will occur at any specific time and place might be taken as a function of the convergence of likely offenders and suitable targets in the absence of capable guardians. Through consideration of how trends and fluctuations in social conditions affect the frequency of this convergence of criminogenic circumstances, an explanation of temporal trends in crime rates can be constructed.

155

The Ecological Nature of Illegal Acts

This ecological analysis of direct-contact predatory violations is intended to be more than metaphorical. In the context of such violations, people, gaining and losing sustenance, struggle among themselves for property, safety, territorial hegemony, sexual outlet, physical control, and sometimes for survival itself. The interdependence between offenders and victims can be viewed as a predatory relationship between functionally dissimilar individuals or groups. Since predatory violations fail to yield any net gain in sustenance for the larger community, they can only be sustained by feeding upon other activities. As offenders cooperate to increase their efficiency at predatory violations and as potential victims organize their resistance to these violations, both groups apply the symbiotic principle to improve their sustenance position. On the other hand, potential victims of predatory crime may take evasive actions which encourage offenders to pursue targets other than their own. Since illegal activities must feed upon other activities, the spatial and temporal structure of routine legal activities should play an important role in determining the location, type and quantity of illegal acts occurring in a given community or society. Moreover, one can analyze how the structure of community organization as well as the level of technology in a society provide the circumstances under which crime can thrive. For example, technology and organization affect the capacity of persons with criminal inclinations to overcome their targets, as well as affecting the ability of guardians to contend with potential offenders by using whatever protective tools, weapons and skills they have at their disposal. Many technological advances designed for legitimate purposes—including the automobile, small power tools, hunting weapons, highways, telephones, etc.—may enable offenders to carry out their own work more effectively or may assist people in protecting their own or someone else's person or property.

Not only do routine legitimate activities often provide the wherewithal to commit offenses or to guard against others who do so, but they also provide offenders with suitable targets. Target suitability is likely to reflect such things as value (i.e., the material or symbolic desirability of a personal or property target for offenders), physical visibility, access, and the inertia of a target against illegal treatment by offenders (including the weight, size, and attached or locked features of property inhibiting its illegal removal and the physical capacity of personal victims to resist attackers with or without weapons). Routine production activities probably affect the suitability of consumer goods for illegal removal by determining their value and weight. Daily activities may affect the location of property and personal targets in visible and accessible places at particular times. These activities also may cause people to have on hand objects that can be used as weapons for criminal acts or self-protection or to be preoccupied with tasks which reduce their capacity to discourage or resist offenders.

While little is known about conditions that affect the convergence of potential offenders, targets and guardians, this is a potentially rich source of propositions about crime rates. For example, daily work activities separate many people from those they trust and the property they value. Routine activities also bring together at various times of day or night persons of different background, sometimes in the presence of facilities, tools or weapons which influence the commission or avoidance of illegal acts. Hence, the timing of work, schooling and leisure may be of central importance for explaining crime rates.

The ideas presented so far are not new, but they frequently are overlooked in the theoretical literature on crime. Although an investigation of the literature uncovers significant examples of descriptive and practical data related to the routine activities upon which illegal behavior feeds, these data seldom are treated within an analytical framework. The next section reviews some of this literature.

◉ Relation of the Routine Activity Approach to Extant Studies

A major advantage of the routine activity approach presented here is that it helps assemble some diverse and previously unconnected criminological analyses into a single substantive framework. this framework also serves to link illegal and legal activities, as illustrated by a few examples of descriptive accounts of criminal activity.

Descriptive Analyses

There are several descriptive analyses of criminal acts in criminological literature. For example, Thomas Reppetto's (1974) study, *Residential Crime*, considers how residents supervise their neighborhoods and streets and limit access of possible offenders. He also considers how distance of households from the central city reduces risks of criminal victimization. Reppetto's evidence—consisting of criminal justice records, observations of comparative features of geographic areas, victimization survey data and offender interviews—indicates that offenders are very likely to use burglary tools and to have at least minimal technical skills, that physical characteristics of dwellings affect their victimization rates, that the rhythms of residential crime rate patterns are marked (often related to travel and work patterns of residents), and that visibility of potential sites of crime affects the risk that crimes will occur there. Similar findings are reported by Pope's (1977a; 1977b) study of burglary in California and by Scarr's (1972) study of burglary in and around the District of Columbia. In addition, many studies report that architectural and environmental design as well as community crime programs serve to decrease target suitability and increase capable guardianship (see, for example, Newman, 1973; Jeffrey, 1971; Washnis, 1976), while many biographical or autobiographical descriptions of illegal activities note that lawbreakers take into account the nature of property and/or the structure of human activities as they go about their illegal work (see, e.g., Chambliss, 1972; Klockars, 1974; Sutherland, 1937; Letkemann, 1973; Jackston, 1969; Martin, 1952; Maurer, 1964; Cameron, 1964; Williamson, 1968).

Evidence that the spatio-temporal organization of society affects patterns of crime can be found in several sources. Strong variations in specific predatory crime rates from hour to hour, day to day, and month to month are reported often (e.g., Wolfgang, 1958; Amir, 1971; Reppetto, 1974; Scarr, 1972; FBI, 1975; 1976), and these variations appear to correspond to the various tempos of the related legitimate activities upon which they feed. Also at a microsociological level, Short and Strodtbeck (1965: chaps. 5 and 11) describe opportunities for violent confrontations of gang boys and other community residents which arise in the context of community leisure patterns, such as "quarter parties" in black communities, and the importance, in the calculus of decision making employed by participants in such episodes, of low probabilities of legal intervention. In addition, a wealth of empirical evidence indicates strong spatial variations over community areas in crime and delinquency rates[3] (for an excellent discussion and review of the literature on ecological studies of crimes, see Wilks, 1967). Recently, Albert Reiss (1976) has argued convincingly that these spatial variations (despite some claims to the contrary) have been supported consistently by both official and unofficial sources of data. Reiss further cites victimization studies which indicate that offenders are very likely to select targets not far from their own residence (see USDJ, 1974a; 1974b; 1974c).

*M*acrolevel *A*nalyses of *C*rime *T*rends and *C*ycles

Although details about how crime occurs are intrinsically interesting, the important analytical task is to learn from these details how illegal activities carve their niche within the larger system of activities. This task is not an easy one. For example, attempts by Bonger (1916), Durkheim (1951; 1966), Henry and Short (1954), and Fleisher (1966) to link the rate of illegal activities to the economic condition of a society have not been completely successful. Empirical tests of the relationships postulated in the above studies have produced inconsistent results which some observers view as an indication that the level of crime is not related systematically to the economic conditions of a society (Mansfield et al., 1974: 463; Cohen and Felson, 1979).

It is possible that the wrong economic and social factors have been employed in these macro studies of crime. Other researchers have provided stimulating alternative descriptions of how social change affects the criminal opportunity structure, thereby influencing crime rates in particular societies. For example, at the beginning of the nineteenth century, Patrick Colquhoun (1800) presented a detailed, lucid description and analysis of crime in the London metropolitan area and suggestions for its control. He assembled substantial evidence that London was experiencing a massive crime wave attributable to a great increment in the assemblage and movement of valuable goods through its ports and terminals.

A similar examination of crime in the period of the English industrial expansion was carried out by a modern historian, J. J. Tobias (1967), whose work on the history of crime in nineteenth century England is perhaps the most comprehensive effort to isolate those elements of social change affecting crime in an expanding industrial nation. Tobias details how far reaching changes in transportation, currency, technology, commerce, merchandising, poverty, housing, and the like, had tremendous repercussions on the amount and type of illegal activities committed in the nineteenth century. His thesis is that structural transformations either facilitated or impeded the opportunities to engage in illegal activities. In one of the few empirical studies of how recent social change affects the opportunity structure for crime in the United States, Leroy Gould (1969) demonstrated that the increase in the circulation of money and the availability of automobiles between 1921 and 1965 apparently led to an increase in the rate of bank robberies and auto thefts, respectively. Gould's data suggest that these relationships are due more to the abundance of opportunities to perpetrate the crimes than to short-term fluctuations in economic activities.

Although the sociological and historical studies cited in this section have provided some useful *empirical* generalizations and important insights into the incidence of crime, it is fair to say that they have not articulated systematically the *theoretical* linkages between routine legal activities and illegal endeavors. Thus, these studies cannot explain how changes in the larger social structure generate changes in the opportunity to engage in predatory crime and hence account for crime rate trends.[4] To do so requires a conceptual framework such as that sketched in the preceding section. Before attempting to demonstrate the feasibility of this approach with macrolevel data, we examine available microlevel data for its consistency with the major assumptions of this approach.

/\\icrolevel /\\ssumptions of the 'Routine /\\ctivity /\\pproach

The theoretical approach taken here specifies that crime rate trends in the post-World War II United States are related to patterns of what we have called routine activities. We define these as any recurrent and prevalent activities which provide for basic population and individual needs, whatever their biological or cultural origins. Thus routine activities would include formalized work, as well as the provision of standard food, shelter, sexual outlet, leisure, social interaction, learning and childrearing. These activities may go well beyond the minimal levels needed to prevent a population's extinction, so long as their prevalence and recurrence makes them a part of everyday life.

Routine activities may occur (1) at home, (2) in jobs away from home, and (3) in other activities away from home. The latter may involve primarily household members or others. We shall argue that, since World War II, the United States has experienced a major shift of routine activities away from the first category into the remaining ones, especially those nonhousehold activities involving nonhousehold members. In particular, we shall argue that this shift in the structure of routine activities increases the probability that motivated offenders will converge in space and time with suitable targets in the absence of capable guardians, hence contributing to significant increases in the direct-contact predatory crime rates over these years.

If the routine activity approach is valid, then we should expect to find evidence for a number of empirical relationships regarding the nature and distribution of predatory violations. For example, we would expect routine activities performed within or near the home and among family or other primary groups to entail lower risk of criminal victimization because they enhance guardianship capabilities. We should also expect that routine daily activities affect the location of property and personal targets in visible and accessible places at particular times, thereby influencing their risk of victimization. Furthermore, by determining their size and weight and in some cases their value, routine production activities should affect the suitability of consumer goods for illegal removal. Finally, if the routine activity approach is useful for explaining the paradox presented earlier, we should find that the circulation of people and property, the size and weight of consumer items etc., will parallel changes in crime rate trends for the post-World War II United States.

The veracity of the routine activity approach can be assessed by analyses of both microlevel and macrolevel interdependencies of human activities. While consistency at the former level may appear noncontroversial, or even obvious, one nonetheless needs to show that the approach does not contradict existing data before proceeding to investigate the latter level.

● Empirical Assessment

Circumstances and Location of Offenses

The routine activity approach specifies that household and family activities entail lower risk of criminal victimization than nonhousehold-nonfamily activities, despite the problems in measuring the former.[5]

National estimates from large-scale government victimization surveys in 1973 and 1974 support this generalization (see methodological information in Hindelang et al., 1976: Appendix 6). Table 1 presents several incident-victimization rates per 100,000 population ages 12 and older. Clearly, the rates in Panels A and B are far lower at or near home than elsewhere and far

TABLE 1 *Incident-Specific Risk Rates for Rape, Robbery, Assault and Personal Larceny with Contact, United States, 1974*

		Rape	Robbery	Assault	Personal Larceny with Contact	Total
A.*						
PLACE OF RESIDENCE	In or near home	63	129	572	75	839
	Elsewhere	119	584	1,897	1,010	3,610
B.*						
VICTIM-OFFENDER RELATIONSHIP	(Lone Offender)					
	Relative	7	13	158	5	183
	Well Known	23	30	333	30	416
	Casual Acquaintance	11	26	308	25	370
	Don't Know/Sight Only	106	227	888	616	1,837
	(Multiple Offender)					
	Any known	10***	68	252	43	373
	All strangers	25***	349	530	366	1,270
C.*						
NUMBER OF VICTIMS	One	170	647	2,116	1,062	4,004
	Two	3	47	257	19	326
	Three	0	13	53	3	09
	Four Plus	0	6	43	1	50
D.**						
LOCATION AND RELATIONSHIP (sole offender only)	Home, Stranger	61	147	345	103	654
	Home, Nonstranger	45	74	620	22	761
	Street, Stranger	1,370	7,743	15,684	7,802	32,460
	Street, Nonstranger	179	735	5,777	496	7,167
	Elsewhere, Stranger	129	513	1,934	2,455	4,988
	Elsewhere, Nonstranger	47	155	1,544	99	1,874

*Calculated from Hindelang et al., 1977: Tables 3.16, 3.18, 3.27, 3.28. Rates are per 100,000 persons ages 12 and over.

**See fn. 6 for source. Rates are per billion person-hours in stated locations.

***Based on white data only due to lack of suitable sample size for nonwhites as victims of rape with multiple offenders.

lower among relatives than others. The data indicate that risk of victimization varies directly with social distance between offender and victim. Panel C of this table indicates, furthermore, that risk of lone victimization far exceeds the risk of victimization for groups. These relationships are strengthened by considering time budget evidence that, on the average, Americans spend 16.26 hours per day at home, 1.38 hours on streets, in parks, etc., and 6.36 hours in other places (Szalai, 1972:795). Panel D of Table 1 presents our estimates of victimization per billion person-hours spent in such locations.[6] For example, personal larceny rates (with contact) are 350 times higher at the hands of strangers in streets than at the heads of nonstrangers at home. Separate computations from 1973 victimization data (USDJ, 1976; Table 48) indicate that there were two motor vehicle thefts per million vehicle-hours parked at or near home, 55 per million vehicle-hours in streets, parks, playgrounds, school grounds or parking lots, and 12 per million vehicle-hours elsewhere. While the direction of these relationships is not surprising, their magnitudes should be noted. It appears that risk of criminal victimization varies dramatically among the circumstances and locations in which people place themselves and their property.

𝒯arget 𝒮uitability

Another assumption of the routine activity approach is that target suitability influences the occurrence of direct-contact predatory violations. Though we lack data to disaggregate all major components of target suitability (i.e., value, visibility, accessibility and inertia), together they imply that expensive and movable durables, such as vehicles and electronic appliances, have the highest risk of illegal removal.

As a specific case in point, we compared the 1975 composition of stolen property reported in the Uniform Crime Report (FBI, 1976: Tables 26–7) with national data on personal consumer expenditures for goods (CEA, 1976: Tables 13–16) and to appliance industry estimates of the value of shipments the same year (*Merchandising Week*, 1976). We calculated that $26.44 in motor vehicles and parts were stolen for each $100 of these goods consumed in 1975, while $6.82 worth of electronic appliances were stolen per $100 consumed. Though these estimates are subject to error in citizen and police estimation, what is important here is their size relative to other rates. For example, only 8¢ worth of nondurables and 12¢ worth of furniture and nonelectronic household durables were stolen per $100 of each category consumed, the motor vehicle risk being, respectively, 330 and 220 times as great. Though we lack data on the "stocks" of goods subject to risk, these "flow" data clearly support our assumption that vehicles and electronic appliances are greatly overrepresented in thefts.

The 1976 Buying Guide issue of *Consumer Reports* (1975) indicates why electronic appliances are an excellent retail value for a thief. For example, a Panasonic car tape player is worth $30 per lb., and a Phillips phonograph cartridge is valued at over $5,000 per lb., while large appliances such as refrigerators and washing machines are only worth $1 to $3 per lb. Not surprisingly, burglary data for the District of Columbia in 1969 (Scarr, 1972: Table 9) indicate that home entertainment items alone constituted nearly four times as many stolen items as clothing, food, drugs, liquor, and tobacco combined and nearly eight times as many stolen items as office supplies and equipment. In addition, 69% of national thefts classified in 1975 (FBI, 1976: Tables 1, 26) involve automobiles, their parts or accessories, and thefts from automobiles or thefts of bicycles. Yet radio and television sets plus electronic components and accessories totaled only 0.10% of the total truckload tonnage terminated in 1973 by intercity motor carriers, while passenger cars, motor vehicle parts and accessories, motorcycles, bicycles, and their parts, totaled only 5.5% of the 410 million truckload tons terminated (ICC, 1974). Clearly, portable and movable durables are reported stolen in great disproprotion to their share of the value and weight of goods circulating in the United States.

𝒥amily 𝒜ctivities and 𝒞rime 𝒯ates

One would expect that persons living in single-adult households and those employed outside the home are less obligated to confine their time to family activities within households. From a routine activity perspective, these persons and their households should have higher rates of predatory criminal victimization. We also expect that adolescents and young adults who are perhaps more likely to engage in peer group activities rather than family activities will have higher rates of criminal victimization. Finally, married persons should have lower rates than others. Tables 2 and 3 largely confirm these expectations (with the exception of personal larceny with contact). Examining these tables, we note that victimization rates appear to be related inversely to age and are lower for persons in "less active" statuses (e.g., keeping house, unable to work, retired) and persons in intact marriages. A notable exception is indicated in Table 2, where persons unable to work appear more likely to be victimized by rape, robbery and personal larceny with contact than are other "inactive persons." Unemployed persons also have unusually high rates of victimization. However, these rates are consistent with the routine activity approach offered here: the high rates of victimization suffered by the unemployed may reflect their residential proximity to high concentrations of potential offenders as well as their age and racial composition, while handicapped persons have high risk of personal victimization because they are less able to resist motivated offenders. Nonetheless, persons who keep house have noticeably lower rates of victimization than those who are employed, unemployed, in school or in the armed forces.

As Table 3 indicates, burglary and robbery victimization rates are about twice as high for persons living in single-adult households as for other persons in each age group examined. Other victimization data (USDJ, 1976: Table 21) indicate that, while household victimization rates tend to vary directly with household size, larger households have lower rates per person. For example, the total household victimization rates (including burglary, household larceny, and motor vehicle theft) per 1,000 households were 168 for single-person households and 326 for households containing six or more persons. Hence, six people distributed over six single-person households experience an average of 1,008 household victimizations, more than three times as many as one six-person household. Moreover, age of household head has a strong relationship to a household's victimization rate for these crimes. For households headed by persons under 20, the motor vehicle theft rate is nine times as high, and the burglary and household larceny rates four times as high as those for households headed by persons 65 and over (USDJ, 1976: Table 9).

While the data presented in this section were not collected originally for the purpose of testing the routine activity approach, our efforts to rework them for these purposes have proven fruitful. The routine activity approach is consistent with the data examined and, in addition, helps to accommodate within a rather simple and coherent analytical framework certain findings which, though not necessarily new, might otherwise be attributed only "descriptive" significance. In the next section, we examine macrosocial trends as they relate to trends in crime rates.

TABLE 2 *Selected Status-Specific Personal Victimization Rates for the United States (Per 100,000 Persons in Each Category)*

Variables and Sources	Victim Category	Rape	Robbery	Personal Assault	Personal Larceny with Contact	Larceny without Contact
A. AGE (Source: Hindelang, et al., 1977: Table 310, 1974 rates	12–15	147	1,267	3,848	311	16,355
	16–19	248	1,127	5,411	370	15,606
	20–24	209	1,072	4,829	337	14,295
	25–34	135	703	3,023	263	10,354
	35–49	21	547	1,515	256	7,667
	50–64	33	411	731	347	4,588
	65+	20	388	492	344	1,845
B. MAJOR ACTIVITY OF VICTIM (Source: Hindelang, et al., 1977: Table 313, 1974 rates)	(Male 16+) Armed Forces	—	1,388	4,153	118	16,274
	Employed	—	807	3,285	252	10,318
	Unemployed	—	2,179	7,984	594	15,905
	Keep house	—	0	2,475	463	3,998
	In school	—	1,362	5,984	493	17,133
	Unable to work	—	1,520	2,556	623	3,648
	Retired	—	578	662	205	2,080
	(Female 16+) Keep house	116	271	978	285	4,433
	Employed	156	529	1,576	355	9,419
	Unemployed	798	772	5,065	461	12,338
	In School	417	430	2,035	298	12,810
	Unable to work	287	842	741	326	1,003
	Retired	120	172	438	831	1,571

TABLE 2 *Continued*

Variables and Sources	Victim Category	Rape	Robbery	Personal Assault	Personal Larceny with Contact	Larceny without Contact
C. MARITAL STATUS (Male 12+)						
(Source: USDJ: 1977, Table 5, 1973 rates)	Never Married	—	1,800	5,870	450	16,450
	Married	—	550	2,170	170	7,660
	Separated/Divorced	—	2,270	5,640	1,040	12,960
	Widowed	—	1,150	1,500	—	4,120
(Female 12+)	Never Married	360	580	2,560	400	12,880
	Married	70	270	910	220	6,570
	Separated/Divorced	540	1,090	4,560	640	9,130
	Widowed	—	450	590	480	2,460

Line indicates too few offenses for accurate estimates of rate. However, rates in these cells are usually small.

167

TABLE 3 *Robbery-Burglary Victimization Rates by Ages and Number of Adults in Household, 1974 and 1976 General Social Survey*

Age	Number of Adults in Household				Ratio
	One		Two or More		
18–35	0.200	(140)	0.095	(985)	2.11
36–55	0.161	(112)	0.079	(826)	2.04
56 and over	0.107	(262)	0.061	(640)	1.76
All Ages	0.144	(514)	0.081	(2451)	1.78

(Numbers in parentheses are the base for computing risk rates.)

Source: Calculated from 1974 and 1976 General Social Survey, National Opinion Research Center, University of Chicago.

● Changing Trends in Routine Activity Structure and Parallel Trends in Crime Rates

The main thesis presented here is that the dramatic increase in the reported crime rates in the U.S. since 1960 is linked to changes in the routine activity structure of American society and to a corresponding increase in target suitability and decrease in guardian presence. If such a thesis has validity, then we should be able to identify these social trends and show how they relate to predatory criminal victimization rates.

Trends in Human Activity Patterns

The decade 1960–1970 experienced noteworthy trends in the activities of the American population. For example, the percent of the population consisting of female college students increased 118% (USBC, 1975: Table 225). Married female labor force participant rates increased 31% (USBC, 1975: Table 563), while the percent of the population living as primary individuals increased by 34% (USBC, 1975: Table 51; see also Kobrin, 1976). We gain some further insight into changing routine activity patterns by comparing hourly data for 1960 and 1971 on households *unattended* by persons ages 14 or over when U.S. census interviewers first called (see Table 4). These data suggest that the proportion of households unattended at 8 A.M. increased by almost half between 1960 and 1971. One also finds increases in rates of out-of-town travel, which provides greater opportunity for both daytime and nighttime burglary of residences. Between 1960 and 1970, there was a 72% increase in state and national park visits per capita (USBC, 1975), an 144% increase in the percent of plant workers eligible for three weeks vacation (BLS, 1975: Table 116), and an 184% increase in over-seas travellers per 100,000 population (USBC, 1975: Table 366). The National Travel Survey, conducted as part of the U.S. Census Bureau's Census of Transportation, confirms the general trends, tallying an 81% increase in the number of vacations taken by Americans from 1967 to 1972, a five-year period (USBC, 1973a: Introduction).

The dispersion of activities away from households appears to be a major recent social change. Although this decade also experienced an important 31% increase in the percent of the population ages 15–24, age structure change was only one of many social trends occurring during the period,

TABLE 4 *Proportion of Households Unattended by Anyone 14 Years Old or Over by Time of Day during First Visit by Census Bureau Interviewer, 1960 and 1971*

Time of day	1960 Census	November, 1971 Current Pop. Survey	Percent Change
8:00– 8:59 a.m.	29%	43	+48.9%
9:00– 9:59 a.m.	29	44	+58
10:00–10:59 a.m.	31	42	+36
11:00–11:59 a.m.	32	41	+28
12:00–12:59 p.m.	32	41	+28
1:00– 1:59 p.m.	31	43	+39
2:00– 2:59 p.m.	33	43	+30
3:00– 3:59 p.m.	30	33	+10
4:00– 4:59 p.m.	28	30	+ 7
5:00– 5:59 p.m.	22	26	+18
6:00– 6:59 p.m.	22	25	+14
7:00– 7:59 p.m.	20	29	+45
8:00– 8:59 p.m.	24	22	- 8

Source: Calculated from USBC (1973b: Table A).

especially trends in the circulation of people and property in American society.[7]

The importance of the changing activity structure is underscored by taking a brief look at demographic changes between the years 1970 and 1975, a period of continuing crime rate increments. Most of the recent changes in age structure relevant to crime rates already had occurred by 1970; indeed, the proportion of the population ages 15–24 increased by only 6% between 1970 and 1975, compared with a 15% increase during the five years 1965 to 1970. On the other hand, major changes in the structure of routine activities continued during these years. For example, in only five years, the estimated proportion of the population consisting of husband-present, married women in the labor force households increased by 11%, while the estimated number of non-husband-wife households per 100,000 population increased from 9,150 to 11,420, a 25% increase (USBC, 1976: Tables 50, 276; USBC, 1970–1975). At the same time, the percent of population enrolled in higher education increased 16% between 1970 and 1975.

𝒯elated 𝒫roperty 𝒯rends and 𝒯heir 𝒯elation to 𝒜uman 𝒜ctivity 𝒫atterns

Many of the activity, trends mentioned above normally involve significant investments in durable goods. For example, the dispersion of population across relatively more households (especially non-husband-wife households) enlarges the market for durable goods such as television sets and automobiles. Women participating in the labor force and both men and women enrolled in college provide a market for automobiles. Both work and travel often involve the purchase of major movable or portable durables and their use away from home.

Considerable data are available which indicate that sales of consumer goods changed dramatically between 1960 and 1970 (as did their size and weight), hence providing more suitable property available for theft. For example, during this decade, constant-dollar personal consumer expenditures in the United States for motor vehicles and parts increased by 71%, while constant-dollar expenditures for other durables increased by 105% (calculated from CEA, 1976: Table B-16), In addition, electronic household appliances and small houseware shipments increased from 56.2 to 119.7 million units (*Electrical Merchandising Week,* 1964; *Merchandising Week,*

1973). During the same decade, appliance imports increased in value by 681% (USBC, 1975: Table 1368).

This same period appears to have spawned a revolution in small durable product design which further feeds the opportunity for crime to occur. Relevant data from the 1960 and 1970 Sears catalogs on the weight of many consumer durable goods were examined. Sears is the nation's largest retailer and its policy of purchasing and relabeling standard manufactured goods makes its catalogs a good source of data on widely merchandised consumer goods. The lightest television listed for sale in 1960 weighed 38 lbs., compared with 15 lbs. for 1970. Thus, the lightest televisions were $2\frac{1}{2}$ times as heavy in 1960 as 1970. Similar trends are observed for dozens of other goods listed in the Sears catalog. Data from *Consumer Reports Buying Guide*, published in December of 1959 and 1969, show similar changes for radios, record players, slide projectors, tape recorders, televisions, toasters and many other goods. Hence, major declines in weight between 1960 and 1970 were quite significant for these and other goods, which suggests that the consumer goods market may be producing many more targets suitable for theft. In general, one finds rapid growth in property suitable for illegal removal and in household and individual exposure to attack during the years 1960–1975.

Related Trends in Business Establishments

Of course, as households and individuals increased their ownership of small durables, businesses also increased the value of the merchandise which they transport and sell as well as the money involved in these transactions. Yet the Census of Business conducted in 1958, 1963, 1967, and 1972 indicate that the number of wholesale, retail, service, and public warehouse establishments (including establishments owned by large organizations) was a nearly constant ratio of one for every 16 persons in the United States. Since more goods and money were distributed over a relatively fixed number of business establishments, the tempo of business activity per establishment apparently was increasing. At the same time, the percent of the population employed as sales clerks or salesmen in retail trade declined from 1.48% to 1.27%, between 1960 and 1970, a 14.7% decline (USBC, 1975: Table 589).

Though both business and personal property increased, the changing pace of activities appears to have exposed the latter to greater relative risk of attack, whether at home or elsewhere, due to the dispersion of goods among many more households, while concentrating goods in business establishments. However, merchandise in retail establishments with heavy volume and few employees to guard it probably is exposed to major increments in risk of illegal removal than is most other business property.

Composition of Crime Trends

If these changes in the circulation of people and property are in fact related to crime trends, the *composition* of the latter should reflect this. We expect relatively greater increases in personal and household victimization as compared with most business victimizations, while shoplifting should increase more rapidly than other types of thefts from businesses. We expect personal offenses at the hands of strangers to manifest greater increases than such offenses at the hands of nonstrangers. Finally, residential burglary rates should increase more in daytime than nighttime.

The available time series on the composition of offenses confirm these expectations. For example, Table 5 shows that commercial burglaries declined from 60% to 36% of the total, while daytime residential burglaries increased from 16% to 33%. Unlike the other crimes against business, shoplifting increased its share. Though we lack trend data on the circumstances of other violent offenses, murder data confirm our expectations. Between 1963 and 1975, felon-type murders increased from 17% to 32% of the total. Compared with a 47% increase in the rate of relative killings in this period, we calculated a 294% increase in the murder rate at the hands of known or suspected felon types.

Thus the trends in the composition of recorded crime rates appear to be highly consistent with the activity structure trends noted earlier. . . .

◉ The Relationship of the Household Activity Ratio to Five Annual Official Index

TABLE 5 *Offense Analysis Trends for Robbery, Burglary, Larceny and Murder; United States, 1960–1975*

A. ROBBERIES[a]	1960	1965	1970	
Highway Robbery	52.6	57.0	59.8	
Residential Robbery	8.0	10.1	13.1	
Commercial Robbery	39.4	32.9	27.1	
Totals	100.0	100.0	100.0	
B. BURGLARIES	1960	1965	1970	1975
Residential	15.6	24.5	31.7	33.2
Residential Nighttime	24.4	25.2	25.8	30.5
Commercial	60.0	50.2	42.5	36.3
Totals	100.0	99.9	100.0	100.0
C. LARCENIES	1960	1965	1970	1975
Shoplifting	6.0	7.8	9.2	11.3
Other	94.0	92.2	90.8	88.7
Totals	100.0	100.0	100.0	100.0
D. MURDERS	1963	1965	1970	1975
Relative Killings	31.0	31.0	23.3	22.4
Romance, Arguments[b]	51.0	48.0	47.9	45.2
Felon Types[c]	17.0	21.0	28.8	32.4
Totals	100.0	100.0	100.0	100.0

Source: Offense Analysis from UCR, various years.

[a]Excluding miscellaneous robberies. The 1975 distribution omitted due to apparent instability of post-1970 data.

[b]Includes romantic triangles, lovers' quarrels and arguments.

[c]Includes both known and suspected felon types.

$\mathcal{C}$rime $\mathcal{R}$ates in the $\mathcal{U}$nited States, 1947–1974

In this selection, we test the hypothesis that aggregate official crime rate trends in the United States vary directly over time with the dispersion of activities away from family and household. The limitations of annual time series data do not allow construction of direct measures of changes in hourly activity patterns, or quantities, qualities and movements of exact stocks of household durable goods, but the Current Population Survey does provide related time series on labor force and household structure. From these data, we calculate annually (beginning in 1947) a household activity ratio by

adding the number of married, husband-present female labor force participants (source: BLS, 1975: Table 5) to the number of non-husband-wife
households (source: USBC, 1947–1976), dividing this sum by the total
number of households in the U.S. (source: USBC, 1947–1976). This calculation provides an estimate of the proportion of American households in
year t expected to be most highly exposed to risk of personal and property
victimization due to the dispersion of their activities away from family and
household and/or their likelihood of owning extra sets of durable subject to
high risk of attack. Hence, the household activity ratio should vary directly
with official index crime rates.

Our empirical goal in this section is to test this relationship, with
controls for those variables which other researchers have linked empirically
to crime rate trends in the United States. Since various researchers have
found such trends to increase with the proportion of the population in teen
and young adult years (Fox, 1976; Land and Felson, 1976; Sagi and
Wellford, 1968; Wellford, 1973), we include the population ages 15–24 per
100,000 resident population in year t as our first control variable (source:
USBC, various years). Others (e.g., Brenner, 1976a; 1976b) have found
unemployment rates to vary directly with official crime rates over time,
although this relationship elsewhere has been shown to be empirically questionable (see Mansfield et al., 1974: 463; Cohen and Felson, 1979). Thus, as
our second, control variable, we take the standard annual unemployment
rate (per 100 persons ages 16 and over) as a measure of the business cycle
(source: BLS, 1975).

Four of the five crime rates that we utilize here (forcible rape, aggravated assault, robbery and burglary) are taken from FBI estimates of offenses
100,000 U.S. population (as revised and reported in OMB, 1973). We
exclude larceny-theft due to a major definitional change in 1960 and auto
theft due to excessive multicollinearity in the analysis.[8] For our homicide
indicator we employ the homicide mortality rate taken from the vital statistics data collected by the Bureau of the Census (various years). The latter rate
has the advantage of being collected separately from the standard crime
reporting system and is thought to contain less measurement error (see
Bowers and Pierce, 1975). Hence, this analysis of official index crime rates
includes three violent offenses (homicide, forcible rape, and aggravated
assault), one property offense (burglary), and one offense which involves
both the removal of property and the threat of violence (robbery). The
analysis thus includes one offense thought to have relatively low reporting

reliability (forcible rape), one thought to have relatively high reliability (homicide), and three others having relatively intermediate levels of reporting quality (Ennis, 1967).

Since official crime rates in year t are likely to reflect some accumulation of criminal opportunity and inclinations over several years, one should not expect these rates to respond solely to the level of the independent variables for year t. A useful model of cumulative social change in circumstances such as this is the difference equation, which can be estimated in two forms (see Goldberg, 1958). One form takes the first difference $(y_t - y_{t-1})$ as the dependent variable—in this case, the change in the official crime rate per 100,000 population between year $t-1$ and year t. Alternatively, one can estimate the difference equation in autoregressive form by taking the official crime rate in year t as a function of the exogenous predictors plus the official crime rate in year $t-1$ on the right-hand side of the equation. (See Land, 1978, for a review of these and other methods and for references to related literature.) Both forms are estimable with ordinary least squares methods, which we employ for the years 1947 through 1974. The N is 28 years for all but the homicide rate, for which publication lags reduce our N to 26.

Even if a positive relationship between the household activity ratio and the official crime rates is observed, with controls for age and unemployment, we are open to the charge that this may be a spurious consequence of autocorrelation of disturbances, that is, the possibility that residuals are systematically related for nearby time points. While spurious relationships are a risk one also takes in cross-sectional regression analysis, time-series analysts have devised a variety of methods for monitoring and adjusting for spuriousness due to this autocorrelation, including the Durbin and Watson (1951) statistic, Durbin's h statistic (Durbin, 1970), the Griliches (1967) criterion, as well as cochrane and Orcutt (1949) corrections. We employ (but do not report in detail) these methods to check for the likelihood that the observed relationship is spurious. (See Land, 1978, for a review of such tests and the related literature on their applicability and robustness; see Theil, 1971, for a methodological review.)

Findings

Our time-series analysis for the years 1947–1974 consistently revealed positive and statistically significant relationships between the household activity ratio and each official crime rate change. Whichever official crime rate is employed, this finding occurs—whether we take the first difference for each crime rate as exogenous or estimate the equation in autoregressive form (with the lagged dependent variable on the right-hand side of the equation); whether we include or exclude the unemployment variable; whether we take the current scales of variables or convert them to natural log values; whether we employ the age structure variable as described or alter the ages examined (e.g., 14–24, 15–19, etc.) In short, the relationship is positive and significant in each case.

Before calculating the difference equations, we regressed each crime rate in year t on the three independent variables for year t. This ordinary structural equation also produced consistent positive and significant coefficients for the routine activity coefficient, the total variance explained ranges from 84% to 97%. However, the Durbin-Watson statistics for these equations indicated high risk of autocorrelation, which is hardly surprising since they ignore lagged effects. Reestimated equations taking first differences as endogenous reduced the rise of autocorrelation significantly (and also reduced variance explained to between 35% and 77%). These equations also consistently produce significant positive coefficients for the household activity variable. When unemployment is included in these equations, its coefficients are all negative and near zero.

The top panel of Table 6 presents regression estimates of first differences for five official crime rates, with the age structure and household activity variables in year t as the only predictors. Again, the household activity coefficients are consistently positive, with t ratios always significant with a one-tailed test. Except for the aggravated assault equation, the household activity variable has a t ratio and standardized coefficient greater than that of the age structure variable. The standardized coefficients for the household activity variable range from .42 to .72, while the age structure coefficients are consistently positive. In general, the household activity variable is a stronger predictor of official crime rate trends than the age structure.

The equation in the top panel of Table 6 generally has lower variance explained but also lower risk of autocorrelation of disturbances than those reported above. For all five equations, the Durbin-Watson statistic allows acceptance of the null hypothesis that autocorrelation is absent at the 1% level. A 5% level (which *increases* the likelihood of proving the statistic nonzero) allows us neither to accept nor reject the null hypothesis that autocorrelation is absent in the homicide and robbery equations.

TABLE 6 *Regression Equations for First Differences in Five Index Crime Rates and Sensitivity Analyses, the United States, 1947–1974*

First Difference Form	(1) Nonnegligent Homicide	(2) Forcible Rape	(3) Aggravated Assault	(4) Robbery	(5) Burglary
Constant	-2.3632	-4.8591	-32.0507	-43.8838	-221.2303
t ratio	.3502	5.3679	7.6567	3.4497	3.7229
Proportion 15–24 (t)					
Standardized	.1667	.1425	.4941	.2320	.1952
Unstandardized	3.2190	6.4685	132.1072	116.7742	486.0806
t ratio	1.0695	.7505	3.3147	.9642	.8591
Household Activity Ratio (t)					
Standardized	.7162	.6713	.4377	.4242	.5106
Unstandardized	4.0676	8.9743	34.4658	62.8834	374.4746
t ratio	4.5959	3.5356	2.9364	1.7629	2.2474
Multiple R^2 Adjusted	.6791	.5850	.7442	.3335	.4058
Degrees of Freedom	23	25	25	25	25
Durbin–Watson Value	2.5455	2.3388	2.3446	1.4548	1.7641
1%	Accept	Accept	Accept	Accept	Accept
5% test	Uncertain	Accept	Accept	Uncertain	Accept

(Continued on next page)

177

TABLE 6 *Regression Equations for First Differences in Five Index Crime Rates and Sensitivity Analyses, the United States, 1947–1974 (Continued)*

First Difference Form	(1) Nonnegligent Homicide	(2) Forcible Rape	(3) Aggravated Assault	(4) Robbery	(5) Burglary
Autoregressive Form					
Multiple R² Adjusted	.9823	.9888	.9961	.9768	.9859
Durbin's h	–1.3751	–.7487	.9709	1.5490	1.1445
–1% test	Accept	Accept	Accept	Accept	Accept
–5% test	Accept	Accept	Accept	Accept	Accept
Griliches Criterion	Accept	Accept	Accept	Accept	Accept
Cochrane-Orcutt Correction, Effect upon Household Activity	Minimal	Minimal	Minimal	Minimal	Minimal
Unemployment Rate as Control, Effect Upon Household Activity	Minimal	Minimal	Minimal	Minimal	Minimal

Though autocorrelation has not been proven to exist in these five equations, its risk may be sufficient in two to motivate further efforts at equation estimation (see bottom panel of Table 6). We estimated the equations in autoregressive form to see if the risk abates. Since the Durbin-Watson statistic was not designed for evaluating autocorrelation in these equations, we calculated Durbin's h, a statistic specifically designed for equations estimated with a lagged dependent variable (Durbin, 1970), and recently found to be robust for small samples (Maddala and Rao, 1973). This statistic allows acceptance of the null hypothesis (at both 1% and 5% levels) that autocorrelation is absent for all five equations. Application of the Griliches (1967) criterion further allows acceptance of each equation as manifesting distributing lags rather than serial correlation. We also employed the Cochrane-Orcutt (1949) iterative procedure to calculate a correction estimate for any autocorrelation present. The resulting correction for the household activity coefficient proves minimal in all five cases. Finally, we calculated each of the above equations for natural log values of the relevant variables, finding again that the household activity coefficient was consistently positive and statistically significant and the risk of autocorrelation reduced still further.

The positive and significant relationship between the household activity variable and the official crime rates is robust and appears to hold for both macro- and microlevel data; it explains five crime rate trends, as well as the changing composition of official crime rates reported in Table 5. These results suggest that routine activities may indeed provide the opportunity for many illegal activities to occur.

◎ Discussion

In our judgment many conventional theories of crime (the adequacy of which usually is evaluated by cross-sectional data, or no data at all) have difficulty accounting for the annual changes in crime rate trends in the post-World War II United States. These theories may prove useful in explaining crime trends during other periods, within specific communities, or in particular subgroups of the population. Longitudinal aggregate data for the United States, however, indicate that the trends for many of the presumed causal variables in these theoretical structures are in a direction opposite to those hypothesized to be the causes of crime. For example, during the decade 19601970, the percent of the population below the low-income level

179

declined 44% and the unemployment rate declined 186%. Central city population as a share of the whole population declined slightly, while the percent of foreign stock declined 0.1%, etc. (see USBC, 1975: 654, 19, 39).

On the other hand, the convergence in time and space of three elements (motivated offenders, suitable targets, and the absence of capable guardians) appears useful for understanding crime rate trends. The lack of any of these elements is sufficient to prevent the occurrence of a successful direct-contact predatory crime. The convergence in time and space of suitable targets and the absence of capable guardians can lead to large increases in crime rates without any increase or change in the structural conditions that motivate individuals to engage in crime. Presumably, had the social indicators of the variables hypothesized to be the causes of crime in conventional theories changed in the direction of favoring increased crime in the post-World War II United States, the increases in crime rates likely would have been even more staggering than those which were observed. In any event, it is our belief that criminologists have underemphasized the importance of the convergence of suitable targets and the absence of capable guardians in explaining recent increases in the crime rate. Furthermore, the effects of the convergence in time and space of these elements may be multiplicative rather than additive. That is, their convergence by a fixed percentage may produce increases in crime rates far greater than that fixed percentage, demonstrating how some relatively modest social trends can contribute to some relatively large changes in crime rate trends. The fact that logged variables improved our equations (moving Durbin-Watson values closer to "ideal" levels) lends support to the argument that such an interaction occurs.

Those few investigations of cross-sectional data which include household indicators produce results similar to ours. For example, Roneck (1975) and Choldin and Roncek (1976) report on block-level data for San Diego, Cleveland and Peoria and indicate that the proportion of a block's households which are primary individual households consistently offers the best or nearly the best predictor of a block's crime rate. This relationship persisted after they controlled for numerous social variables, including race, density, age and poverty. Thus the association between household structure and risk of criminal victimization has been observed in individual-level and block-level cross-sectional data, as well as aggregate national time-series data.

Without denying the importance of factors motivating offenders to engage in crime, we have focused specific attention upon violations themselves and the prerequisites for their occurrence. However, the routine activity approach might in the future be applied to the analysis of offenders and their inclinations as well. For example, the structure of primary group activity may affect the likelihood that cultural transmission or social control of criminal inclinations will occur, while the structure of the community may affect the tempo of criminogenic peer group activity. We also may expect that circumstances favorable for carrying out violations contribute to criminal inclinations in the long run by rewarding these inclinations.

We further suggest that the routine activity framework may prove useful in explaining why the criminal justice system, the community and the family have appeared so ineffective in exerting social control since 1960. Substantial increases in the opportunity to carry out predatory violations may have undermined society's mechanisms for social control. For example, it may be difficult for institutions seeking to increase the certainty, celerity and severity of punishment to compete with structural changes resulting in vast increases in the certainty, celerity and value of rewards to be gained from illegal predatory acts.

It is ironic that the very factors which increase the opportunity to enjoy the benefits of life also may increase the opportunity for predatory violations. For example, automobiles provide freedom of movement to offenders as well as average citizens and offer vulnerable targets for theft. College enrollment, female labor force participation, urbanization, suburbanization, vacations and new electronic durables provide various opportunities to escape the confines of the household while they increase the risk of predatory victimization. Indeed, the opportunity for predatory crime appears to be enmeshed in the opportunity structure for legitimate activities to such an extent that it might be very difficult to root out substantial amounts of crime without modifying much of our way of life. Rather than assuming that predatory crime is simply an indicator of social breakdown, one might take it as a byproduct of freedom and prosperity as they manifest themselves in the routine activities of everyday life.

Endnotes

[1]Though official data severely underestimate crime, they at least provide a rough indicator of trends over time in the volume of several major felonies. The possibility that these data also reflect trends in rates at which offenses are reported to the police has motivated extensive victimology research (see Nettler, 1974; and Hindelang, 1976, for a review). This work consistently finds that seriousness of

offense is the strongest determinant of citizen reporting to law enforcement officials (Skogan, 1976: 145; Hindelang, 1976: 401). Hence the upward trend in official crime rates since 1960 in the U.S. may reflect increases in both the volume and seriousness of offenses. Though disaggregating these two components may not be feasible, one may wish to interpret observed trends as generated largely by both.

[2]The analytical distinction between target and guardian is not important in those cases where a personal target engages in self-protection from direct-contact predatory violations. We leave open for the present the question of whether a guardian is effective or ineffective in all situations. We also allow that various guardians may primarily supervise offenders, targets or both. These are questions for future examination.

[3]One such ecological study by Sarah Boggs (1965) presents some similar ideas in distinguishing *familiarity* of offenders with their targets as two offenders with their targets and *profitability* of targets as two elements of crime occurrence. Boggs' work stands apart from much research on the ecology of crime in its consideration of crime occurrence rates separately from offender rates. The former consist of the number of offenses committed in a given area per number of suitable targets within that area (as estimated by various indicators). The latter considers the residence of offenders in computing the number of offenders per unit population. Boggs examines the correlations between crime occurrence rates and offender rates for several offenses in St. Louis and shows that the two are often independent. It appears from her analysis that *both* target and offender characteristics play a central role in the location of illegal activity.

[4]The concept of the opportunity for crime contained in the above research and in this study differs considerably from the traditional sociological usage of the *differential opportunity* concept. For example, Cloward and Ohlin (1960) employed this term in discussing how legitimate and illegitimate opportunities affect the resolution of adjustment problems leading to gang delinquency. From their viewpoint, this resolution depends upon the kind of social support for one or another type of illegitimate activity that is given at different points in the social structure (Cloward and Ohlin, 1960: 151). Rather than circumstantial determinants of crime, they use differential opportunity to emphasize structural features which motivate offenders to perpetrate certain types of crimes. Cloward and Ohlin are largely silent on the interaction of the motivation with target suitability and guardianship as this interaction influences crime rates.

[5]Recent research indicates the existence of substantial quantities of family violence which remains outside of UCR data (see annotated bibliography of family violence in Lystad, 1974). While we cannot rule out the likelihood that much family violence is concealed from victimization surveys, the latter capture infor-

mation absent from police data and still indicate that nonfamily members are usually much more dangerous than family members are to each other (see text). Also, when family violence leads to death, its suppression becomes quite difficult. The murder circumstances data indicate that about two-thirds of killings involve nonrelatives. Without denying the evidence that the level of family violence is far greater than police reports would indicate, available data also suggest that time spent in family activities within households incurs less risk of victimization than many alternative activities in other places. In addition, many of the most *common* offenses (such as robbery and burglary) always have been recognized as usually involving nonfamily members.

[6]Billion person-hours can easily be conceptualized as 1,000,000 persons spending 1,000 hours each (or about 42 days) in a given location (Szalai, 1972:795). Fox obtained these data from a 1966 time budget study in 44 American cities. The study was carried out by the Survey Research Center, the University of Michigan. We combined four subsamples in computing our figures. We combined activities into three locations, as follows: (1) at or just outside home; (2) at another's home, restaurants or bars, or indoor leisure; (3) in streets, parks, or outdoor leisure. Our computing formula was

$$Q = [(R \div 105) \div (A \cdot 365)] \cdot 10^9,$$

where Q is the risk per billion person-hours; R is the victimization rate, reported per 10^5 persons in Hindelang et al. (1976: Table 318); A is the hours spent per location calculated from Szalai (1972: 795); 365 is the multiplier to cover a year's exposure to risk; and 10^9 converts risk per person-hour to billion person-hours.

[7]While the more sophisticated treatments of the topic have varied somewhat in their findings, most recent studies attempting to link crime rate increases to the changing age structure of the American population have found that the latter account for a relatively limited proportion of the general crime trend (see, for example, Sagi and Wellford, 1968; Ferdinand, 1970; and Wellford, 1973).

[8]The auto theft rate lagged one year correlated quite strongly with the predictor variables. This multicollinearity impaired our difference equation analysis, although we again found consistently positive coefficients for the house hold activity ration. We were able to remove autocorrelation by logging all variables and including the unemployment as a control, but do not report these equation.

References

Amir, Menachem. 1971. Patterns of Forcible Rape. Chicago: University of Chicago Press.

Boggs, Sarah. 1965. "Urban crime patterns." American Sociological Review 30:899–905.

Bonger, W. A. 1916. Criminality and Economic Conditions. Boston: Little, Brown.

Bowers, W. J. and Glen L. Pierce. 1975. "The illusion of deterrence of Isaac Ehrlich's research on capital punishment." Yale Law Journal 85:187–208.

Brenner, Harvey. 1976a. Estimating the Social Costs of National Economic Policy: Implications for Mental and Physical Health and Criminal Aggression. Paper no. 5, Joint Economic Committee, Congress of the United States. Washington, D.C.: U.S. Government Printing Office.

————. 1976b. Effects of the National Economy on Criminal Aggression II. Final Report to National Institute of Mental Health. Contract #282–76–0355FS.

Bureau of Labor Statistics (BLS). 1975. Handbook of Labor Statistics 1975— Reference Edition. Washington, D.C.: U.S. Government Printing Office.

Cameron, Mary Owen. 1964. The Booster and the Snitch. New York: Free Press.

Chambliss, William J. 1972. Boxman: A Professional Thief's Journey. New York: Harper and Row.

Choldin, Harvey M. and Dennis W. Roncek. 1976. "Density, population potentia-land pathology: a block-level analysis." Public Data Use 4:19–30.

Cloward, Richard and Lloyd Ohlin. 1960. Delinquency and Opportunity. New York: Free Press.

Cochrane, D., and G. H. Orcutt. 1949. "Application of least squares regression to relationship containing autocorrelated error terms." Journal of the American Statistical Association 44:32–61.

Cohen, Lawrence E. and Marcus Felson. 1979. "On estimating the social costs of national economic policy: a critical examination of the Brenner study." Social Indicators Research. In press.

Colquhoun, Patrick. 1800. Treatise on the Police of the Metropolis. London: Baldwin.

Consumer Reports Buying Guide. 1959. Consumer Reports (December). Mt. Vernon: Consumers Union.

————. 1969. Consumer Reports (December). Mt. Vernon: Consumers Union.

————. 1975. Consumer Reports (December). Mt. Vernon: Consumers Union.

Council of Economic Advisors (CEA). 1976. The Economic Report of the President. Washington, D.C.: U.S. Government Printing Office.

Durbin, J. 1970. "Testing for serial correlation when least squares regressors are lagged dependent variables." Econometrica 38:410–21.

Durbin, J., and G. S. Watson. 1951. "Testing for serial correlation in least squares regression, II." Biometrika 38:410–21.

Durkheim, Emile. 1951. Suicide: A Study in Sociology. New York: Free Press.

————. 1966. The Division of Labor in Society. New York: Free Press.

Electrical Merchandising Week. 1964. Statistical and Marketing Report (January). New York: Billboard Publications.

Ennis, Philip H. 1967. "Criminal victimization in the U.S.: a report of a national survey, field surveys II." The President's Commission on Law Enforcement and the Administration of Justice. Washington, D.C.: U.S. Government Printing Office.

Federal Bureau of Investigation (FBI). 1975. Crime in the U.S.: Uniform Crime Report. Washington, D.C.: U.S. Government Printing Office.

————. 1976. Crime in the U.S.: Uniform Crime Report. Washington, D.C.: U.S. Government Printing Office.

Ferdinand, Theodore N. 1970. "Demographic shifts and criminality." British Journal of Criminology 10:169–75.

Fleisher, Belton M. 1966. The Economics of Delinquency. Chicago: Quadrangle.

Fox, James A. 1976. An Econometric Analysis of Crime Data. Ph.D. dissertation, Department of Sociology, University of Pennsylvania. Ann Arbor: University Microfilms.

Glaser, Daniel. 1971. Social Deviance. Chicago: Markham.

Goldberg, Samuel. 1958. Introduction to Difference Equations. New York: Wiley.

Gould, Leroy. 1969. "The changing structure of property crime in an affluent society." Social Forces 48:50–0.

Griliches, Z. 1967. "Distributed lags: a survey." Econometrica 35:16–49.

Guerry, A. M. 1833. "Essai sur la statistique morale de la France." Westminister Review 18:357.

Hawley, Amos. 1950. Human Ecology: A Theory of Community Structure. New York: Ronald.

Henry, A. F., and J. F. Short. 1954. Suicide and Homicide. New York: Free Press.

Hindelang, Michael J. 1976. Criminal Victimization in Eight American Cities: A Descriptive Analysis of Common Theft and Assault. Cambridge: Ballinger.

Hindelang, Michael J., Christopher S. Dunn, Paul Sutton and Alison L. Aumick. 1976. Sourcebook of Criminal Justice Statistics—1975. U.S. Dept. of Justice, Law Enforcement Assistance Administration. Washington, D.C.: U.S. Government Printing Office.

_____. 1977. Sourcebook of Criminal Justice Statistics—1976. U.S. Dept. of Justice, Law Enforcement Assistance Administration. Washington, D.C.: U.S. Government Printing Office.

Interstate Commerce Commission (ICC). 1974. Annual Report: Freight Commodity Statistics of Class I Motor Carriers of Property Operative in Intercity Service. Washington, D.C.: U.S. Government Printing Office.

Jackson, Bruce. 1969. A Thief's Primer. New York: Macmillan.

Jeffery, C. R. 1971. Crime Prevention Through Environmental Design. Beverly Hills: Sage.

Klockars, Carl B. 1974. The Professional Fence. New York: Free Press.

Kobrin, Frances E. 1976. "The primary individual and the family: changes in living agreements in the U.S. since 1940." Journal of Marriage and the Family 38:233–9.

Land, Kenneth C. 1978. "Modelling macro social change." Paper presented at annual meeting of the American Sociological Association, San Francisco.

Land, Kenneth C. and Marcus Felson. 1976. "A general framework for building dynamic macro social indicator models: including an analysis of changes in crime rates and police expenditures." American Journal of Sociology 82:565–604.

Letkemann, Peter. 1973. Crime As Work. Englewood Cliffs: Prentice-Hall.

Lystad, Mary. 1974. An Annotated Bibliography: Violence at Home. DHEW Publication No. (ADM 75–136). Washington, D.C.: U.S. Government Printing Office.

Maddala, G. S., and A. S. Rao. 1973. "Tests for serial correlation in regression models with lagged dependent variables and serially correlated errors." Econometrica 41:761–74.

Mansfield, Roger, Leroy Gould, and J. Zvi Namenwirth. 1974. "A socioeconomic model for the prediction of societal rates of property theft." Social Forces 52:462–72.

Martin, John Bower. 1952. My Life in Crime. New York: Harper.

Maurer, David W. 1964. Whiz Mob. New Haven: College and University Press.

Merchandising Week. 1973. Statistical and Marketing Report (February). New York: Billboard Publications.

_____. 1976. Statistical and Marketing Report (March). New York: Billboard Publications.

National Commission on the Causes and Prevention of Violence. 1969. Crimes of Violence. Vol. 13. Washington, D.C.: U.S. Government Printing Office.

Nettler, Gwynn. 1974. Explaining Crime. New York: McGraw-Hill.

Newman, Oscar. 1973. Defensible Space: Crime Prevention Through Urban Design. New York: Macmillan.

Office of Management and the Budget (OMB). 1973. Social Indicators 1973. Washington, D.C: U.S. Government Printing Office.

Pope, Carl E. 1977a. Crime-Specific Analysis: The Characteristics of Burglary Incidents. U.S. Dept. of Justice, Law Enforcement Assistance Administration. Analytic Report 10. Washington, D.C.: U.S Government Printing Office.

_____. 1977b. Crime-Specific Analysis: An Empirical Examination of Burglary Offense and Offender Characteristics. U.S. Dept. of Justice, Law Enforcement Assistance Administration. Analytical Report 12. Washington, D.C.: U.S. Government Printing Office.

Quètelet, Adolphe. 1842. A Treatise on Man. Edinburgh: Chambers.

Reiss, Albert J. 1976. "Settling the frontiers of a pioneer in American criminology: Henry McKay." Pp. 64–88 in James F. Short, Jr. (ed.), Delinquency, Crime, and Society. Chicago: University of Chicago Press.

Reppetto, Thomas J. 1974. Residential Crime. Cambridge: Ballinger.

Roncek, Dennis. 1975. Crime Rates and Residential Densities in Two Large Cities. Ph.D. dissertation, Department of Sociology, University of Illinois, Urbana.

Sagi, Phillip C. and Charles E. Wellford. 1968. "Age composition and patterns of change in criminal statistics." Journal of Criminal Law, Criminology and Police Science 59:29–36.

Scarr, Harry A. 1972. Patterns of Burglary. U.S. Dept. of Justice, Law Enforcement Assistance Administration. Washington, D.C.: U.S. Government Printing Office.

Sears Catalogue. 1960. Chicago: Sears.

_____. 1970. Chicago: Sears.

Shaw, Clifford R., Henry D. McKay, Frederick Zorbaugh and Leonard S. Cottrell. 1929. Delinquency Areas. Chicago: University of Chicago Press.

Short, James F., and Fred Strodtbeck. 1965. Group Process and Gang Delinquency. Chicago: University of Chicago Press.

Skogan, Wesley G. 1976. "The victims of crime: some material findings." Pp. 131–48 in Anthony L. Guenther (ed.), Criminal Behavior in Social Systems. Chicago: Rand McNally.

Sutherland, Edwin H. 1937. The Professional Thief. Chicago: University of Chicago Press.

Szalai, Alexander (ed.). 1972. The Use of Time: Daily Activities of Urban and Suburban Populations in Twelve Countries. The Hague: Mouton.

Theil, Henri. 1971. Principles of Econometrics. New York: Wiley.

Tobias, J. J. 1967. Crime and Industrial Society in the Nineteenth Century. New York: Schocken Books.

U.S. Bureau of the Census (USBC). 1973a. Census of Transportation, 1972. U.S. Summary. Washington, D.C.: U.S. Government Printing Office.

_____. 1973b. Who's Home When. Working Paper 37. Washington, D.C.: U.S. Government Printing Office.

_____. 1975–1976. Statistical Abstract of the U.S. Washington, D.C.: U.S. Government Printing Office.

_____. 1947–1976. Current Population Studies. P-25 Ser. Washington, C.D.: U.S. Government Printing Office.

U.S. Department of Justice (USDJ). 1974a. Preliminary Report of the Impact Cities, Crime Survey Results. Washington, D.C.: Law Enforcement Assistance Administration (NCJISS).

_____. 1974b. Crime in the Nation's Five Largest Cities: Advance Report. Washington, D.C.: Law Enforcement Assistance Admnistration (NCJISS).

_____. 1974c. Crime and Victims: A Report on the Dayton-San Jose Pilot Survey of Victimization. Washington, D.C.: Law Enforcement Assistance Administration.

_____. 1976. Criminal Victimizations in the U.S., 1973. Washington, D.C.: Law Enforcement Assistance Administration (NCJISS).

_____. 1977. Criminal Victimizations in the U.S.: A Comparison of 1974 and 1975 Findings. Washington, D.C.: Law Enforcement Assistance Administration (NCJISS).

Washnis, George J. 1976. Citizen Involvement in Crime Prevention. Lexington: Heath.

Wellford, Charles F. 1973. "Age composition and the increase in recorded crime." Criminology 11:61–70.

Wilks, Judith A. 1976. "Ecological correlates of crime and delinquency." Pp. 138–56 in President's Commission on Law Enforcement and the Administrtion of Justice Task Force Report. Crime and Its Impace—An Assessment. Appendix A. Washington, D.C.: U.S. Government Printing Office.

Williamson, Henry. 1968. Hustler! New York: Doubleday.

Wolfgang, Marvin E. 1958. Patterns fo Criminal Homicide. Philadelphia: University of Pennsylvania Press.

❧ ❧ ❧

Questions

1. What are "routine activities"? How do they influence rates of crime?

2. According to Cohen and Felson, which societal changes brought about increased crime rates in the United States in the 1960s and 1970s?

3. How would the routine activities theory apply to crimes not involving direct social contact, such as public drunkenness?

4. Many areas of the United States witnessed sharp declines in predatory, direct-contact crime in the 1990s. How would you explain these declines using the routine activity approach?

Broken Windows

JAMES Q. WILSON AND GEORGE L. KELLING

In this groundbreaking article, James Q. Wilson and George L. Kelling advance their theory about the impact of a single broken window in a neighborhood. Just as a broken window invites further vandalism, they argue, so disorderly behavior in public creates an atmosphere in which crime flourishes. As such, the conditions of a neighborhood, and not just the people who inhabit it, influence its crime rate. Thus, police can help prevent or reduce crime by enforcing less-serious public-order laws.

*I*n the mid-1970s, the state of New Jersey announced a "Safe and Clean Neighborhoods Program," designed to improve the quality of community life in twenty-eight cities. As part of that program, the state provided money to help cities take police officers out of their patrol cars and assign them to walking beats. The governor and other state officials were enthusiastic about using foot patrol as a way of cutting crime, but many police chiefs were skeptical. Foot patrol, in their eyes, had been pretty much discredited. It reduced the mobility of the police, who thus had difficulty responding to citizen calls for service, and it weakened headquarters control over patrol officers.

Many police officers also disliked foot patrol, but for different reasons: it was hard work, it kept them outside on cold, rainy nights, and it reduced their chances for making a "good pinch." In some departments, assigning officers to foot patrol had been used as a form of punishment. And academic experts on policing doubted that foot patrol would have any impact on crime rates; it was, in the opinion of most, little more than a sop to public opinion. But since the state was paying for it, the local authorities were willing to go along.

Five years after the program started, the Police Foundation, in Washington, D.C., published an evaluation of the foot-patrol project. Based on its analysis of a carefully controlled experiment carried out chiefly in Newark, the foundation concluded, to the surprise of hardly anyone, that

"Broken Windows," by James Q. Wilson and George L. Kelling, reprinted from *The Atlantic Monthly*, March 1982, pp. 29–38.

foot patrol had not reduced crime rates. But residents of the foot-patrolled neighborhoods seemed to feel more secure than persons in other areas, tended to believe that crime had been reduced, and seemed to take fewer steps to protect themselves from crime (staying at home with the doors locked, for example). Moreover, citizens in the foot-patrol areas had a more favorable opinion of the police than did those living elsewhere. And officers walking beats had higher morale, greater job satisfaction, and a more favorable attitude toward citizens in their neighborhoods than did officers assigned to patrol cars.

These findings may be taken as evidence that the skeptics were right—foot patrol has no effect on crime; it merely fools the citizens into thinking that they are safer. But in our view, and in the view of the authors of the Police Foundation study (of whom Kelling was one), the citizens of Newark were not fooled at all. They knew what the foot-patrol officers were doing, they knew it was different from what motorized officers do, and they knew that having officers walk beats did in fact make their neighborhoods safer.

But how can a neighborhood be "safer" when the crime rate has not gone down—in fact, may have gone up? Finding the answer requires first that we understand what most often frightens people in public places. Many citizens, of course, are primarily frightened by crime, especially crime involving a sudden, violent attack by a stranger. This risk is very real, in Newark as in many large cities. But we tend to overlook or forget another source of fear—the fear of being bothered by disorderly people. Not violent people, nor, necessarily, criminals, but disreputable or obstreperous or unpredictable people: panhandlers, drunks, addicts, rowdy teenagers, prostitutes, loiterers, the mentally disturbed.

What foot-patrol officers did was to elevate, to the extent they could, the level of public order in these neighborhoods. Though the neighborhoods were predominantly black and the foot patrolmen were mostly white, this "order-maintenance" function of the police was performed to the general satisfaction of both parties.

One of us (Kelling) spent many hours walking with Newark foot-patrol officers to see how they defined "order" and what they did to maintain it. One beat was typical: a busy but dilapidated area in the heart of Newark, with many abandoned buildings, marginal shops (several of which prominently displayed knives and straight-edged razors in their windows), one large department store, and, most important, a train station and several major bus stops. Though the area was run-down, its streets were filled with people, because it was a major transportation center. The good order of this area was important not only to those who lived and worked there but also to many others, who had to move through it on their way home, to supermarkets, or to factories.

The people on the street were primarily black; the officer who walked the street was white. The people were made up of "regulars" and "strangers." Regulars included both "decent folk" and some drunks and derelicts who were always there but who "knew their place." Strangers were, well, strangers, and viewed suspiciously, sometimes apprehensively. The officer—call him Kelly—knew who the regulars were, and they knew him. As he saw his job, he was to keep an eye on strangers, and make certain that the disreputable regulars observed some informal but widely understood rules. Drunks and addicts could sit on the stoops, but could not lie down. People could drink on side streets, but not at the main intersection. Bottles had to be in paper bags. Talking to, bothering, or begging from people waiting at the bus stop was strictly forbidden. If a dispute erupted between a businessman and a customer, the businessman was assumed to be right, especially if the customer was a stranger. If a stranger loitered, Kelly would ask him if he had any means of support and what his business was; if he gave unsatisfactory answers, he was sent on his way. Persons who broke the informal rules, especially those who bothered people waiting at bus stops, were arrested for vagrancy. Noisy teenagers were told to keep quiet.

These rules were defined and enforced in collaboration with the "regulars" on the street. Another neighborhood might have different rules, but these, everybody understood, were the rules for *this* neighborhood. If someone violated them, the regulars not only turned to Kelly for help but also ridiculed the violator. Sometimes what Kelly did could be described as "enforcing the law," but just as often it involved taking informal or extralegal steps to help protect what the neighborhood had decided was the appropriate level of public order. Some of the things he did probably would not withstand a legal challenge.

A determined skeptic might acknowledge that a skilled foot-patrol officer can maintain order but still insist that this sort of "order" has little to do with the real sources of community fear—that is, with violent crime. To a degree, that is true. But two things must be borne in mind. First, outside observers should not assume that they know how much of the anxiety now endemic in many big-city neighborhoods stems from a fear of "real" crime and how much from a sense that the street is disorderly, a source of distasteful, worrisome encounters. The people of Newark, to judge from their behavior and their remarks to interviewers, apparently assign a high value to public older, and feel relieved and reassured when the police help them maintain that order.

Second, at the community level, disorder and crime are usually inextricably linked, in a kind of developmental sequence. Social psychologists and police officers tend to agree that if a window in a building is broken *and is left unrepaired,* all the rest of the windows will soon be broken. This is as true in nice neighborhoods as in run-down ones. Window-breaking does not necessarily occur on a large scale because some areas are inhabited by determined window-breakers whereas others are populated by window-lovers; rather, one unrepaired broken window is a signal that no one cares, and so breaking more windows costs nothing. (It has always been fun.)

Philip Zimbardo, a Stanford psychologist, reported in 1969 on some experiments testing the broken-window theory. He arranged to have an automobile without license plates parked with its hood up on a street in the Bronx and a comparable automobile on a street in Palo Alto, California. The car in the Bronx was attacked by "vandals" within ten minutes of its "abandonment." The first to arrive were a family—father, mother, and young son—who removed the radiator and battery. Within twenty-four hours, virtually everything of value had been removed. Then random destruction began—windows were smashed, parts torn off, upholstery ripped. Children began to use the car as a playground. Most of the adult "vandals" were well-dressed, apparently clean-cut whites. The car in Palo Alto sat untouched for more than a week. Then Zimbardo smashed part of it with a sledgehammer. Soon, passersby were joining in. Within a few hours, the car had been turned upside down and utterly destroyed. Again, the "vandals" appeared to be primarily respectable whites.

Untended property becomes fair game for people out for fun or plunder, and even for people who ordinarily would not dream of doing such things and who probably consider themselves law-abiding. Because of the nature of community life in the Bronx—its anonymity, the frequency with which cars are abandoned and things are stolen or broken, the past experience of "no one caring"—vandalism begins much more quickly than it does in staid Palo Alto, where people have come to believe that private possessions are cared for, and that mischievous behavior is costly. But vandalism can occur anywhere once communal barriers—the sense of mutual regard and the obligations of civility—are lowered by actions that seem to signal that "no one cares."

We suggest that "untended" behavior also leads to the breakdown of community controls. A stable neighborhood of families who care for their homes, mind each other's children, and confidently frown on unwanted intruders can change, in a few years or even a few months, to an inhospitable and frightening jungle. A piece of property is abandoned, weeds grow up, a window is smashed. Adults stop scolding rowdy children; the children, emboldened, become more rowdy. Families move out, unattached adults move in. Teenagers gather in front of the corner store. The merchant asks them to move; they refuse. Fights occur. Litter accumulates. People start drinking in front of the grocery; in time, an inebriate slumps to the sidewalk and is allowed to sleep it off. Pedestrians are approached by panhandlers.

At this point it is not inevitable that serious crime will flourish or violent attacks on strangers will occur. But many residents will think that crime, especially violent crime, is on the rise, and they will modify their behavior accordingly. They will use the streets less often, and when on the streets will stay apart from their fellows, moving with averted eyes, silent lips, and hurried steps. "Don't get involved." For some residents, this growing atomization will matter little, because the neighborhood is not their "home" but "the place where they live." Their interests are elsewhere; they are cosmopolitans. But it will matter greatly to other people, whose lives derive meaning and satisfaction from local attachments rather than worldly involvement; for them, the neighborhood will cease to exist except for a few reliable friends whom they arrange to meet.

Such an area is vulnerable to criminal invasion. Though it is not inevitable, it is more likely that here, rather than in places where people are confident they can regulate public behavior by informal controls, drugs will change hands, prostitutes will solicit, and cars will be stripped. That the drunks will be robbed by boys who do it as a lark, and the prostitutes' customers will be robbed by men who do it purposefully and perhaps violently. That muggings will occur.

Among those who often find it difficult to move away from this are the elderly. Surveys of citizens suggest that the elderly are much less likely to be the victims of crime than younger persons, and some have inferred from this that the well-known fear of crime voiced by the elderly is an exaggeration: perhaps we ought not to design special programs to protect older persons; perhaps we should even try to talk them out of their mistaken fears. This argument misses the point. The prospect of a confrontation with an obstreperous teenager or a drunken panhandler can be as fear-inducing for defenseless persons as the prospect of meeting an actual robber; indeed, to a defenseless person, the two kinds of confrontation are often indistinguishable. Moreover, the lower rate at which the elderly are victimized is a measure of the steps they have already taken—chiefly, staying behind locked doors—to minimize the risks they face. Young men are more frequently attacked than older women, not because they are easier or more lucrative targets but because they are on the street more.

Nor is the connection between disorderliness and fear made only by the elderly. Susan Estrich, of the Harvard Law School, has recently gathered together a number of surveys on the sources of public fear. One, done in Portland, Oregon, indicated that three fourths of the adults interviewed cross to the other side of a street when they see a gang of teenagers; another survey, in Baltimore, discovered that nearly half would cross the street to avoid even a single strange youth. When an interviewer asked people in a housing project where the most dangerous spot was, they mentioned a place where young persons gathered to drink and play music, despite the fact that not a single crime had occurred there. In Boston public housing projects, the greatest fear was expressed by persons living in the buildings where disorderliness and incivility, not crime, were the greatest. Knowing this helps one understand the significance of such otherwise harmless displays as subway graffiti. As Nathan Glazer has written, the proliferation of graffiti, even when not obscene, confronts the subway rider with the "inescapable knowledge that the environment he must endure for an hour or more a day is uncontrolled and uncontrollable, and that anyone can invade it to do whatever damage and mischief the mind suggests."

In response to fear, people avoid one another, weakening controls. Sometimes they call the police. Patrol cars arrive, an occasional arrest occurs, but crime continues and disorder is not abated. Citizens complain to the police chief, but he explains that his department is low on personnel and that the courts do not punish petty or first-time offenders. To the residents, the police who arrive in squad cars are either ineffective or uncaring; to the police, the residents are animals who deserve each other. The citizens may soon stop calling the police, because "they can't do anything."

The process we call urban decay has occurred for centuries in every city. But what is happening today is different in at least two important respects. First, in the period before, say, World War II, city dwellers—because of

195

money costs, transportation difficulties, familial and church connections—could rarely move away from neighborhood problems. When movement did occur, it tended to be along public-transit routes. Now mobility has become exceptionally easy for all but the poorest or those who are blocked by racial prejudice. Earlier crime waves had a kind of built-in self-correcting mechanism: the determination of a neighborhood or community to reassert control over its turf. Areas in Chicago, New York, and Boston would experience crime and gang wars, and then normalcy would return, as the families for whom no alternative residences were possible reclaimed their authority over the streets.

Second, the police in this earlier period assisted in that reassertion of authority by acting, sometimes violently, on behalf of the community. Young toughs were roughed up, people were arrested "on suspicion" or for vagrancy, and prostitutes and petty thieves were routed. "Rights" were something enjoyed by decent folk, and perhaps also by the serious professional criminal, who avoided violence and could afford a lawyer.

This pattern of policing was not an aberration or the result of occasional excess. From the earliest days of the nation, the police function was seen primarily as that of a night watchman: to maintain order against the chief threats to order—fire, wild animals, and disreputable behavior. Solving crimes was viewed not as a police responsibility but as a private one. In the March, 1969, *Atlantic,* one of us (Wilson) wrote a brief account of how the police role had slowly changed from maintaining order to fighting crimes. The change began with the creation of private detectives (often ex-criminals), who worked on a contingency-fee basis for individuals who had suffered losses. In time, the detectives were absorbed into municipal police agencies and paid a regular salary; simultaneously, the responsibility for prosecuting thieves was shifted from the aggrieved private citizen to the professional prosecutor. This process was not complete in most places until the twentieth century.

In the 1960s, when urban riots were a major problem, social scientists began to explore carefully the order-maintenance function of the police, and to suggest ways of improving it—not to make streets safer (its original function) but to reduce the incidence of mass violence. Order-maintenance became, to a degree, coterminous with "community relations." But, as the crime wave that began in the early 1960s continued without abatement throughout the decade and into the 1970s, attention shifted to the role of the police as crime-fighters. Studies of police behavior ceased, by and large, to be accounts of the order-maintenance function and became, instead, efforts to propose and test ways whereby the police could solve more crimes, make more arrests, and gather better evidence. If these things could be done, social scientists assumed, citizens would be less fearful.

A great deal was accomplished during this transition, as both police chiefs and outside experts emphasized the crime-fighting function in their plans, in the allocation of resources, and in deployment of personnel. The police may well have become better crime-fighters as a result. And doubtless they remained aware of their responsibility for order. But the link between order-maintenance and crime-prevention, so obvious to earlier generations, was forgotten.

That link is similar to the process whereby one broken window becomes many. The citizen who fears the ill-smelling drunk, the rowdy teenager, or the importuning beggar is not merely expressing his distaste for unseemly behavior; he is also giving voice to a bit of folk wisdom that happens to be a correct generalization—namely, that serious street crime flourishes in areas in which disorderly behavior goes unchecked. The unchecked panhandler is, in effect, the first broken window. Muggers and robbers, whether opportunistic or professional, believe they reduce their chances of being caught or even identified if they operate on streets where potential victims are already intimidated by prevailing conditions. If the neighborhood cannot keep a bothersome panhandler from annoying passersby, the thief may reason, it is even less likely to call the police to identify a potential mugger or to interfere if the mugging actually takes place.

Some police administrators concede that this process occurs, but argue that motorized-patrol officers can deal with it as effectively as foot-patrol officers. We are not so sure. In theory, an officer in a squad car can observe as much as an officer on foot; in theory, the former can talk to as many people as the latter. But the reality of police-citizen encounters is powerfully altered by the automobile. An officer on foot cannot separate himself from the street people; if he is approached, only his uniform and his personality can help him manage whatever is about to happen. And he can never be certain what that will be—a request for directions, a plea for help, an angry denunciation, a teasing remark, a confused babble, a threatening gesture.

In a car, an officer is more likely to deal with street people by rolling down the window and looking at them. The door and the window exclude the approaching citizen; they are a barrier. Some officers take advantage of this barrier, perhaps unconsciously, by acting differently if in the car than they would on foot. We have seen this countless times. The police car pulls up to a corner where teenagers are gathered. The window is rolled down. The officer stares at the youths. They stare back. The officer says to one, "C'mere." He saunters over, conveying to his friends by his elaborately casual style the idea that he is not intimidated by authority. "What's your name?" "Chuck." "Chuck who?" "Chuck Jones." "What'ya doing, Chuck?" "Nothin'." "Got a P.O. [parole officer]?" "Nah." "Sure?" "Yeah." "Stay out of trouble, Chuckie." Meanwhile, the other boys laugh and exchange comments among themselves, probably at the officer's expense. The officer stares harder. He cannot be certain what is being said, nor can he join in and, by displaying his own skill at street banter, prove that he cannot be "put down." In the process, the officer has learned almost nothing, and the boys have decided the officer is an alien force who can safely be disregarded, even mocked.

Our experience is that most citizens like to talk to a police officer. Such exchanges give them a sense of importance, provide them with the basis for gossip, and allow them to explain to the authorities what is worrying them (whereby they gain a modest but significant sense of having "done something" about the problem). You approach a person on foot more easily, and talk to him more readily, than you do a person in a car. Moreover, you can more easily retain some anonymity if you draw an officer aside for a private chat. Suppose you want to pass on a tip about who is stealing handbags, or who offered to sell you a stolen TV. In the inner city, the culprit, in all likelihood, lives nearby. To walk up to a marked patrol car and lean in the window is to convey a visible signal that you are a "fink."

The essence of the police role in maintaining order is to reinforce the informal control mechanisms of the community itself. The police cannot, without committing extraordinary resources, provide a substitute for that informal control. On the other hand, to reinforce those natural forces the police must accommodate them. And therein lies the problem.

Should police activity on the street be shaped, in important ways, by the standards of the neighborhood rather than by the rules of the state? Over the past two decades, the shift of police from order-maintenance to law-enforcement has brought them increasingly under the influence of legal restrictions, provoked by media complaints and enforced by court decisions and departmental orders. As a consequence, the order-maintenance functions of the police are now governed by rules developed to control police relations with suspected criminals. This is, we think, an entirely new development. For centuries, the role of the police as watchmen was judged primarily not in terms of its compliance with appropriate procedures but rather in terms of its attaining a desired objective. The objective was order, an inherently ambiguous term but a condition that people in a given community recognized when they saw it. The means were the same as those the community itself would employ, if its members were sufficiently determined, courageous, and authoritative. Detecting and apprehending criminals, by contrast, was a means to an end, not an end in itself; a judicial determination of guilt or innocence was the hoped-for result of the law-enforcement mode. From the first, the police were expected to follow rules defining that process, though states differed in how stringent the rules should be. The criminal-apprehension process was always understood to involve individual rights, the violation of which was unacceptable because it meant that the violating officer would be acting as a judge and jury—and that was not his job. Guilt or innocence was to be determined by universal standards under special procedures.

Ordinarily, no judge or jury ever sees the persons caught up in a dispute over the appropriate level of neighborhood order. That is true not only because most cases are handled informally on the street but also because no universal standards are available to settle arguments over disorder, and thus a judge may not be any wiser or more effective than a police officer. Until quite recently in many states, and even today in some places, the police make arrests on such charges as "suspicious person" or "vagrancy" or "public drunkenness"—charges with scarcely any legal meaning. These charges exist not because society wants judges to punish vagrants or drunks but because it wants an officer to have the legal tools to remove undesirable persons from a neighborhood when informal efforts to preserve order in the streets have failed.

Once we begin to think of all aspects of police work as involving the application of universal rules under special procedures, we inevitably ask what constitutes an "undesirable person" and why we should "criminalize" vagrancy or drunkenness. A strong and commendable desire to see that people are treated fairly makes us worry about allowing the police to rout persons who are undesirable by some vague or parochial standard. A growing and not-so-commendable utilitarianism leads us to doubt that any behavior that does not "hurt" another person should be made illegal. And thus many of us who watch over the police are reluctant to allow them to perform, in the only way they can, a function that every neighborhood desperately wants them to perform.

This wish to "decriminalize" disreputable behavior that "harms no one"—and thus remove the ultimate sanction the police can employ to maintain neighborhood older—is, we think, a mistake. Arresting a single drunk or a single vagrant who has harmed no identifiable person seems unjust, and in a sense it is. But failing to do anything about a score of drunks or a hundred vagrants may destroy an entire community. A particular rule that seems to make sense in the individual case makes no sense when it is made a universal rule and applied to all cases. It makes no sense because it fails to take into account the connection between one broken window left untended and a thousand broken windows. Of course, agencies other than the police could attend to the problems posed by drunks or the mentally ill, but in most communities—especially where the "deinstitutionalization" movement has been strong—they do not.

The concern about equity is more serious. We might agree that certain behavior makes one person more undesirable than another, but how do we ensure that age or skin color or national origin or harmless mannerisms will not also become the basis for distinguishing the undesirable from the desirable? How do we ensure, in short, that the police do not become the agents of neighborhood bigotry?

We can offer no wholly satisfactory answer to this important question. We are not confident that there is a satisfactory answer, except to hope that by their selection, training, and supervision, the police will be inculcated with a clear sense of the outer limit of their discretionary authority. That limit, roughly, is this—the police exist to help regulate behavior, not to maintain the racial or ethnic purity of a neighborhood.

Consider the case of the Robert Taylor Homes in Chicago, one of the largest public-housing projects in the country. It is home for nearly 20,000 people, all black, and extends over ninety-two acres along South State Street. It was named after a distinguished black who had been, during the 1940s, chairman of the Chicago Housing Authority. Not long after it opened, in 1962, relations between project residents and the police deteriorated badly. The citizens felt that the police were insensitive or brutal; the police, in turn, complained of unprovoked attacks on them. Some Chicago officers tell of times when they were afraid to enter the Homes. Crime rates soared.

Today, the atmosphere has changed. Police-citizen relations have improved—apparently both sides learned something from the earlier experience. Recently, a boy stole a purse and ran off. Several young persons who saw the theft voluntarily passed along to the police information on the identity and residence of the thief, and they did this publicly, with friends and neighbors looking on. But problems persist, chief among them the presence of youth gangs that terrorize residents and recruit members in the project. The people expect the police to "do something" about this, and the police are determined to do just that.

But do what? Though the police can obviously make arrests whenever a gang member breaks the law, a gang can form, recruit, and congregate without breaking the law. And only a tiny fraction of gang-related crimes can be solved by an arrest; thus, if an arrest is the only recourse for the police, the residents' fears will go unassuaged. The police will soon feel helpless, and the residents will again believe that the police "do nothing." What the police in fact do is to chase known gang members out of the project. In the words of one officer, "We kick ass." Project residents both know and approve of this. The tacit police-citizen alliance in the project is reinforced by the police view that the cops and the gangs are the two rival sources of power in the area, and that the gangs are not going to win.

None of this is easily reconciled with any conception of due process or fair treatment. Since both residents and gang members are black, race is not a factor. But it could be. Suppose a white project confronted a black gang, or vice versa. We would be apprehensive about the police taking sides. But the substantive problem remains the same: how can the police strengthen the informal social-control mechanisms of natural communities in order to minimize fear in public places? Law enforcement, per se, is no answer. A gang can weaken or destroy a community by standing about in a menacing fashion and speaking rudely to passersby without breaking the law.

We have difficulty thinking about such matters, not simply because the ethical and legal issues are so complex but because we have become accustomed to thinking of the law in essentially individualistic terms. The law defines *my* rights, punishes *his* behavior, and is applied by *that* officer because of *this* harm. We assume, in thinking this way, that what is good for the individual will be good for the community, and what doesn't matter when it happens to one person won't matter if it happens to many. Ordinarily, those are plausible assumptions. But in cases where behavior that is tolerable to one person is intolerable to many others, the reactions of the others—fear, withdrawal, flight—may ultimately make matters worse for everyone, including the individual who first professed his indifference.

It may be their greater sensitivity to communal as opposed to individual needs that helps explain why the residents of small communities are more satisfied with their police than are the residents of similar neighborhoods in big cities. Elinor Ostrom and her co-workers at Indiana University compared the perception of police services in two poor, all-black Illinois towns—Phoenix and East Chicago Heights—with those of three comparable all-black neighborhoods in Chicago. The level of criminal victimization and the quality of police-community relations appeared to be about the same in the towns and the Chicago neighborhoods. But the citizens living in their own villages were much more likely than those living in the Chicago neighborhoods to say that they do not stay at home for fear of crime, to agree that the local police have "the right to take any action necessary" to deal with problems, and to agree that the police "look out for the needs of the average citizen." It is possible that the residents and the police of the small towns saw themselves as engaged in a collaborative effort to maintain a certain standard of communal life, whereas those of the big city felt themselves to be simply requesting and supplying particular services on an individual basis.

If this is true, how should a wise police chief deploy his meager forces? The first answer is that nobody knows for certain, and the most prudent course of action would be to try further variations on the Newark experiment, to see more precisely what works in what kinds of neighborhood. The second answer is also a hedge—many aspects of order-maintenance in neighborhoods can probably best be handled in ways that involve the police minimally, if at all. A busy, bustling shopping center and a quiet, well-tended suburb may need almost no visible police presence. In both cases, the ratio of respectable to disreputable people is ordinarily so high as to make informal social control effective.

Even in areas that are in jeopardy from disorderly elements, citizen action without substantial police involvement may be sufficient. Meetings between teenagers who like to hang out on a particular corner and adults who want to use that corner might well lead to an amicable agreement on a set of rules about how many people can be allowed to congregate, where, and when.

Where no understanding is possible—or if possible, not observed—citizen patrols may be a sufficient response. There are two traditions of communal involvement in maintaining order. One, that of the "community watchmen," is as old as the first settlement of the New World. Until well into the nineteenth century, volunteer watchmen, not policemen, patrolled their communities to keep order. They did so, by and large, without taking the law into their own hands—without, that is, punishing persons or using force. Their presence deterred disorder or alerted the community to disorder that could not be deterred. There are hundreds of such efforts today in communities all across the nation. Perhaps the best known is that of the Guardian Angels, a group of unarmed young persons in distinctive berets and T-shirts, who first came to public attention when they began patrolling the New York City subways but who claim now to have chapters in more than thirty American cities. Unfortunately, we have little information about the effect of these groups on crime. It is possible, however, that whatever their effect on crime, citizens find their presence reassuring, and that they thus contribute to maintaining a sense of order and civility.

The second tradition is that of the "vigilante." Rarely a feature of the settled communities of the East, it was primarily to be found in those frontier towns that grew up in advance of the reach of government. More than 350 vigilante groups are known to have existed; their distinctive feature was that their members did take the law into their own hands, by acting as judge, jury, and often executioner as well as policeman. Today, the vigilante movement is conspicuous by its rarity, despite the great fear expressed by citizens that the older cities are becoming "urban frontiers." But some community-watchmen groups have skirted the line, and others may cross it in the future. An ambiguous case, reported in *The Wall Street Journal,* involved a citizens' patrol in the Silver Lake area of Belleville, New Jersey A leader told the reporter, "We look for outsiders." If a few teenagers from outside the neighborhood enter it, "we ask them their business," he said. "If they say they're going down the street to see Mrs. Jones, fine, we let them pass. But then we follow them down the block to make sure they're really going to see Mrs. Jones."

Though citizens can do a great deal, the police are plainly the key to order-maintenance. For one thing, many communities, such as the Robert Taylor Homes, cannot do the job by themselves. For another, no citizen in a neighborhood, even an organized one, is likely to feel the sense of responsibility that wearing a badge confers. Psychologists have done many studies on why people fail to go to the aid of persons being attacked or seeking help, and they have learned that the cause is not "apathy" or "selfishness" but the absence of some plausible grounds for feeling that one must personally accept responsibility. Ironically, avoiding responsibility is easier when a lot of people are standing about. On streets and in public places, where order is so important, many people are likely to be "around," a fact that reduces the chance of any one person acting as the agent of the community. The police officer's uniform singles him out as a person who must accept responsibility if asked. In addition, officers, more easily than their fellow citizens, can be expected to distinguish between what is necessary to protect the safety of the street and what merely protects its ethnic purity.

But the police forces of America are losing, not gaining, members. Some cities have suffered substantial cuts in the number of officers available for duty. These cuts are not likely to be reversed in the near future. Therefore, each department must assign its existing officers with great care. Some neighborhoods are so demoralized and crime-ridden as to make foot patrol useless; the best the police can do with limited resources is respond to the enormous number of calls for service. Other neighborhoods are so stable and serene as to make foot patrol unnecessary. The key is to identify neighborhoods at the tipping point—where the public order is deteriorating but not unreclaimable, where the streets are used frequently but by apprehensive people, where a window is likely to be broken at any time, and must quickly be fixed if all are not to be shattered.

Most police departments do not have ways of systematically identifying such areas and assigning officers to them. Officers are assigned on the basis of crime rates (meaning that marginally threatened areas are often stripped so that police can investigate crimes in areas where the situation is hopeless) or on the basis of calls for service (despite the fact that most citizens do not call the police when they are merely frightened or annoyed). To allocate patrol wisely, the department must look at the neighborhoods and decide, from first-hand evidence, where an additional officer will make the greatest difference in promoting a sense of safety.

One way to stretch limited police resources is being tried in some public-housing projects. Tenant organizations hire off-duty police officers for patrol work in their buildings. The costs are not high (at least not per resident), the officer likes the additional income, and the residents feel safer. Such arrangements are probably more successful than hiring private watchmen, and the Newark experiment helps us understand why. A private security guard may deter crime or misconduct by his presence, and he may go to the aid of persons needing help, but he may well not intervene—that is, control or drive away—someone challenging community standards. Being a sworn officer—a "real cop"—seems to give one the confidence, the sense of duty and the aura of authority necessary to perform this difficult task.

Patrol officers might be encouraged to go to and from duty stations on public transportation and, while on the bus or subway car, enforce rules about smoking, drinking, disorderly conduct, and the like. The enforcement need involve nothing more than ejecting the offender (the offense, after all, is not one with which a booking officer or a judge wishes to be bothered). Perhaps the random but relentless maintenance of standards on buses would lead to conditions on buses that approximate the level of civility we now take for granted on airplanes.

But the most important requirement is to think that to maintain order in precarious situations is a vital job. The police know this is one of their functions, and they also believe, correctly, that it cannot be done to the exclusion of criminal investigation and responding to calls. We may have encouraged them to suppose, however, on the basis of our oft-repeated concerns about serious, violent crime, that they will be judged exclusively on their capacity as crime-fighters. To the extent that this is the case, police administrators will continue to concentrate police personnel in the highest-crime areas (though not necessarily in the areas most vulnerable to criminal invasion), emphasize their training in the law and criminal apprehension (and not their training in managing street life), and join too quickly in campaigns to decriminalize "harmless" behavior (though public drunkenness, street prostitution, and pornographic displays can destroy a community more quickly than any team of professional burglars).

Above all, we must return to our long-abandoned view that the police ought to protect communities as well as individuals. Our crime statistics and victimization surveys measure individual losses, but they do not measure communal losses. Just as physicians now recognize the importance of fostering health rather than simply treating illness, so the police—and the rest of us—ought to recognize the importance of maintaining, intact, communities without broken windows.

● ● ●

Questions

1. How exactly does public disorder encourage criminal activity?

2. Does public disorder increase the crimes committed by neighborhood residents, outsiders—or both?

3. According to Wilson and Kelling, which kind of police patrols prevent crime more effectively: car patrols or foot patrols? Why?

4. What do the authors recommend for reducing crime rates?

5. How might the policy recommendations advanced here violate individuals' rights?

Racial Politics, Racial Disparities, and the War on Crime

Michael Tonry

Why are so many more African-Americans in prison than are whites? In this article, Tonry reviews data on racial trends in arrests, jailing, and imprisonment. He then argues that racial disparities in the justice system have worsened since 1980 because of the "war on drugs." This war, launched during the Reagan and Bush presidential administrations, is conducted from a foundation of racially motivated political decisions, Tonry maintains. These decisions in turn have spurred the imprisonment of African-Americans in the last two decades.

Racial disparities in arrests, jailing, and imprisonment steadily worsened after 1980 for reasons that have little to do with changes in crime patterns and almost everything to do with two political developments. First, conservative Republicans in national elections "played the race card" by using anticrime slogans (remember Willie Horton?) as a way to appeal to anti-Black sentiments of White voters. Second, conservative politicians of both parties promoted and voted for harsh crime control and drug policies that exacerbated existing racial disparities.

The worsened disparities might have been ethically defensible if they had been based on good faith beliefs that some greater policy good would thereby have been achieved. Sometimes unwanted side effects of social policy are inevitable. Traffic accidents and fatalities are a price we pay for the convenience of automobiles. Occupational injuries are a price we pay for engaging in the industries in which they occur.

The principal causes of worse racial disparities have been the War on Drugs launched by the Bush and Reagan administrations, characterized by

"Racial Politics, Racial Disparities, and the War on Crime," by Michael Tonry, reprinted from *Crime & Delinquency*, vol. 40, no. 4, 1994, pp. 475–494.

vast increases in arrests and imprisonment of street-level drug dealers, and the continuing movement toward harsher penalties. Policies toward drug offenders are a primary cause of recent increases in jail and prison admissions and populations. Racial disparities among drug offenders are worse than among other offenders.

It should go without saying in the late 20th century that governments detest racial injustice and desire racial justice, and that racial disparities are tolerable only if they are unavoidable or are outweighed by even more important social gains. There are no offsetting gains that can justify the harms done to Black Americans by recent drug and crime control policies.

This article presents data on racial trends in arrests, jailing, and imprisonment; examines the rationales for the policies that have produced those trends; and considers whether the adoption of policies known to have disparate adverse effects on Blacks can be ethically justified. First, the evidence concerning the effectiveness of recent drug and crime control policies that have exacerbated racial disparities is examined. Next, data on arrests, jail, and imprisonment trends are presented and demonstrate that racial disparities have worsened, but not because Blacks are committing larger proportions of the serious offenses (homicide, rape, robbery, aggravated assault) for which offenders were traditionally sent to prison. Finally, the reasons why recent policies were adopted and whether they can be ethically justified are considered.

● Crime Reduction Effects of Crime Control Policy

There is no basis for a claim that recent harsh crime control policies or the enforcement strategies of the War on Drugs were based on good faith beliefs that they would achieve their ostensible purposes. In this and other countries, practitioners and scholars have long known that manipulation of penalties has few, if any, effects on crime rates.

Commissions and expert advisory bodies have been commissioned by the federal government repeatedly over the last 30 years to survey knowledge of the effects of crime control policies, and consistently they have concluded that there is little reason to believe that harsher penalties significantly enhance public safety. In 1967, the President's Commission on Law Enforcement and Administration of Justice observed that crime control efforts can have little effect on crime rates without much larger efforts being directed at crime's underlying social and economic causes. "The Commission . . . has no doubt whatever that the most significant action that can be taken against crime is action designed to eliminate slums and ghettos, to improve education, to provide jobs . . . . We shall not have dealt effectively with crime until we have alleviated the conditions that stimulate it."

In 1978, the National Academy of Sciences Panel on Research on Deterrent and Incapacitative Effects, funded by President Ford's department of justice and asked to examine the available evidence on the crime-reductive effects of sanctions, concluded: "In summary, we cannot assert that the evidence warrants an affirmative conclusion regarding deterrence" (Blumstein, Cohen, and Nagin 1978). Fifteen years later, the National Academy of Sciences Panel on the Understanding and Control of Violent Behavior, created and paid for with funds from the Reagan and Bush administration departments of justice, surveyed knowledge of the effects of harsher penalties on violent crime (Reiss and Roth 1993). A rhetorical question and answer in the panel's final report says it all: "What effect has increasing the prison population had on violent crime? Apparently very little. . . . If tripling the average length of sentence of incarceration per crime [between 1976 and 1989] had a strong preventive effect," reasoned the panel, "then violent crime rates should have declined" (p. 7). They had not.

I mention that the two National Academy of Sciences panels were created and supported by national Republican administrations to demonstrate that skepticism about the crime-preventive effects of harsher punishments is not a fantasy of liberal Democrats. Anyone who has spent much time talking with judges or corrections officials knows that most, whatever their political affiliations, do not believe that harsher penalties significantly enhance public safety. Likewise, outside the United States, conservative governments in other English-speaking countries have repudiated claims that harsher penalties significantly improve public safety. In Margaret Thatcher's England, for example, a 1990 White Paper (an official policy statement of the government), based on a 3-year study, expressed its skepticism about the preventive effects of sanctions:

> Deterrence is a principle with much immediate appeal. . . . But much crime is committed on impulse, given the opportunity presented by an open window or an unlocked door, and it is committed by offenders who live from moment to moment; their crimes are as impulsive as the rest of their

feckless, sad, or pathetic lives. It is unrealistic to construct sentencing arrangements on the assumption that most offenders will weigh up the possibilities in advance and base their conduct on rational calculation. (Home Office 1990)

Canada is the other English-speaking country that has recently had a conservative government. In Brian Mulroney's Canada, the Committee on Justice and the Solicitor General (in American terms, the judiciary committee) proposed in 1993 that Canada shift from an American-style crime control system to a European-style preventive approach. In arguing for the shift in emphasis, the committee observed that "the United States affords a glaring example of the limited effect that criminal justice responses may have on crime. . . . If locking up those who violate the law contributed to safer societies then the United States should be the safest country in the world" (Standing Committee on Justice and the Solicitor General 1993). Six years earlier, the Canadian Sentencing Commission (1987) had reached similar conclusions: "Deterrence cannot be used, with empirical justification, to guide the imposition of sanctions."

There is no better evidentiary base to justify recent drug control policies. Because no other western country has adopted drug policies as harsh as those of the United States, a bit of background may be useful before I show why there was no reasonable basis for believing recent policies would achieve their ostensible goals. In drug policy jargon, the United States has adopted a prohibitionistic rather than a harm-reduction strategy and has emphasized supply-side over demand-side tactics (Wilson 1990). This strategic choice implies a preference for legal threats and moral denunciation of drug use and users instead of a preference for minimizing net costs and social harms to the general public, the law enforcement system, and drug users. The tactical choice is between a law enforcement emphasis on arrest and punishment of dealers, distributors, and importers, interdiction, and source-country programs or a prevention emphasis on drug treatment, drug-abuse education in schools, and mass media programs aimed at public education. The supply-side bias in recent American policies was exemplified throughout the Bush administration by its insistence that 70% of federal antidrug funds be devoted to law enforcement and only 30% to treatment and education (Office of National Drug Control Policy 1990).

It has been a long time since most researchers and practitioners believed that current knowledge justifies recent American drug control policies. Because the potential income from drug dealing means that willing aspirants are nearly always available to replace arrested street-level dealers, large-scale arrests have repeatedly been shown to have little or no effect on the volume of drug trafficking or on the retail prices of drugs (e.g., Chaiken 1988; Sviridoff, Sadd, Curtis, and Grinc 1992). Because the United States has long and porous borders, and because an unachievably large proportion of attempted smuggling would have to be stopped to affect drug prices significantly, interdiction has repeatedly been shown to have little or no effect on volume or prices (Reuter 1988). Because cocaine, heroin, and marijuana can be grown in many parts of the world in which government controls are weak and peasant farmers' incentives are strong, source-country programs have seldom been shown to have significant influence on drug availability or price in the United States (Moore 1990).

The evidence in support of demand-side strategies is far stronger. In December 1993, the President's Commission on Model State Drug Laws, appointed by President Bush, categorically concluded, "Treatment works." That conclusion is echoed by more authoritative surveys of drug treatment evaluations by the U.S. General Accounting Office (1990), the National Institute of Medicine (Gerstein and Jarwood 1990), and in *Crime and Justice* by Anglin and Hser (1990). Because drug use and offending tend to coincide in the lives of drug-using offenders, the most effective and cost-effective way to deal with such offenders is to get and keep them in well-run treatment programs.

A sizable literature now also documents the effectiveness of school-based drug education in reducing drug experimentation and use among young people (e.g., Botvih 1990; Ellickson and Bell 1990). Although there is no credible literature that documents the effects of mass media campaigns on drug use, a judge could take judicial notice of their ubiquity. It is not unreasonable to believe that such campaigns have influenced across-the-board declines in drug use in the United States since 1980 (a date, incidentally, that precedes the launch of the War on Drugs by nearly 8 years).

That the preceding summary of our knowledge of the effectiveness of drug control methods is balanced and accurate is shown by the support it receives from leading conservative scholars. Senator-scholar Daniel Patrick Moynihan (1993) has written, "Interdiction and 'drug busts' are probably necessary symbolic acts, but nothing more." James Q. Wilson (1990), for two decades America's leading conservative crime control scholar, observed that "significant reductions in drug abuse will come only from reducing demand for those drugs. . . . The marginal product of further investment in supply reduction is likely to be small" (p. 534). He reports that "I know of no serious law-enforcement official who disagrees with this conclusion. Typically, police officials tell interviewers that they are fighting either a losing war or, at best, a holding action" (p. 534).

Thus a fair-minded survey of existing knowledge provides no grounds for believing that the War on Drugs or the harsh policies exemplified by "three strikes and you're out" laws and evidenced by a tripling in America's prison population since 1980 could achieve their ostensible purposes. If such policies cannot be explained in instrumental terms, how can they be explained? The last section answers that question, but first a summary of recent data on racial trends in arrests, jailing, and incarceration.

● Racial Disparities in Arrests, Jail, and Prison

Racial disparities, especially affecting Blacks, have long bedeviled the criminal justice system. Many hundreds of studies of disparities have been conducted and there is now widespread agreement among researchers about causes. Racial bias and stereotyping no doubt play some role, but they are not the major cause. In the longer term, disparities in jail and prison are mainly the result of racial differences in offending patterns. In the shorter term, the worsening disparities since 1980 are not primarily the result of racial differences in offending but were foreseeable effects of the War on Drugs and the movement toward increased use of incarceration. These patterns can best be seen by approaching the recent increases in racial disparities in imprisonment as a mystery to be solved. (Because of space limitations, jail data are not discussed here at length, but the trends parallel those for prisons. Between 1980 and 1991, e.g., the percentage of jail inmates who were Black increased from 40% to 48%.)

Figure 1, showing the percentages of prison inmates who were Black or White from 1960 to 1991, reveals two trends. First, for as long as prison population data have been compiled, the percentage of inmates who are Black has by several times exceeded the percentage of Americans who are Black (10% to 13% during the relevant period). Second, since 1980 the Black percentage among prisoners has increased sharply.

Racial disproportions among prison inmates are inherently undesirable, and considerable energy has been expended on efforts to understand them.

FIGURE 1 *Prisoners In State and Federal Prisons on Census Date by Race, 1960–1991*

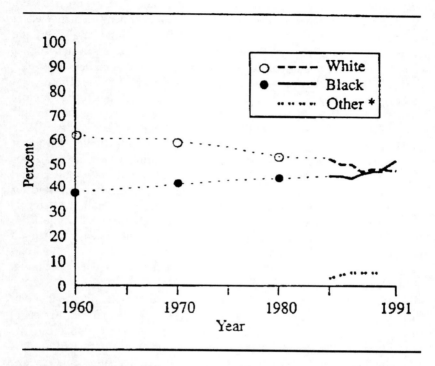

Sources: For 1960, 1970, 1980: Cahalan 1986, table 3.31; for 1985–1991: Bureau of Justice Statistics 1993, 1991a, 1991b, 1989a, 1989b, 1987.

* = Hispanics in many states, Asians, Native Americans.

In 1982, Blumstein showed that around 80% of the disproportion could be explained on the basis of racial differences in arrest patterns. Of the unexplained 20%, Blumstein argued, some might represent bias and some might reflect racial differences in criminal history or arguably valid case-processing differences. Some years earlier, Hindelang (1976, 1978) had demonstrated that racial patterns in victims' identifications of their assailants closely resembled racial differences in arrests. Some years later, Langan (1985) skipped over the arrest stage altogether and showed that racial patterns in victims' identifications of their assailants explained about 80% of disparities in prison admissions. In 1990, Klein, Petersilia, and Turner showed that, after criminal history and other legitimate differences between cases were taken into account, the offender's race had no independent predictive effect in California on whether he was sent to prison or for how long. There the matter rests. Blumstein (1993a) updated his analysis and reached similar conclusions (with one important exception that is discussed below).

Although racial crime patterns explain a large part of racial imprisonment patterns, they do not explain why the Black percentage rose so rapidly after 1980. Table 1 shows Black and White percentages among people arrested for the eight serious FBI Index Crimes at 3-year intervals from 1976 to 1991 and for 1992. Within narrow bands of fluctuation, racial arrest percentages have been stable since 1976. Comparing 1976 with 1992, for example, Black percentages among people arrested for murder, robbery, and burglary were slightly up and Black percentages among those arrested for rape, aggravated assault, and theft were slightly down. Overall, the percentage among those arrested for violent crimes who were Black fell from 47.5% to 44.8%. Because prison sentences have traditionally been imposed on people convicted of violent crimes, Blumstein's and the other analyses suggest that the Black percentage among inmates should be flat or declining. That, however, is not what Figure 1 shows. Why not?

Part of the answer can be found in prison admissions. Figure 2 shows racial percentages among prison admissions from 1960 to 1992. Arrests of Blacks for violent crimes may not have increased since 1980, but the percentage of Blacks among those sent to prison has increased starkly, reaching 54% in 1991 and 1992. Why? The main explanation concerns the War on Drugs.

Table 2 shows racial percentages among persons arrested for drug crimes between 1976 and 1992. Blacks today make up about 13% of the U.S. population and, according to National Institute on Drug Abuse (1991) surveys of Americans' drug use, are no more likely than Whites ever to have used most drugs of abuse. Nonetheless, the percentages of Blacks among drug arrestees were in the low 20% range in the late 1970s, climbing to around 30% in the early 1980s and peaking at 42% in 1989. The number of drug arrests of Blacks more than doubled between 1985 and 1989, whereas White drug arrests increased only by 27%. Figure 3 shows the stark differences in drug arrest trends by race from 1976 to 1991.

TABLE 1 Percentage Black and White Arrests for Index I Offenses 1976–1991 (3-year intervals)[a]

	1976		1979		1982		1985		1988		1991		1992	
	White	Black	White	Black	White	Black	White	Black	White	Black	White	Black	White	Black
Murder and nonnegligent manslaughter	45.0	53.5	49.4	47.7	48.8	49.7	50.1	48.4	45.0	53.5	43.4	54.8	43.5	55.1
Forcible rape	51.2	46.6	50.2	47.7	48.7	49.7	52.2	46.5	52.7	45.8	54.8	43.5	55.5	42.8
Robbery	38.9	59.2	41.0	56.9	38.2	60.7	37.4	61.7	36.3	62.6	37.6	61.1	37.7	60.9
Aggravated assault	56.8	41.0	60.9	37.0	59.8	38.8	58.0	40.4	57.6	40.7	60.0	38.3	59.5	38.8
Burglary	69.0	29.2	69.5	28.7	67.0	31.7	69.7	28.9	67.0	31.3	68.8	29.3	67.8	30.4
Larceny-theft	65.7	32.1	67.2	30.2	64.7	33.4	67.2	30.6	65.6	32.2	66.6	30.9	66.2	31.4
Motor vehicle theft	71.1	26.2	70.0	27.2	66.9	31.4	65.8	32.4	58.7	39.5	58.5	39.3	58.4	39.4
Arson	—	—	78.9	19.2	74.0	24.7	75.7	22.8	73.5	25.0	76.7	21.5	76.4	21.9
Violent crime[b]	50.4	47.5	53.7	44.1	51.9	46.7	51.5	47.1	51.7	46.8	53.6	44.8	53.6	44.8
Property crime[c]	67.0	30.9	68.2	29.4	65.5	32.7	67.7	30.3	65.3	32.6	66.4	31.3	65.8	31.8
Total crime index	64.1	33.8	65.3	32.4	62.7	35.6	64.5	33.7	62.4	35.7	63.2	34.0	62.7	35.2

Sources: *Sourcebook of Criminal Justice Statistics.* Various years. Washington, DC: Department of Justice, Bureau of Justice Statistics; FBI 1993, Table 43.

a. Because of rounding, the percentages may not add to total.

b. Violent crimes are offenses of murder, forcible rape, robbery, and aggravated assault.

c. Property crimes are offenses of burglary, larceny-theft, motor vehicle theft, and arson.

FIGURE 2 *Admissions to Federal and State Prisons by Race, 1960–1992*

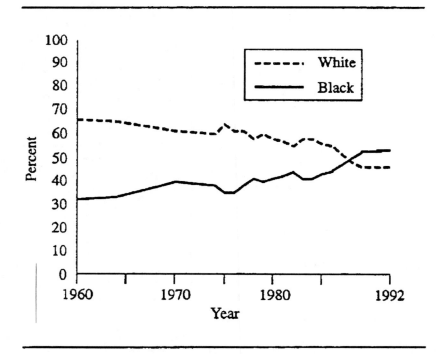

Sources: Langan 1991; Gilliard 1992; Perkins 1992, 1993; Perkins and Gilliard 1992.
Note: Hispanics are included in Black and White populations.

Drug control policies are a major cause of worsening racial disparities in prison. In the federal prisons, for example, 22% of new admissions and 25% of the resident population were drug offenders in 1980. By 1990, 42% of new admissions were drug offenders as in 1992 were 58% of the resident population. In state prisons, 5.7% of inmates in 1979 were drug offenders, a figure that by 1991 had climbed to 21.3% to become the single largest category of prisoners (robbers, burglars, and murderers were next at 14.8%, 12.4%, and 10.6%, respectively) (Beck et al. 1993).

TABLE 2 *U.S. Drug Arrests by Race, 1976–1992*

Year	Total Violations	White	White %	Black	Black %
1976	475,209	366,081	77	103,615	22
1977	565,371	434,471	77	122,594	22
1978	592,168	462,728	78	127,277	21
1979	516,142	396,065	77	112,748	22
1980	531,953	401,979	76	125,607	24
1981	584,776	432,556	74	146,858	25
1982	562,390	400,683	71	156,369	28
1983	615,081	423,151	69	185,601	30
1984	560,729	392,904	70	162,979	29
1985	700,009	482,486	69	210,298	30
1986	688,815	463,457	67	219,159	32
1987	809,157	511,278	63	291,177	36
1988	844,300	503,125	60	334,015	40
1989	1,074,345	613,800	57	452,574	42
1990	860,016	503,315	59	349,965	41
1991	763,340	443,596	58	312,997	41
1992	919,561	546,430	59	364,546	40

Sources: FBI 1993. Table 43; *Sourcebook of Criminal Justice Statistics—1978–1992*. Various tables. Washington, DC: U.S. Department of Justice. Bureau of Justice Statistics.

The effect of drug policies can be seen in prison data from a number of states. Figure 4 shows Black and White prison admissions in North Carolina from 1970 to 1990. White rates held steady; Black rates doubled between 1980 and 1990, rising most rapidly after 1987. Figure 5 shows prison admissions for drug crimes in Virginia from 1983 to 1989; the racial balance flipped from two-thirds White, one-third non-White in 1983 to the reverse in 1989. Similarly, in Pennsylvania, Clark (1992) reports, Black male prison admissions for drug crimes grew four times faster (up 1,613%) between 1980 and 1990 than did White male admissions (up 477%). In California, according to Zimring and Hawkins (1994), the number of males in prison for drug crimes grew 15 fold between 1980 and 1990 and "there were more people in prison in California for drug offences in 1991 than there were for *all* offences in California at the end of 1979" (p. 89; emphasis in original).

Why, if Blacks in their lives are no more likely than Whites to use illicit drugs, are Blacks so much more likely to be arrested and imprisoned? One possible answer, which is almost certainly wrong, is that Blacks are propor-

FIGURE 3 *Arrest Rates for Drug Offenses by Race, 1965–1991*

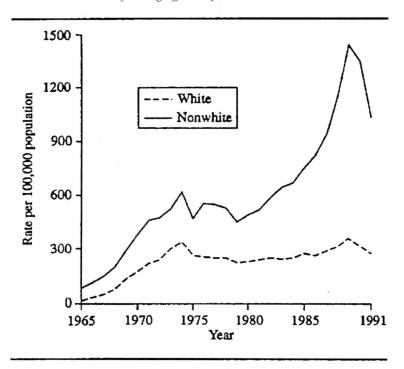

Source: Blumstein 1993b.

tionately more likely to sell drugs. We have no representative surveys of drug dealers and so cannot with confidence paint demographic pictures. However, there is little reason to suspect that drug crimes are more interracial than are most other crimes. In addition, the considerations that make arrests of Black dealers relatively easy make arrests of White dealers relatively hard.

Drug arrests are easier to make in socially disorganized inner-city minority areas than in working- or middle-class urban or suburban areas for a number of reasons. First, although drug sales in working- or middle-class areas are likely to take place indoors and in private spaces where they are difficult to observe, drug sales in poor minority areas are likely to take place

FIGURE 4 Prison Admissions per 100,000 General Population, North Carolina, by Race, 1970–1990.

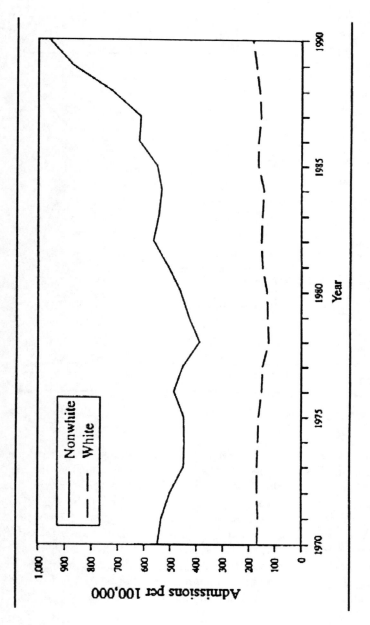

Source: Clarke 1992.

219

FIGURE 5 *Percentage of New Drug Commitments by Race, Virginia, Fiscal Years 1983–1989*

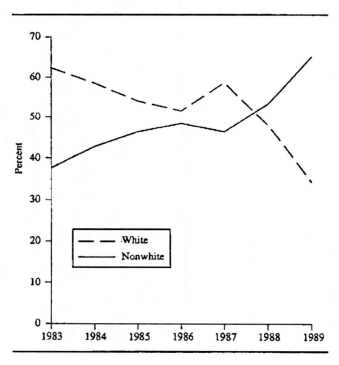

Source: Austin and McVey 1989.

outdoors in streets, alleys, or abandoned buildings, or indoors in public places like bars. Second, although working- or middle-class drug dealers in stable areas are unlikely to sell drugs to undercover strangers, dealers in disorganized areas have little choice but to sell to strangers and new acquaintances. These differences mean that it is easier for police to make arrests and undercover purchases in urban minority areas than elsewhere. Because arrests are fungible for purposes of both the individual officer's personnel file and the department's year-to-year statistical comparisons, more easy arrests look better than fewer hard ones. And because, as ethnographic studies of drug trafficking make clear (Fagan 1993; Padilla 1992), arrested drug dealers in disadvantaged urban minority communities are generally replaced within days, there is a nearly inexhaustible potential supply of young minority Americans to be arrested.

There is another reason why the War on Drugs worsened racial disparities in the justice system. Penalties for drug crimes were steadily made harsher since the mid-1980s. In particular, purveyors of crack cocaine, a drug used primarily by poor urban Blacks and Hispanics, are punished far more severely than are purveyors of powder cocaine, a pharmacologically indistinguishable drug used primarily by middle-class Whites. The most notorious disparity occurs under federal law which equates 1 gram of crack with 100 grams of powder. As a result, the average prison sentence served by Black federal prisoners is 40% longer than the average sentence for Whites (McDonald and Carlson 1993). Although the Minnesota Supreme Court and two federal district courts have struck down the 100-to-1 rule as a denial of constitutional equal protection to Blacks, at the time of writing, every federal court of appeals that had considered the question had upheld the provision.

The people who launched the drug wars knew all these things—that the enemy troops would mostly be young minority males, that an emphasis on supply-side antidrug strategies, particularly use of mass arrests, would disproportionately ensnare young minority males, that the 100-to-1 rule would disproportionately affect Blacks, and that there was no valid basis for believing that any of these things would reduce drug availability or prices.

Likewise, as the first section showed, there was no basis for a good faith belief that the harsher crime control policies of recent years—more and longer mandatory minimum sentences, tougher and more rigid sentencing guidelines, and three-strikes-and-you're-out laws—would reduce crime rates, and there was a good basis for predicting that they would disproportionately damage Blacks. If Blacks are more likely than Whites to be arrested, especially for drug crimes, the greater harshness of toughened penalties will disproportionately be borne by Blacks. Because much crime is intraracial, concern for Black victims might justify harsher treatment of Black offenders if there were any reason to believe that harsher penalties would reduce crime rates. Unfortunately, as the conservative national governments of Margaret Thatcher and Brian Mulroney and reports of National Academy of Sciences Panels funded by the administrations of Republican Presidents Ford, Reagan, and Bush all agree, there is no reason to believe that harsher penalties significantly reduce crime rates.

◎ Justifying the Unjustifiable

There is no valid policy justification for the harsh drug and crime control policies of the Reagan and Bush administrations, and for their adverse differential effect on Blacks. The justification, such as it is, is entirely political. Crime is an emotional subject and visceral appeals by politicians to people's fears and resentments are difficult to counter.

It is easy to seize the low ground in political debates about crime policy. When one candidate campaigns with pictures of clanging prison gates and grief-stricken relatives of a rape or murder victim, and with disingenuous promises that newer, tougher policies will work, it is difficult for an opponent to explain that crime is a complicated problem, that real solutions must be long term, and that simplistic toughness does not reduce crime rates. This is why, as a result, candidates often compete to establish which is tougher in his views about crime. It is also why less conservative candidates often try to preempt their more conservative opponents by adopting a tough stance early in the campaign. Finally, it is why political pundits congratulate President Clinton on his acumen in proposing federal crime legislation as or more harsh than his opponents. He has, it is commonly said, "taken the crime issue away from the Republicans."

Conservative Republican politicians have, since the late 1960s, used welfare, especially Aid to Families with Dependent Children, and crime as symbolic issues to appeal to anti-Black sentiments and resentments of White voters, as Thomas and Mary Edsall's *Chain Reaction: The Impact of Race, Rights, and Taxes on American Politics* (1991) makes clear. The Edsalls provide a history, since the mid-1960s, of "a conservative politics that had the effect of polarizing the electorate along racial lines." Anyone who observed Ronald Reagan's portrayal in several campaigns of Linda Evans, a Black Chicago woman, as the "welfare queen" or George Bush's use of Black murderer Willie Horton to caricature Michael Dukakis's criminal justice policies knows of what the Edsalls write.

The story of Willie Horton is the better known and makes the Edsalls' point. Horton, who in 1975 had been convicted of the murder of a 17-year-old boy, failed to return from a June 12, 1986, furlough. The following April, he broke into a home in Oxon Hill, Maryland, where he raped a woman and stabbed her companion.

Lee Atwater, Bush's campaign strategist, after testing the visceral effects of Willie Horton's picture and story on participants in focus groups, decided a year later to make Horton a wedge issue for Republicans. Atwood reportedly told a group of Republican activists that Bush would win the presidency "if I can make Willie Horton a household name." He later told a Republican gathering in Atlanta, "there's a story about a fellow named Willie Horton who, for all I know, may end up being Dukakis's running mate." Atwood for a time denied making both remarks but in 1991, dying of cancer, recanted: "In 1988, fighting Dukakis, I said that I would . . . make Willie Horton his running mate. I am sorry."

The sad reality is that tragedies like the crimes of Willie Horton are inevitable. So are airplane crashes, 40,000 to 50,000 traffic fatalities per year, and defense department cost overruns. Every person convicted of a violent crime cannot be held forever. Furloughs are used in most corrections systems as a way to ease offenders back into the community and to test their suitability for eventual release on parole or commutation. Horton had successfully completed nine previous furloughs, from each of which he had returned without incident, under a program established in 1972 not by Michael Dukakis but by Governor Francis Sargent, a Republican.

Public discourse about criminal justice issues has been debased by the cynicism that made Willie Horton a major participant in the 1988 presidential election. That cynicism has made it difficult to discuss or develop sensible public policies, and that cynicism explains why conservative politicians have been able year after year successfully to propose ever harsher penalties and crime control and drug policies that no informed person believes can achieve their ostensible goals.

Three final points, arguments that apologists for current policies sometimes make, warrant mention. First, it is sometimes said to be unfair to blame national Republican administrations for the failures and disparate impacts of recent crime control policies. This ignores the efforts of the Reagan and Bush administrations to encourage and, through federal mandates and funding restrictions, to coerce states to follow the federal lead. Attorney General William Barr (e.g., 1992) made the most aggressive efforts to compel state adoption of tougher criminal justice policies, and the Bush administration's final proposed crime bills restricted eligibility for federal funds to states that, like the federal government, abolished parole release and adopted sentencing standards no less severe than those in the federal sentencing guidelines. In any case, as the Edsalls' book makes clear, the use of crime control issues (among others including welfare reform and affirmative action) to elicit anti-Black sentiments from White voters has long been a stratagem of both state and federal Republican politicians.

Second, sometimes it is argued that political leaders have merely followed the public will; voters are outraged by crime and want tougher policies (DiIulio 1991). This is a half-truth that gets the causal order backwards. Various measures of public sentiment, including both representative surveys like Gallup and Harris polls and work with focus groups, have for many years consistently shown that the public is of two minds about crime (Roberts 1992). First, people are frustrated and want offenders to be punished. Second, people believe that social adversity, poverty, and a troubled home life are the principal causes of crime, and they believe government should work to rehabilitate offenders. A number of surveys have found that respondents who would oppose a tax increase to pay for more prisons would support a tax increase to pay for rehabilitative programs. These findings of voter ambivalence about crime should not be surprising. Most people have complicated views about complicated problems. For example, most judges and corrections officials have the same ambivalent feelings about offenders that the general public has. Conservative politicians have seized upon public support of punishment and ignored public support of rehabilitation and public recognition that crime presents complex, not easy, challenges. By presenting crime control issues only in emotional, stereotyped ways, conservative politicians have raised its salience as a political issue but made it impossible for their opponents to respond other than in the same stereotyped ways.

Third, sometimes it is argued that disparate impacts on Black offenders are no problem and that, because much crime is intraracial, failure to adopt tough policies would disserve the interests of Black victims. As former Attorney General Barr (1992) put it, perhaps in ill-chosen words, "the benefits of increased incarceration would be enjoyed disproportionately by Black Americans" (p. 17). This argument also is based on a half-truth. No one wants to live in unsafe neighborhoods or to be victimized by crime, and in a crisis, people who need help will seek it from the police, the public agency of last resort. Requesting help in a crisis and supporting harsh policies with racially disparate effects are not the same thing. The relevant distinction is between acute and chronic problems. A substantial body of public opinion research (e.g., National Opinion Research Center surveys conducted throughout the 1980s summarized in Wood 1990) shows that Blacks far more than Whites support establishment of more generous social welfare policies, full employment programs, and increased social spending. The congressional Black and Hispanic caucuses have consistently opposed bills calling for tougher sanctions and supported bills calling for increased spending on social programs aimed at improving conditions that cause crime. Thus, in claiming to be concerned about Black victims, conservative politicians are responding to natural human calls for help in a crisis while ignoring evidence that Black citizens would rather have government support efforts to ameliorate the chronic social conditions that cause crime and thereby make calls for help in a crisis less necessary.

The evidence on the effectiveness of recent crime control and drug abuse policies, as the first section demonstrated, cannot justify their racially disparate effects on Blacks, nor, as this section demonstrates, can the claims that such policies merely manifest the peoples' will or respect the interests of Black victims. All that is left is politics of the ugliest kind. The War on Drugs and the set of harsh crime control policies in which it was enmeshed were adopted to achieve political, not policy, objectives, and it is the adoption for political purposes of policies with foreseeable disparate impacts, the use of disadvantaged Black Americans as means to the achievement of White politicians' electoral ends, that must in the end be justified. It cannot.

References

Anglin, M. Douglas and Yih-Ing Hser. 1990. "Treatment of Drug Abuse." In *Drugs and Crime*, edited by M. Tonry and J. Q. Wilson. Chicago: University of Chicago Press.

Austin, James and Aaron David McVey. 1989. *The Impact of the War on Drugs.* San Francisco: National Council on Crime and Delinquency.

Barr, William P. 1992. "The Case for More Incarceration." Washington, DC: U.S. Department of Justice, Office of Policy Development.

Beck, Allen et al.1993. *Survey of State Prison Inmates, 1991.* Washington, DC: Bureau of Justice Statistics.

Blumstein, Alfred. 1982. "On the Racial Disproportionality of United States' Prison Populations." *Journal of Criminal Law and Criminology* 73:1259–81.

_____. 1993a. "Racial Disproportionality of U.S. Prison Populations Revisited." *University of Colorado Law Review* 64:743–60.

_____. 1993b. "Making Rationality Relevant The American Society of Criminology 1992 Presidential Address." *Criminology* 31:1–16.

Blumstein, Alfred, Jacqueline Cohen, and Daniel Nagin. 1978. *Deterrence and Incapacitation.* Report of the National Academy of Sciences Parcel on Research on Deterrent and Incapacitative Effects. Washington, DC: National Academy Press.

Botvin, Gilbert J. 1990. "Substance Abuse Prevention: Theory, Practice, and Effectiveness." In *Drugs and Crime,* edited by M. Tonry and J. Q. Wilson. Chicago: University of Chicago Press.

Bureau of Justice Statistics. 1987. *Correctional Populations in the United States, 1985.* Washington, DC: U.S. Department of Justice, Bureau of Justice Statistics.

_____. 1989a. *Correctional Populations in the United States, 1987.* Washington, DC: U.S. Department of Justice, Bureau of Justice Statistics.

_____. 1989b. *Correctional Populations in the United States, 1986.* Washington, DC: U.S. Department of Justice, Bureau of Justice Statistics.

_____. 1991a. *Correctional Populations in the United States, 1989.* Washington, DC: U.S. Department of Justice, Bureau of Justice Statistics.

_____. 1991b. *Correctional Populations in the United States, 1988.* Washington, DC: U.S. Department of Justice, Bureau of Justice Statistics.

_____. 1993. *Correctional Populations in the United States, 1991.* Washington, DC: U.S. Department of Justice, Bureau of Justice Statistics.

Cahalan, Margaret Werner. 1986. *Historical Corrections Statistics in the United States, 1850–1984.* Washington, DC: U.S. Department of Justice, Bureau of Justice Statistics.

Canadian Sentencing Commission. 1987. *Sentencing Reform: A Canadian Approach.* Ottawa: Canadian Government Publishing Centre.

Chaiken, Marcia, ed. 1988. *Street Level Enforcement: Examining the Issues.* Washington, DC: U.S. Government Printing Office.

Clark, Stover. 1992. "Pennsylvania Corrections in Context." *Overcrowded Times* 3:4–5.

Clarke, Stevens H. 1992. "North Carolina Prisons Growing." *Overcrowded Times* 3:1, 11–13.

DiIulio, John J. 1991. *No Escape: The Future of American Corrections.* New York: Basic Books.

Edsall, Thomas and Mary Edsall. 1991. *Chain Reaction: The Impact of Race, Rights, and Taxes on American Politics.* New York: Norton.

Ellickson, Phyllis L. and Robert M. Bell. 1990. *Prospects for Preventing Drug Use Among Young Adolescents.* Santa Monica, CA: RAND.

Fagan, Jeffrey. 1993. "The Political Economy of Drug Dealing Among Urban Gangs." In *Drugs and the Community,* edited by R. C. Davis, A. J. Lurigio, and D. P. Rosenbaum. Springfield, IL: Charles C. Thomas.

Federal Bureau of Investigation. 1993. *Uniform Crime Reports for the United States— 1992.* Washington, DC: U.S. Government Printing Office.

Gerstein, Dean R. and Henrik J. Jarwood, eds. 1990. *Treating Drug Problems.* Report of the Committee for Substance Abuse Coverage Study, Division of Health Care Services, National Institute of Medicine. Washington, DC: National Academy Press.

Gilliard, Darrell K. 1992. *National Corrections Reporting Program, 1987.* Washington, DC: U.S. Department of Justice, Bureau of Justice Statistics.

Hindelang, Michael. 1976. *Criminal Victimization in Eight American Cities: A Descriptive Analysis of Common Theft and Assault.* Washington, DC: Law Enforcement Assistance Administration.

––––––––. 1978. "Race and Involvement in Common Law Personal Crimes." *American Sociological Review* 43:93–108.

Home Office. 1990. *Protecting the Public.* London: H. M. Stationery Office.

Klein, Stephen, Joan Petersilia, and Susan Turner. 1990. "Race and Imprisonment Decisions in California." *Science* 247:812–16.

Langan, Patrick A. 1985. "Racism on Trial: New Evidence to Explain the Racial Composition of Prisons in the United States." *Journal of Criminal Law and Criminology* 76:666–83.

––––––––. 1991. *Race of Persons Admitted to State and Federal Institutions, 1926–86.* Washington, DC: U.S. Department of Justice, Bureau of Justice Statistics.

McDonald, Douglas and Ken Carlson. 1993. *Sentencing in the Federal Courts: Does Race Matter?* Washington, DC: U.S. Department of Justice, Bureau of Justice Statistics.

Moore, Mark H. 1990. "Supply Reduction and Drug Law Enforcement." In *Drugs and Crime,* edited by M. Tonry and J. Q. Wilson. Chicago: University of Chicago Press.

Moynihan, Daniel Patrick. 1993. "Iatrogenic Government—Social Policy and Drug Research." *American Scholar* 62:351–62.

National Institute on Drug Abuse. 1991. *National Household Survey on Drug Abuse: Population Estimates 1990.* Washington, DC: U.S. Government Printing Office.

Office of National Drug Control Policy. 1990. *National Drug Control Strategy—January 1990*. Washington, DC: Author.

Padilla, Felix. 1992. *The Gang as an American Enterprise*. New Brunswick, NJ: Rutgers University Press.

Perkins, Craig. 1992. *National Corrections Reporting Program, 1989*. Washington, DC: U.S., Department of Justice, Bureau of Justice Statistics.

————. 1993. *National Corrections Reporting Program, 1990*. Washington, DC: U.S. Department of Justice, Bureau of Justice Statistics.

Perkins, Craig and Darrell K. Gilliard. 1992. *National Corrections Reporting Program, 1988*. Washington, DC: U.S. Department of Justice, Bureau of Justice Statistics.

President's Commission on Law Enforcement and Administration of Justice. 1967. *The Challenge of Crime in a Free Society*. Washington, DC: U.S. Government Printing Office.

President's Commission on Model State Drug Laws. 1993. *Final Report*. Washington, DC: U.S. Government Printing Office.

Reiss, Albert J., Jr. and Jeffrey Roth. 1993. *Understanding and Controlling Violence. Report of the National Academy of Sciences Panel on the Understanding and Control of Violence*. Washington, DC: National Academy Press.

Reuter, Peter. 1988. "Can the Borders Be Sealed?" *Public Interest* 92:51–65.

Roberts, Julian V. 1992. "Public Opinion, Crime, and Criminal Justice." In *Crime and Justice: A Review of Research*, vol. 16, edited by M. Tonry. Chicago: University of Chicago Press.

Sourcebook of Criminal Justice Statistics. 1978–1992. Washington, DC: Department of Justice, Bureau of Justice Statistics.

Standing Committee on Justice and the Solicitor General. 1993. *Crime Prevention in Canada: Toward a National Strategy*. Ottawa: Canada Communication Group.

Sviridoff, Michele, Susan Sadd, Richard Curtis, and Randolph Grinc. 1992. *The Neighborhood Effects of Street-Level Drug Enforcement*. New York: Vera Institute of Justice.

Tonry, Michael. 1994. *Malign Neglect: Race, Crime, and Punishment in America*. New York: Oxford University Press.

U.S. General Accounting Office. 1990. *Drug Abuse: Research on Treatment May Not Address Current Needs*. Washington, DC: U.S. General Accounting Office.

Wilson, James Q. 1990. "Drugs and Crime." In *Drugs and Crime*, edited by M. Tonry and J. Q. Wilson. Chicago: University of Chicago Press.

Wood, Floris W. 1990. *An American Profile: Opinions and Behavior, 1972–1989*. New York: Gale Research.

Zimring, Franklin E. and Gordon Hawkins. 1994. "The Growth of Imprisonment in California." *British Journal of Criminology* 34:83–95.

● ● ●

Questions

1. According to Tonry, why have rates of African-American imprisonment increased so dramatically since 1980?

2. Do African-Americans and whites differ in their rates of criminal behavior? If so, how much does this difference contribute to inequities in imprisonment rates for the two races?

3. In what ways has the "war on drugs" targeted African-Americans?

4. How could policy makers change drug laws so that the laws no longer discriminate by race?

Girls' Crime and Woman's Place: Toward a Feminist Model of Female Delinquency

Meda Chesney-Lind

Almost everything we know about crime and delinquency in the United States applies primarily to boys. Sociologists have historically studied boys' delinquency, generated theories from these studies, and tested the theories' applicability on samples of boys. Therefore, the sanctions and social-control methods that most program initiatives and juvenile-justice systems implement are applicable to only one-half of the youth population. Meda Chesney-Lind recognizes this problem. In this article, she criticizes the current literature for failing to account for the unique social context in which girls are situated in U.S. society. What are the consequences of gender bias in the study of delinquency, and what can be done to acknowledge gender differences in theory and practice? Consider these questions as you read this selection.

I ran away so many times. I tried anything man, and they wouldn't believe me. . . . As far as they are concerned they think I'm the problem. You know, runaway, bad label. (Statement of a 16-year-old girl who, after having been physically and sexually assaulted, started running away from home and was arrested as a "runaway" in Hawaii.)

You know, one of these days I'm going to have to kill myself before you guys are gonna listen to me. I can't stay at home. (Statement of a 16-year-old Tucson runaway with a long history of physical abuse [Davidson, 1982, p. 26].)

"Girls' Crime and Woman's Place: Toward a Feminist Model of Female Delinquency," by Meda Chesney-Lind, reprinted from *Crime and Delinquency*, vol. 35, no. 1. 1989, pp. 5–29.

*W*ho is the typical female delinquent? What causes her to get into trouble? What happens to her if she is caught? These are questions that few members of the general public could answer quickly. By contrast, almost every citizen can talk about "delinquency," by which they generally mean male delinquency, and can even generate some fairly specific complaints about, for example, the failure of the juvenile justice system to deal with such problems as "the alarming increase in the rate of serious juvenile crime" and the fact that the juvenile courts are too lenient on juveniles found guilty of these offenses (Opinion Research Corporation, 1982).

This situation should come as no surprise since even the academic study of delinquent behavior has, for all intents and purposes, been the study of male delinquency. "The delinquent is a rogue male" declared Albert Cohen (1955, p. 140) in his influential book on gang delinquency. More than a decade later, Travis Hirschi, in his equally important book entitled *The Causes of Delinquency*, relegated women to a footnote that suggested, somewhat apologetically, that "in the analysis that follows, the 'non-Negro' becomes 'white,' and the girls disappear."

This pattern of neglect is not all that unusual. All areas of social inquiry have been notoriously gender blind. What is perhaps less well understood is that theories developed to describe the misbehavior of working- or lower-class male youth fail to capture the full nature of delinquency in America; and, more to the point, are woefully inadequate when it comes to explaining female misbehavior and official reactions to girls' deviance.

To be specific, delinquent behavior involves a range of activities far broader than those committed by the stereotypical street gang. Moreover, many more young people than the small visible group of "troublemakers" that exist on every intermediate and high school campus commit some sort of juvenile offense and many of these youth have brushes with the law. One study revealed, for example, that 33% of all the boys and 14% of the girls born in 1958 had at least one contact with the police before reaching their eighteenth birthday (Tracy, Wolfgang, and Figlio, 1985, p. 5). Indeed, some forms of serious delinquent behavior, such as drug and alcohol abuse, are far more frequent than the stereotypical delinquent behavior of gang fighting and vandalism and appear to cut across class and gender lines.

Studies that solicit from youth themselves the volume of their delinquent behavior consistently confirm that large numbers of adolescents engage in at least some form of misbehavior that could result in their arrest. As a consequence, it is largely trivial misconduct, rather than the commission of serious crime, that shapes the actual nature of juvenile delinquency. One national study of youth aged 15–21, for example, noted that only 5% reported involvement in a serious assault, and only 6% reported having participated in a gang fight. In contrast, 81% admitted to having used alcohol, 44% admitted to having used marijuana, 37% admitted to having been publicly drunk, 42% admitted to having skipped classes (truancy), 44% admitted having had sexual intercourse, and 15% admitted to having stolen from the family (McGarrell and Flanagan, 1985, p. 363). Clearly, not all of these activities are as serious as the others. It is important to remember that young people can be arrested for all of these behaviors.

Indeed, one of the most important points to understand about the nature of delinquency, and particularly female delinquency, is that youth can be taken into custody for both criminal acts and a wide variety of what are often called "status offenses." These offenses, in contrast to criminal violations, permit the arrest of youth for a wide range of behaviors that are violations of parental authority: "running away from home," "being a person in need of supervision," "minor in need of supervision," being "incorrigible," "beyond control," truant, in need of "care and protection," and so on. Juvenile delinquents, then, are youths arrested for either criminal or noncriminal status offenses; and, as this discussion will establish, the role played by uniquely juvenile offenses is by no means insignificant, particularly when considering the character of female delinquency.

Examining the types of offenses for which youth are actually arrested, it is clear that again most are arrested for the less serious criminal acts and status offenses. Of the one and a half million youth arrested in 1983, for example, only 4.5% of these arrests were for such serious violent offenses as murder, rape, robbery, or aggravated assault (McGarrell and Flanagan, 1985, p. 479). In contrast, 21% were arrested for a single offense (larceny theft) much of which, particularly for girls, is shoplifting (Shelden and Horvath, 1986).

Table 1 presents the five most frequent offenses for which male and female youth are arrested and from this it can be seen that while trivial offenses dominate both male and female delinquency, trivial offenses, particularly status offenses, are more significant in the case of girls' arrests; for example the five offenses listed in Table 1 account for nearly three-quarters of female offenses and only slightly more than half of male offenses.

More to the point, it is clear that, though routinely neglected in most delinquency research, status offenses play a significant role in girls' official

TABLE 1 *Rank Order of Adolescent Male and Female Arrests for Specific Offenses, 1977 and 1986*

	Male				Female			
	1977	% of Total Arrests	1986	% of Total Arrests	1977	% of Total Arrests	1986	% of Total Arrests
(1)	Larceny-Theft	18.4	Larceny-Theft	20.4	Larceny-Theft	27.0	Larceny-Theft	25.7
(2)	Other Offenses	14.5	Other Offenses	16.5	Runaway	22.9	Runaway	20.5
(3)	Burglary	13.0	Burglary	9.1	Other Offenses	14.2	Other Offenses	14.8
(4)	Drug Abuse Violations	6.5	Vandalism	7.0	Liquor Laws	5.5	Liquor Laws	8.4
(5)	Vandalism	6.4	Vandalism	6.3	Curfew & Loitering Violations	4.0	Curfew & Loitering Violations	4.7

	Male			Female		
	1977	1986	% N Change	1977	1986	% N Change
Arrests for Serious Violent Offenses[a]	+4.2%	+4.7%	2.3	1.8%	2.0%	+1.7
Arrests of All Violent Offenses[b]	7.6%	9.6%	+10.3	5.1%	7.1%	+26.0
Arrests for Status Offenses[c]	8.8%	8.3%	-17.8	26.9%	25.2%	-14.7

SOURCE: Compiled from Federal Bureau of Investigation (1987, p. 169).

a. Arrests for murder and nonnegligent manslaughter, robbery, forcible rape, and aggravated assault.

b. Also includes arrests for other assaults.

c. Arrests for curfew and loitering law violation and runaway.

delinquency. Status offenses accounted for about 25.2% of all girls' arrests in 1986 (as compared to 26.9% in 1977) and only about 8.3% of boys' arrests (compared to 8.8% in 1977). These figures are somewhat surprising since dramatic declines in arrests of youth for these offenses might have been expected as a result of the passage of the Juvenile Justice and Delinquency Prevention Act in 1974, which, among other things, encouraged jurisdictions to divert and deinstitutionalize youth charged with noncriminal offenses. While the figures in Table 1 do show a decline in these arrests, virtually all of this decline occurred in the 1970s. Between 1982 and 1986 girls' curfew arrests increased by 5.1% and runaway arrests increased by a striking 24.5%. And the upward trend continues; arrests of girls for running away increased by 3% between 1985 and 1986 and arrests of girls for curfew violations increased by 12.4% (Federal Bureau of Investigation, 1987, p. 171).

Looking at girls who find their way into juvenile court populations, it is apparent that status offenses continue to play an important role in the character of girls' official delinquency. In total, 34% of the girls, but only 12% of the boys, were referred to court in 1983 for these offenses (Snyder and Finnegan, 1987, pp. 6-20). Stating these figures differently, they mean that while males constituted about 81% of all delinquency referrals, females constituted 46% of all status offenders in courts (Snyder and Finnegan, 1987, p. 20). Similar figures were reported for 1977 by Black and Smith (1981). Fifteen years earlier, about half of the girls and about 20% of the boys were referred to court for these offenses (Children's Bureau, 1965). These data do seem to signal a drop in female status offense referrals, though not as dramatic a decline as might have been expected.

For many years statistics showing large numbers of girls arrested and referred for status offenses were taken to be representative of the different types of male and female delinquency. However, self-report studies of male and female delinquency do not reflect the dramatic differences in misbehavior found in official statistics. Specifically, it appears that girls charged with these noncriminal status offenses have been and continue to be significantly overrepresented in court populations.

Teilmann and Landry (1981) compared girls' contribution to arrests for runaway and incorrigibility with girls' self-reports of these two activities, and found a 10.4% overrepresentation of females among those arrested for runaway and a 30.9% overrepresentation in arrests for incorrigibility. From these data they concluded that girls are "arrested for status offenses at a higher rate than boys, when contrasted to their self-reported delinquency rates" (Teilmann and Landry, 1981, pp. 74–75). These findings were confirmed in another recent self-report study. Figueira-McDonough(1985, p. 277) analyzed the delinquent conduct of 2,000 youths and found "no evidence of greater involvement of females in status offenses." Similarly, Canter (1982) found in the National Youth Survey that there was no evidence of greater female involvement, compared to males, in any category of delinquent behavior. Indeed, in this sample, males were significantly more likely than females to report status offenses.

Utilizing Canter's national data on the extensiveness of girls self-reported delinquency and comparing these figures to official arrests of girls (see Table 2) reveals that girls are underrepresented in every arrest category with the exception of status offenses and larceny theft. These figures strongly suggest that official practices tend to exaggerate the role played by status offenses in girls' delinquency.

Delinquency theory, because it has virtually ignored female delinquency, failed to pursue anomalies such as these found in the few early studies examining gender differences in delinquent behavior. Indeed, most delinquency theories have ignored status offenses. As a consequence, there is considerable question as to whether existing theories that were admittedly developed to explain male delinquency can adequately explain female delinquency. Clearly, these theories were much influenced by the notion that class and protest masculinity were at the core of delinquency. Will the "add women and stir approach" be sufficient? Are these really theories of delinquent behavior as some (Simons, Miller, and Aigner, 1980) have argued?

This article will suggest that they are not. The extensive focus on male delinquency and the inattention to the role played by patriarchal arrangements in the generation of adolescent delinquency and conformity has rendered the major delinquency theories fundamentally inadequate to the task of explaining female behavior. There is, in short, an urgent need to rethink current models in light of girls' situation in patriarchal society.

To understand why such work must occur, it is first necessary to explore briefly the dimensions of the androcentric bias found in the dominant and influential delinquency theories. Then the need for a feminist model of female delinquency will be explored by reviewing the available evidence on girls' offending. This discussion will also establish that the proposed overhaul of delinquency theory is not, as some might think, solely an academic exercise. Specifically, it is incorrect to assume that because girls

TABLE 2 *Comparison of Sex Differences in Self-Reported and Official Delinquency for Selected Offenses*

	Self-Report[a] M/F Ratios (1976)	1976	Official Statistics[b] M/F Arrest Ratio 1986
Theft	3.5:1 (Felony Theft) 3.4:1 (Minor Theft)	2.5:1	2.7:1
Drug Violation	1:1 (Hard Drug Use)	5.1:1	6.0:1 (Drug Abuse Violations)
Vandalism	5.1:1	12.3:1	10.0:1
Disorderly Conduct	2.8:1	4.5:1	4.4:1
Serious Assault	3.5:1 (Felony Assault)	5.6:1	5.5:1 (Aggravated Assault)
Minor Assault	3.4:1	3.8:1	3.4:1
Status Offenses	1.6:1	1.3:1	1.1:1 (Runaway, Curfew)

a. Extracted from Rachelle Canter (1982, p. 383).
b. Compiled from Federal Bureau of Investigation (1986, p. 173).

are charged with less serious offenses, they actually have few problems and are treated gently when they are drawn into the juvenile justice system. Indeed, the extensive focus on disadvantaged males in public settings has meant that girls' victimization and the relationship between that experience and girls' crime has been systematically ignored. Also missed has been the central role played by the juvenile justice system in the sexualization of girls' delinquency and the criminalization of girls' survival strategies. Finally, it will be suggested that the official actions of the juvenile justice system should be understood as major forces in girls' oppression as they have historically served to reinforce the obedience of all young women to demands of patriarchal authority no matter how abusive and arbitrary.

● The Romance of the Gang or The West Side Story Syndrome

From the start, the field of delinquency research focused on visible lower-class male delinquency, often justifying the neglect of girls in the most cavalier of terms. Take, for example, the extremely important and influential work of Clifford R. Shaw and Henry D. McKay who, beginning in 1929, utilized an ecological approach to the study of juvenile delinquency. Their impressive work, particularly *Juvenile Delinquency in Urban Areas* (1942) and intensive biographical case studies such as Shaw's *Brothers in Crime* (1938) and *The Jackroller* (1930), set the stage for much of the subcultural research on gang delinquency. In their ecological work, however, Shaw and McKay analyzed only the official arrest data on male delinquents in Chicago and repeatedly referred to these rates as "delinquency rates" (though they occasionally made parenthetical reference to data on female delinquency) (see Shaw and McKay, 1942, p. 356). Similarly, their biographical work traced only male experiences with the law; in *Brothers in Crime*, for example, the delinquent and criminal careers of five brothers were followed for fifteen years. In none of these works was any justification given for the equation of male delinquency with delinquency.

Early fieldwork on delinquent gangs in Chicago set the stage for another style of delinquency research. Yet here too researchers were interested only in talking to and following the boys. Thrasher studied over a thousand juvenile gangs in Chicago during roughly the same period as Shaw and McKay's more quantitative work was being done. He spent approximately one page out of 600 on the five of six female gangs he encountered in his field observation of juvenile gangs. Thrasher (1927, p. 228) did mention, in passing, two factors he felt accounted for the lower number of girl gangs: "First, the social patterns for the behavior of girls, powerfully backed by the great weight of tradition and custom, are contrary to the gang and its activities; and secondly, girls, even in urban disorganized areas, are much more closely supervised and guarded than boys and usually well incorporated into the family groups or some other social structure."

Another major theoretical approach to delinquency focuses on the subculture of lower-class communities as a generating milieu for delinquent behavior. Here again, noted delinquency researchers concentrated either exclusively or nearly exclusively on male lower-class culture. For example, Cohen's work on the subculture of delinquent gangs, which was written nearly twenty years after Thrasher's, deliberately considers only boys' delinquency. His justification for the exclusion of the girls is quite illuminating:

> My skin has nothing of the quality of down or silk, there is nothing limpid or flute-like about my voice, I am a total loss with needle and thread, my posture and carriage are wholly lacking in grace. These imperfections cause me no distress—if anything, they are gratifying—because I conceive myself to be a man and want people to recognize me as a full-fledged, unequivocal representative of my sex. My wife, on the other hand, is not greatly embarrassed by her inability to tinker with or talk about the internal organs of a car, by her modest attainments in arithmetic or by her inability to lift heavy objects. Indeed, I am reliably informed that many women—I do not suggest that my wife is among them—often affect ignorance, frailty and emotional instability because to do otherwise would be out of keeping with a reputation for indubitable femininity. In short, people do not simply want to excel; they want to excel as a man or as a woman [Cohen, 1955, p. 138].

From this Cohen (1955, p. 140) concludes that the delinquent response "however it may be condemned by others on moral grounds, has at least one virtue: it incontestably confirms, in the eyes of all concerned, his essential masculinity." Much the same line of argument appears in Miller's influential paper on the "focal concerns" of lower-class life with its emphasis on importance of trouble, toughness, excitement, and so on. These, the author concludes, predispose poor youth (particularly male youth) to criminal misconduct. However, Cohen's comments are notable in their candor and probably capture both the allure that male delinquency has had for at least some male theorists as well as the fact that sexism has rendered the female delinquent as irrelevant to their work.

Emphasis on blocked opportunities (sometimes the "strain" theories) emerged out of the work of Robert K. Merton (1938) who stressed the need to consider how some social structures exert a definite pressure upon certain persons in the society to engage in nonconformist rather than conformist conduct. His work influenced research largely through the efforts of Cloward and Ohlin who discussed access to "legitimate" and "illegitimate" opportunities for male youth. No mention of female delinquency can be found in their *Delinquency and Opportunity* except that *women are blamed for male delinquency*. Here, the familiar notion is that boys, "engulfed by a feminine world and uncertain of their own identification . . . tend to 'protest' against femininity" (Cloward and Ohlin, 1960, p. 49). Early efforts by Ruth Morris to test this hypothesis utilizing different definitions of success based on the gender of respondents met with mixed success. Attempting to assess boys' perceptions about access to economic power status while for girls the variable concerned itself with the ability or inability of girls to maintain effective relationships, Morris was unable to find a clear relationship between "female" goals and delinquency (Morris, 1964).

The work of Edwin Sutherland emphasized the fact that criminal behavior was teamed in intimate personal groups. His work, particularly the nation of differential association, which also influenced Cloward and Ohlin's work, was similarly male oriented as much of his work was affected by case studies he conducted of male criminals. Indeed, in describing his notion of how differential association works, he utilized male examples (e.g., "In an area where the delinquency rate is high a boy who is sociable, gregarious, active, and athletic is very likely to come in contact with the other boys, in the neighborhood, learn delinquent behavior from them, and become a gangster" [Sutherland, 1978, p. 131]). Finally, the work of Travis Hirschi on the social bonds that control delinquency ("social control theory") was, as was stated earlier, derived out of research on male delinquents (though he, at least, studied delinquent behavior as reported by youth themselves rather than studying only those who were arrested).

Such a persistent focus on social class and such an absence of interest in gender in delinquency is ironic for two reasons. As even the work of Hirschi demonstrated, and as later studies would validate, a clear relationship between social class position and delinquency is problematic, while it is clear that gender has a dramatic and consistent effect on delinquency causation (Hagan, Gillis, and Simpson, 1985). The second irony, and one that consistently eludes even contemporary delinquency theorists, is the fact that while the academics had little interest in female delinquents, the same could not be said for the juvenile justice system. Indeed, work on the early history of the separate system for youth, reveals that concerns about girls' immoral conduct were really at the center of what some have called the "childsaving movement" (Platt, 1969) that set up the juvenile justice system.

⊘ "The Best Place to Conquer Girls"

The movement to establish separate institutions for youthful offenders was part of the larger Progressive movement, which among other things was keenly concerned about prostitution and other "social evils" (white slavery and the like) (Schlossman and Wallach, 1978; Rafter, 1985, p. 54). Childsaving was also a celebration of women's domesticity, though ironically women were influential in the movement (Platt, 1969; Rafter, 1985). In a sense, privileged women found, in the moral purity crusades and the establishment of family courts, a safe outlet for their energies. As the legitimate guardians of the moral sphere, women were seen as uniquely suited to patrol the normative boundaries of the social order. Embracing rather than challenging these stereotypes, women carved out for themselves a role in the policing of women and girls (Feinman, 1980; Freedman, 1981; Messerschmidt, 1987). Ultimately, many of the early childsavers' activities revolved around the monitoring of young girls', particularly immigrant girls', behavior to prevent their straying from the path.

This state of affairs was the direct consequence of a disturbing coalition between some feminists and the more conservative social purity movement. Concerned about female victimization and distrustful of male (and to some degree female) sexuality, notable women leaders, including Susan B. Anthony, found common cause with the social purists around such issues as opposing the regulation of prostitution and raising the age of consent (see Messerschmidt, 1987). The consequences of such a partnership are an important lesson for contemporary feminist movements that are, to some extent, faced with the same possible coalitions.

Girls were the clear losers in this reform effort. Studies of early family court activity reveal that virtually all the girls who appeared in these courts were charged for immorality or waywardness (Chesney-Lind, 1971; Schlossman and Wallach, 1978; Shelden, 1981). More to the point, the sanctions for such misbehavior were extremely severe. For example, in Chicago (where the first family court was founded), one-half of the girl delinquents, but only one-fifth of the boy delinquents, were sent to reformatories between 1899–1909. In Milwaukee, twice as many girls as boys were committed to training schools (Schlossman and Wallach, 1978, p. 72);

and in Memphis females were twice as likely as males to be committed to training schools (Shelden, 1981, p. 70).

In Honolulu, during the period 1929–1930, over half of the girls referred to court were charged with "immorality," which meant evidence of sexual intercourse. In addition, another 30% were charged with "wayward-ness." Evidence of immorality was vigorously pursued by both arresting officers and social workers through lengthy questioning of the girl and, if possible, males with whom she was suspected of having sex. Other evidence of "exposure" was provided by gynecological examinations that were routinely ordered in virtually all girls' cases. Doctors, who understood the purpose of such examinations, would routinely note the condition of the hymen: "admits intercourse hymen rupture," "no laceration," "hymen ruptured" are typical of the notations on the forms. Girls during this period were also twice as likely as males to be detained where they spent five times as long on the average as their male counterparts. They were also nearly three times more likely to be sentenced to the training school (Chesney-Lind, 1971). Indeed, girls were half of those committed to training schools in Honolulu well into the 1950s (Chesney-Lind, 1973).

Not surprisingly, large numbers of girl's reformatories and training schools were established during this period as well as places of "rescue and reform." For example, Schlossman and Wallach note that 23 facilities for girls were opened during the 1910–1920 decade (in contrast to the 1850–1910 period where the average was 5 reformatories per decade [Schlossman and Wallach, 1985, p. 70]), and these institutions did much to set the tone of official response to female delinquency. Obsessed with preco-cious female sexuality, the institutions set about to isolate the females from all contact with males while housing them in bucolic settings. The intention was to hold the girls until marriageable age and to occupy them in domes-tic pursuits during their sometimes lengthy incarceration.

The links between these attitudes and those of juvenile courts some decades later are, of course, arguable; but an examination of the record of the court does not inspire confidence. A few examples of the persistence of what might be called a double standard of juvenile justice will suffice here.

A study conducted in the early 1970s in a Connecticut training school revealed large numbers of girls incarcerated "for their own protection." Explaining this pattern, one judge explained, "Why most of the girls I commit are for status offenses. I figure if a girl is about to get pregnant, we'll keep her until she's sixteen and then ADC (Aid to Dependent Children) will pick her up" (Rogers, 1972). For more evidence of official concern with adolescent sexual misconduct, consider Linda Hancock's (1981) content analysis of police referrals in Australia. She noted that 40% of the referrals of girls to court made specific mention of sexual and moral conduct compared to only 5% of the referrals of boys. These sorts of results suggest that all youthful female misbehavior has traditionally been subject to surveillance for evidence of sexual misconduct.

Gelsthorpe's (1986) field research on an English police station also revealed how everyday police decision making resulted in disregard of complaints about male problem behavior in contrast to active concern about the "problem behavior" of girls. Notable, here, was the concern about the girl's sexual behavior. In one case, she describes police persistence in pursuing a "moral danger" order for a 14-year-old picked up in a truancy run. Over the objections of both the girl's parents and the Social Services Department and in the face of a written confirmation from a surgeon that the girl was still premenstrual, the officers pursued the application because, in one officers words, "I know her sort . . . free and easy. I'm still suspicious that she might be pregnant. Anyway, if the doctor can't provide evidence we'll do her for being beyond the care and control of her parents, no one can dispute that. Running away is proof" (Gelsthorpe, 1986, p. 136). This sexualization of female deviance is highly significant and explains why criminal activities by girls (particularly in past years) were overlooked so long as they did not appear to signal defiance of parental control (see Smith, 1978).

In their historic obsession about precocious female sexuality, juvenile justice workers rarely reflected on the broader nature of female misbehavior or on the sources of this misbehavior. It was enough for them that girls' parents reported them out of control. Indeed, court personnel tended to "sexualize" virtually all female defiance that lent itself to that construction and ignore other misbehavior (Chesney-Lind, 1973, 1977; Smith, 1978). For their part, academic students of delinquency were so entranced with the notion of the delinquent as a romantic rogue male challenging a rigid and unequal class structure, that they spent little time on middle-class delinquency, trivial offenders, or status offenders. Yet it is clear that the vast bulk of delinquent behavior is of this type.

Some have argued that such an imbalance in theoretical work is appropriate as minor misconduct, while troublesome, is not a threat to the safety and well-being of the community. This argument might be persuasive if two additional points could be established. One, that some small number of youth "specialize" in serious criminal behavior while the rest commit only minor acts, and, two, that the juvenile court rapidly releases those youth that come into its purview for these minor offenses, thus reserving resources for the most serious youthful offenders.

The evidence is mixed on both of these points. Determined efforts to locate the "serious juvenile offender" have failed to locate a group of offenders who specialize only in serious violent offenses. For example, in a recent analysis of a national self-report data set, Elliott and his associates noted "there is little evidence for specialization in serious violent offending; to the contrary, serious violent offending appears to be embedded in a more general involvement in a wide range of serious and non-serious offenses" (Elliott, Huizinga, and Morse, 1987). Indeed, they went so far as to speculate that arrest histories that tend to highlight particular types of offenders reflect variations in police policy, practices, and processes of uncovering crime as well as underlying offending patterns.

More to the point, police and court personnel are, it turns out, far more interested in youth they charge with trivial or status offenses than anyone imagined. Efforts to deinstitutionalize "status offenders," for example, ran afoul of juvenile justice personnel who had little interest in releasing youth guilty of noncriminal offenses (Chesney-Lind, 1988). As has been established, much of this is a product of the system's history that encouraged court officers to involve themselves in the noncriminal behavior of youth in order to "save" them from a variety of social ills.

Indeed, parallels can be found between the earlier Progressive period and current national efforts to challenge the deinstitutionalization components of the Juvenile Justice and Delinquency Prevention Act of 1974. These come complete with their celebration of family values and concerns about youthful independence. One of the arguments against the act has been that it allegedly gave children the "freedom to run away" (Office of Juvenile Justice and Delinquency Prevention, 1985) and that it has hampered "reunions" of "missing" children with their parents (Office of Juvenile Justice, 1986). Suspicions about teen sexuality are reflected in excessive concern about the control of teen prostitution and child pornography.

Opponents have also attempted to justify continued intervention into the lives of status offenders by suggesting that without such intervention, the youth would "escalate" to criminal behavior. Yet there is little evidence that status offenders escalate to criminal offenses, and the evidence is particularly weak when considering female delinquents (particularly white female delinquents) (Datesman and Aickin, 1984). Finally, if escalation is occurring, it is likely the product of the justice system's insistence on enforcing status offense laws, thereby forcing youth in crisis to live lives of escaped criminals.

The most influential delinquency theories, however, have largely ducked the issue of status and trivial offenses and, as a consequence, neglected the role played by the agencies of official control (police, probation officers, juvenile court judges, detention home workers, and training school personnel) in the shaping of the "delinquency problem." When confronting the less than distinct picture that emerges from the actual distribution of delinquent behavior, however, the conclusion that agents of social control have considerable discretion in labeling or choosing not to label particular behavior as "delinquent" is inescapable. This symbiotic relationship between delinquent behavior and the official response to that behavior is particularly critical when the question of female delinquency is considered.

● Toward a Feminist Theory of Delinquency

To sketch out completely a feminist theory of delinquency is a task beyond the scope of this article. It may be sufficient, at this point, simply to identify a few of the most obvious problems with attempts to adapt male-oriented theory to explain female conformity and deviance. Most significant of these is the fact that all existing theories were developed with no concern about gender stratification.

Note that this is not simply an observation about the power of gender roles (though this power is undeniable). It is increasingly clear that gender stratification in patriarchal society is as powerful a system as is class. A feminist approach to delinquency means construction of explanations of female behavior that are sensitive to its patriarchal context. Feminist analysis of delinquency would also examine ways in which agencies of social control—the police, the courts, and the prisons—act in ways to reinforce woman's place in male society (Harris, 1977; Chesney-Lind, 1986). Efforts to construct a feminist model of delinquency must first and foremost be sensitive to the situations of girls. Failure to consider the existing empirical evidence on girls' lives and behavior can quickly lead to stereotypical thinking and theoretical dead ends.

An example of this sort of flawed theory building was the early fascination with the notion that the women's movement was causing an increase in women's crime; a notion that is now more or less discredited (Steffensmeier, 1980; Gora, 1982). A more recent example of the same sort of thinking can be found in recent work on the "power-control" model of delinquency (Hagan, Simpson, and Gillis, 1987). Here, the authors speculate that girls commit less delinquency in part because their behavior is more closely controlled by the patriarchal family. The authors' promising beginning quickly gets bogged down in a very limited definition of patriarchal control (focusing on parental supervision and variations in power within the family). Ultimately, the authors' narrow formulation of patriarchal control results in their arguing that mother's work force participation (particularly in high status occupations) leads to increases in daughters' delinquency since these girls find themselves in more "egalitarian families."

This is essentially a not-too-subtle variation on the earlier "liberation" hypothesis. Now, mother's liberation causes daughter's crime. Aside from the methodological problems with the study (e.g., the authors argue that female-headed households are equivalent to upper-status "egalitarian" families where both parents work, and they measure delinquency using a six-item scale that contains no status offense items), there is a more fundamental problem with the hypothesis. There is no evidence to suggest that as women's labor force participation has increased, girls' delinquency has increased. Indeed, during the last decade when both women's labor force participation accelerated and the number of female-headed households soared, aggregate female delinquency measured both by self-report and official statistics either declined or remained stable (Ageton, 1983; Chilton and Datesman, 1987; Federal Bureau of Investigation, 1987).

By contrast, a feminist model of delinquency would focus more extensively on the few pieces of information about girls' actual lives and the role played by girls' problems, including those caused by racism and poverty, in their delinquency behavior. Fortunately, a considerable literature is now developing on girls' lives and much of it bears directly on girls' crime.

● Criminalizing Girls' Survival

It has long been understood that a major reason for girls' presence in juvenile courts was the fact that their parents insisted on their arrest. In the early years, conflicts with parents were by far the most significant referral source;

in Honolulu 44% of the girls who appeared in court in 1929 through 1930 were referred by parents.

Recent national data, while slightly less explicit, also show that girls are more likely to be referred to court by "sources other than law enforcement agencies" (which would include parents). In 1983, nearly a quarter (23%) of all girls but only 16% of boys charged with delinquent offenses were referred to court by non-law enforcement agencies. The pattern among youth referred for status offenses (for which girls are overrepresented) was even more pronounced. Well over half (56%) of the girls charged with these offenses and 45% of the boys were referred by sources other than law enforcement (Snyder and Finnegan, 1987, p. 21; see also Pope and Feyerherm, 1982).

The fact that parents are often committed to two standards of adolescent behavior is one explanation for such a disparity—and one that should not be discounted as a major source of tension even in modern families. Despite expectations to the contrary, gender-specific socialization patterns have not changed very much and this is especially true for parents' relationships with their daughters (Katz, 1979). It appears that even parents who oppose sexism in general feel "uncomfortable tampering with existing traditions" and "do not want to risk their children becoming misfits" (Katz, 1979, p. 24). Clearly, parental attempts to adhere to and enforce these traditional notions will continue to be a source of conflict between girls and their elders. Another important explanation for girls' problems with their parents, which has received attention only in more recent years, is the problem of physical and sexual abuse. Looking specifically at the problem of childhood sexual abuse, it is increasingly clear that this form of abuse is a particular problem for girls.

Girls are, for example, much more likely to be the victims of child sexual abuse than are boys. Finkelhor and Baron estimate from a review of community studies that roughly 70% of the victims of sexual abuse are female (Finkelhor and Baron, 1986, p. 45). Girls' sexual abuse also tends to start earlier than boys (Finkelhor and Baron, 1986, p. 48); they are more likely than boys to be assaulted by a family member (often a stepfather) (DeJong, Hervada, and Emmett, 1983; Russell, 1986), and, as a consequence, their abuse tends to last longer than male sexual abuse (DeJong, Hervada, and Emmett, 1983). All of these factors are associated with more severe trauma—causing dramatic short- and long-term effects in victims (Adams-Tucker, 1982). The effects noted by researchers in this area move from the more well known "fear, anxiety, depression, anger and hostility, and inappropriate sexual behavior" (Browne and Finkelhor, 1986, p. 69) to behaviors of greater familiarity to criminologists, including running away from home, difficulties in school, truancy, and early marriage (Browne and Finkelhor, 1986).

Herman's study of incest survivors in therapy found that they were more likely to have run away from home than a matched sample of women whose fathers were "seductive" (33% compared to 5%). Another study of women patients found that 50% of the victims of child sexual abuse, but only 20% of the nonvictim group, had left home before the age of 18 (Meiselman, 1978).

Not surprisingly, then, studies of girls on the streets or in court populations are showing high rates of both physical and sexual abuse. Silbert and Pines (1981, p. 409) found, for example, that 60% of the street prostitutes they interviewed had been sexually abused as juveniles. Girls at an Arkansas diagnostic unit and school who had been adjudicated for either status or delinquent offenses reported similarly high levels of sexual abuse as well as high levels of physical abuse; 53% indicated they had been sexually abused, 25% recalled scars, 38% recalled bleeding from abuse, and 51% recalled bruises (Mouzakitas, 1981).

A sample survey of girls in the juvenile justice system in Wisconsin (Phelps et al., 1982) revealed that 79% had been subjected to physical abuse that resulted in some form of injury, and 32% had been sexually abused by parents or other persons who were closely connected to their families. Moreover, 50% had been sexually assaulted ("raped" or forced to participate in sexual acts) (Phelps et al., 1982, p. 66). Even higher figures were reported by McCormack and her associates (McCormack, Janus, and Burgess, 1986) in their study of youth in a runaway shelter in Toronto. They found that 73% of the females and 38% of the males had been sexually abused. Finally, a study of youth charged with running away, truancy, or listed as missing persons in Arizona found that 55% were incest victims (Reich and Gutierres, 1979).

Many young women, then, are running away from profound sexual victimization at home, and once on the streets they are forced further into crime in order to survive. Interviews with girls who have run away from home show, very clearly, that they do not have a lot of attachment to their delinquent activities. In fact, they are angry about being labeled as delinquent, yet all engaged in illegal acts (Koroki and Chesney-Lind, 1985). The

Wisconsin study found that 54% of the girls who ran away found it necessary to steal money, food, and clothing in order to survive. A few exchanged sexual contact for money, food, and/or shelter (Phelps et al., 1982, p. 67). In their study of runaway youth, McCormack, Janus, and Burgess (1986, pp. 392-393) found that sexually abused female runaways were significantly more likely than their nonabused counterparts to engage in delinquent or criminal activities such as substance abuse, petty theft, and prostitution. No such pattern was found among male runaways.

Research (Chesney-Lind and Rodriguez, 1983) on the backgrounds of adult women in prison underscores the important links between women's childhood victimizations and their later criminal careers. The interviews revealed that virtually all of this sample were the victims of physical and/or sexual abuse as youngsters; over 60% had been sexually abused and about half had been raped as young women. This situation prompted these women to run away from home (three-quarters had been arrested for status offenses) where once on the streets they began engaging in prostitution and other forms of petty property crime. They also begin what becomes a lifetime problem with drugs. As adults, the women continue in these activities since they possess truncated educational backgrounds and virtually no marketable occupational skills (see also Miller, 1986).

Confirmation of the consequences of childhood sexual and physical abuse on adult female criminal behavior has also recently come from a large quantitative study of 908 individuals with substantiated and validated histories of these victimizations. Widom (1988) found that abused or neglected females were twice as likely as a matched group of controls to have an adult record (16% compared to 7.5). The difference was also found among men, but it was not as dramatic (42% compared to 33%). Men with abuse backgrounds were also more likely to contribute to the "cycle of violence" with more arrests for violent offenses as adult offenders than the control group. In contrast, when women with abuse backgrounds did become involved with the criminal justice system, their arrests tended to involve property and order offenses (such as disorderly conduct, curfew, and loitering violations) (Widom, 1988, p. 17).

Given this information, a brief example of how a feminist perspective on the causes of female delinquency might look seems appropriate. First, like young men, girls are frequently the recipients of violence and sexual abuse. But unlike boys, girls' victimization and their response to that victimization is specifically shaped by their status as young women. Perhaps because of the gender and sexual scripts found in patriarchal families, girls are much more likely than boys to be victim of family-related sexual abuse. Men, particularly men with traditional attitudes toward women, are likely to define their daughters or stepdaughters as their sexual property (Finkelhor, 1982). In a society that idealizes inequality in male/female relationships and venerates youth in women, girls are easily defined as sexually attractive by older men (Bell, 1984). In addition, girls' vulnerability to both physical and sexual abuse is heightened by norms that require that they stay at home where their victimizers have access to them.

Moreover, their victimizers (usually males) have the ability to invoke official agencies of social control in their efforts to keep young women at home and vulnerable. That is to say, abusers have traditionally been able to utilize the uncritical commitment of the juvenile justice system toward parental authority to force girls to obey them. Girls' complaints about abuse were, until recently, routinely ignored. For this reason, statutes that were originally placed in law to "protect" young people have, in the case of girls' delinquency, criminalized their survival strategies. As they run away from abusive homes, parents have been able to employ agencies to enforce their return. If they persisted in their refusal to stay in that home, however intolerable, they were incarcerated.

Young women, a large number of whom are on the run from homes characterized by sexual abuse and parental neglect, are forced by the very statutes designed to protect them into the lives of escaped convicts. Unable to enroll in school or take a job to support themselves because they fear detection, young female runaways are forced into the streets. Here they engage in panhandling, petty theft, and occasional prostitution in order to survive. Young women in conflict with their parents (often for very legitimate reasons) may actually be forced by present laws into petty criminal activity, prostitution, and drug use.

In addition, the fact that young girls (but not necessarily young boys) are defined as sexually desirable and, in fact, more desirable then their older sisters due to the double standard of aging means that their lives on the streets (and their survival strategies) take on unique shape—one again shaped by patriarchal values. It is no accident that girls on the run from abusive homes, or on the streets because of profound poverty, get involved in criminal activities that exploit their sexual object status. American society has defined as desirable youthful, physically perfect women. This means that girls on the streets, who have little else of value to trade, are encouraged to utilize this "resource" (Campagna and Poffenberger, 1988). It also means that the criminal subculture views them from this perspective (Miller, 1986).

❧ Female Delinquency, Patriarchal Authority, and Family Courts

The early insights into male delinquency were largely gleaned by intensive field observation of delinquent boys. Very little of this sort of work has been done in the case of girls' delinquency, though it is vital to an understanding of girls' definitions of their own situations, choices, and behavior (for exceptions to this see Campbell, 1984; Peacock, 1981;Miller, 1986; Rosenberg and Zimmerman, 1977). Time must be spent listening to girls. Fuller research on the settings, such as families and schools, that girls find themselves in and the impact of variations in those settings should also be undertaken (see Figueira-McDonough, 1986). A more complete understanding of how poverty and racism shape girls' lives is also vital (see Messerschmidt, 1986; Campbell, 1984). Finally, current qualitative research on the reaction of official agencies to girls' delinquency must be conducted. This latter task, admittedly more difficult, is particularly critical to the development of delinquency theory that is as sensitive to gender as it is to race and class.

It is clear that throughout most of the court's history, virtually all female delinquency has been placed within the larger context of girls' sexual behavior. One explanation for this pattern is that familial control over girls' sexual capital has historically been central to the maintenance of patriarchy (Lerner, 1986). The fact that young women have relatively more of this capital has been one reason for the excessive concern that both families and official agencies of social control have expressed about youthful female defiance (otherwise much of the behavior of criminal justice personnel makes virtually no sense). Only if one considers the role of women's control over their sexuality at the point in their lives that their value to patriarchal society is so pronounced, does the historic pattern of jailing of huge numbers of girls guilty of minor misconduct make sense.

This framework also explains the enormous resistance that the movement to curb the juvenile justice system's authority over status offenders encountered. Supporters of the change were not really prepared for the

250

political significance of giving youth the freedom to run. Horror stories told by the opponents of deinstitutionalization about victimized youth, youthful prostitution, and youthful involvement in pornography (Office of Juvenile Justice and Delinquency Prevention, 1985) all neglect the unpleasant reality that most of these behaviors were often in direct response to earlier victimization, frequently by parents, that officials had, for years, routinely ignored. What may be at stake in efforts to roll back deinstitutionalization efforts is not so much "protection" of youth as it is curbing the right of young women to defy patriarchy.

In sum, research in both the dynamics of girl's delinquency and official reactions to that behavior is essential to the development of theories of delinquency that are sensitive to its patriarchal as well as class and racial context.

References

Adams-Tucker, Christine. 1982. "Proximate Effects of Sexual Abuse in Childhood." *American Journal of Psychiatry* 193:1252–1256.

Ageton, Suzanne S. 1983. "The Dynamics of Female Delinquency, 1976–1980." *Criminology* 21:555–584.

Bell, Inge Powell. 1984. "The Double Standard: Age." In *Women: A Feminist Perspective*, edited by Jo Freeman. Palo Alto, CA: Mayfield.

Black, T. Edwin and Charles P. Smith. 1981. *A Preliminary National Assessment of the Number and Characteristics of Juveniles Processed in the Juvenile Justice System*. Washington, DC: Government Printing Office.

Browne, Angela and David Finkelhor. 1986. "Impact of Child Sexual Abuse: A Review of Research." *Psychological Bulletin* 99:66–77.

Campagna, Daniel S. and Donald L. Poffenberger. 1988. *The Sexual Trafficking in Children*. Dover, DE: Auburn House.

Campbell, Ann. 1984. *The Girls in the Gang*. Oxford: Basil Blackwell.

Canter, Rachelle J. 1982. "Sex Differences in Self-Report Delinquency." *Criminology* 20:373–393.

Chesney-Lind, Meda. 1971. *Female Juvenile Delinquency in Hawaii*. Master's thesis, University of Hawaii.

_____. 1973. "Judicial Enforcement of the Female Sex Role." *Issues in Criminology* 3:51–71.

_____. 1978. "Young Women in the Arms of the Law." In *Women, Crime and the Criminal Justice System*, edited by Lee H. Bowker. Boston: Lexington.

_____. 1986. "Women and Crime: The Female Offender." *Signs* 12:78–96.

_____. 1988. "Girls and Deinstitutionalization: Is Juvenile Justice Still Sexist?" *Journal of Criminal Justice Abstracts* 20:144–165.

_____ and Noelie Rodriguez. 1983. "Women Under Lock and Key." *Prison Journal* 63:47–65.

Children's Bureau, Department of Health, Education and Welfare. 1965. *1964 Statistics on Public Institutions for Delinquent Children*. Washington, DC: Government Printing Office.

Chilton, Roland and Susan K. Datesman. 1987. "Gender, Race and Crime: An Analysis of Urban Arrest Trend, 1960–1980." *Gender and Society* 1:152–171.

Cloward, Richard A. and Lloyd E. Ohlin. 1960. *Delinquency and Opportunity*. New York: Free Press.

Cohen, Albert K. 1955. *Delinquent Boys: The Culture of the Gang*. New York: Free Press.

Datesman, Susan and Mikel Aickin. 1984. "Offense Specialization and Escalation Among Status Offenders." *Journal of Criminal Law and Criminology* 75:1246–1275.

Davidson, Sue, ed. 1982. *Justice for Young Women*. Tucson, AZ: New Directions for Young Women.

DeJong, Allan R., Arturo R. Hervada, and Gary A. Emmett. 1983. "Epidemiologic Variations in Childhood Sexual Abuse." *Child Abuse and Neglect* 7:155–162.

Elliott, Delbert, David Huizinga, and Barbara Morse. 1987. "A Career Analysis of Serious Violent Offenders." In *Violent Juvenile Crime: What Can We Do About It?* edited by Ira Schwartz. Minneapolis, MN: Hubert Humphrey Institute.

Federal Bureau of Investigation. 1987. *Crime in the United States 1986*. Washington, DC: Government Printing Office.

Feinman, Clarice. 1980. *Women in the Criminal Justice System*. New York: Praeger.

Figueira-McDonough, Josefina. 1985. "Are Girls Different? Gender Discrepancies Between Delinquent Behavior and Control." *Child Welfare* 64:273–289.

_____. 1986. "School Context, Gender, and Delinquency." *Journal of Youth and Adolescence* 15:79–98.

Finkelhor, David. 1982. "Sexual Abuse: A Sociological Perspective." *Child Abuse and Neglect* 6:95–102.

_____ and Larry Baron. 1986. "Risk Factors for Child Sexual Abuse." *Journal of Interpersonal Violence* 1:43–71.

Freedman, Estelle. 1981. *Their Sisters' Keepers*. Ann Arbor: University of Michigan Press.

Gelsthorpe, Loraine. 1986. "Towards a Skeptical Look at Sexism." *International Journal of the Sociology of Law* 14:125–152.

Gora, JoAnn. 1982. *The New Female Criminal: Empirical Reality or Social Myth*. New York: Praeger.

Hagan, John, A. R. Gillis, and John Simpson. 1985. "The Class Structure of Gender and Delinquency: Toward a Power-Control Theory of Common Delinquent Behavior." *American Journal of Sociology* 90:1151–1178.

Hagan, John, John Simpson, and A. R. Gillis. 1987. "Class in the Household: A Power-Control Theory of Gender and Delinquency." *American Journal of Sociology* 92:788–816.

Hancock, Linda. 1981. "The Myth that Females are Treated More Leniently than Males in the Juvenile Justice System." *Australian and New Zealand Journal of Criminology* 16:4–14.

Harris, Anthony. 1977. "Sex and Theories of Deviance." *American Sociological Review* 42:3–16.

Herman, Julia L. 1981. *Father-Daughter Incest*. Cambridge, MA: Harvard University Press.

Katz, Phyllis A. 1979. "The Development of Female Identity." In *Becoming Female: Perspectives on Development*, edited by Claire B. Kopp. New York: Plenum.

Koroki, Jan and Meda Chesney-Lind. 1985. *Everything Just Going Down the Drain*. Hawaii: Youth Development and Research Center.

Lerner, Gerda. 1986. *The Creation of Patriarchy*. New York: Oxford.

McCormack, Arlene, Mark-David Janus, and Ann Wolbert Burgess. 1986. "Runaway Youths and Sexual Victimization: Gender Differences in an Adolescent Runaway Population." *Child Abuse and Neglect* 10:387–395.

McGarrell, Edmund F. and Timothy J. Flanagan, eds. 1985. *Sourcebook of Criminal Justice Statistics—1984*. Washington, DC: Government Printing Office.

Meiselman, Karen. 1978. *Incest*. San Francisco: Jossey-Bass.

Merton, Robert K. 1938. "Social Structure and Anomie." *American Sociological Review* 3(October): 672–682.

Messerschmidt, James. 1986. *Capitalism, Patriarchy, and Crime: Toward a Socialist Feminist Criminology*. Totowa, NJ: Rowman & Littlefield.

_____. 1987. "Feminism, Criminology, and the Rise of the Female Sex Delinquent, 1880–1930." *Contemporary Crises* 11:243–263.

Miller, Eleanor. 1986. *Street Woman*. Philadelphia: Temple University Press.

Miller, Walter B. 1958. "Lower Class Culture as the Generating Milieu of Gang Delinquency." *Journal of Social Issues* 14:5–19.

Morris, Ruth. 1964. "Female Delinquency and Relational Problems." *Social Forces* 43:82–89.

Mouzakitas, C. M. 1981. "An Inquiry into the Problem of Child Abuse and Juvenile Delinquency." In *Exploring the Relationship Between Child Abuse and Delinquency*, edited by R. J. Hunner and Y. E. Walkers. Montclair, NJ: Allanheld, Osmun.

National Female Advocacy Project. 1981. *Young Women and the Justice System: Basic Facts and Issues.* Tucson, AZ: New Directions for Young Women.

Office of Juvenile Justice and Delinquency Prevention. 1985. *Runaway Children and the Juvenile Justice and Delinquency Prevention Act: What is the Impact?* Washington, DC: Government Printing Office.

———. 1986. *America's Missing and Exploited Children. Report and Recommendations of the U.S. Attorney General's Advisory Board on Missing Children.* Washington, DC: Government Printing Office.

Opinion Research Corporation. 1982. "Public Attitudes Toward Youth Crime: National Public Opinion Poll." Mimeographed. Minnesota: Hubert Humphrey Institute of Public Affairs, University of Minnesota.

Peacock, Carol. 1981. *Hand Me Down Dreams.* New York: Schocken.

Phelps, R. J. et al. 1982. *Wisconsin Female Juvenile Offender Study Project Summary Report.* Wisconsin: Youth Policy and Law Center, Wisconsin Council on Juvenile Justice.

Platt, Anthony M. 1969. *The Childsavers.* Chicago: University of Chicago Press.

Pope, Carl and William H. Feyerherm. 1982. "Gender Bias in Juvenile Court Dispositions." *Social Service Review* 6:1–17.

Rafter, Nicole Hahn. 1985. *Partial Justice.* Boston: Northeastern University Press.

Reich, J. W. and S. E. Gutierres. 1979. "Escape/Aggression Incidence in Sexually Abused Juvenile Delinquents." *Criminal Justice and Behavior* 6:239–243.

Rogers, Kristine. 1972. "'For Her Own Protection . . . . Conditions of Incarceration for Female Juvenile Offenders in the State of Connecticut." *Law and Society Review* (Winter):223–246.

Rosenberg, Debby and Carol Zimmerman. 1977. *Are My Dreams Too Much To Ask For?* Tucson, AZ: New Directions for Young Women.

Russell, Diana E. 1986. *The Secret Trauma: Incest in the Lives of Girls and Women.* New York: Basic Books.

Schlossman, Steven and Stephanie Wallach. 1978. "The Crime of Precocious Sexuality: Female Juvenile Delinquency in the Progressive Era." *Harvard Educational Review* 48:65–94.

Shaw, Clifford R. 1930. *The Jack-Roller.* Chicago: University of Chicago Press.

_____. 1938. *Brother in Crime*. Chicago: University of Chicago Press.

_____ and Henry D. McKay. 1942. *Juvenile Delinquency in Urban Areas*. Chicago: University of Chicago Press.

Shelden, Randall. 1981. "Sex Discrimination in the Juvenile Justice System: Memphis, Tennessee, 1900–1917." In *Comparing Female and Male Offenders*, edited by Marguerite Q. Warren. Beverly Hills, CA: Sage.

_____ and John Horvath. 1986. "Processing Offenders in a Juvenile Court: A Comparison of Males and Females." Paper presented at the annual meeting of the Western Society of Criminology, Newport Beach, CA, February 27–March 2.

Silbert, Mimi and Ayala M. Pines. 1981. "Sexual Child Abuse as an Antecedent to Prostitution." *Child Abuse and Neglect* 5:407–411.

Simons, Ronald L., Martin G. Miller, and Stephen M. Aigner. 1980. "Contemporary Theories of Deviance and Female Delinquency: An Empirical Test." *Journal of Research in Crime and Delinquency* 17:42–57.

Smith, Lesley Shacklady. 1978. "Sexist Assumptions and Female Delinquency." In *Women, Sexuality and Social Control*, edited by Carol Smart and Barry Smart. London: Routledge A Kegan Paul.

Snyder, Howard N. and Terrence A. Finnegan. 1987. *Delinquency in the United States*. Washington, DC: Department of Justice.

Steffensmeier, Darrell J. 1980. "Sex Differences in Patterns of Adult Crime, 1965–1977." *Social Forces* 58:1080–1109.

Sutherland, Edwin. 1978. "Differential Association." In *Children of Ishmael: Critical Perspectives on Juvenile Justice*, edited by Barry Krisberg and James Austin. Palo Alto, CA: Mayfield.

Teilmann, Katherine S. and Pierre H. Landry, Jr. 1981. "Gender Bias in Juvenile Justice." *Journal of Research in Crime and Delinquency* 18:47–80.

Thrasher, Frederic M. 1927. *The Gang*. Chicago: University of Chicago Press.

Tracy, Paul E., Marvin E. Wolfgang, and Robert M. Figlio. 1985. *Delinquency in Two Birth Cohorts: Executive Summary*. Washington, DC: Department of Justice.

Widom, Cathy Spatz. 1988. "Child Abuse, Neglect, and Violent Criminal Behavior." Unpublished manuscript.

◉ ◉ ◉

Questions

1. What gender differences exist in the kinds and rates of delinquency among young people?

2. What are "status offenses"? How can they help us understand how girls' and boys' delinquency varies?

3. What does Chesney-Lind mean when she states that the study of crime and delinquency has an "androcentric" focus? How does this focus manifest itself in theories of delinquency? How does it manifest itself in the criminal-justice and court systems?

4. How has the study of crime and delinquency failed to account for the patriarchal nature of U.S. society? Why is it important to account for patriarchy when we try to understand girls' crime and delinquency?

5. Do you agree with the author that the differences in types of crime and delinquency committed by boys and girls, types of punishments given to boys and girls, and lack of attention to social context still exist? Why or why not?